Women's War

Women's War

Fighting and Surviving the American Civil War

Stephanie McCurry

The Belknap Press of
Harvard University Press

Cambridge, Massachusetts
London, England
2019

First printing

Library of Congress Cataloging-in-Publication Data
Names: McCurry, Stephanie, author.
Title: Women's war : fighting and surviving the American Civil War /
Stephanie McCurry.
Description: Cambridge, Massachusetts : The Belknap Press of Harvard
University Press, 2019. | Includes bibliographical references and index.
Identifiers: LCCN 2018045331 | ISBN 9780674987975 (alk. paper)
Subjects: LCSH: United States—History—Civil War, 1861–1865—Women. |
Spies—Confederate States of America. | Women spies—Confederate States
of America. | Women slaves—United States—History—19th century. |
Fugitive slaves—United States—History—19th century. | Civil-military
relations—United States—History—19th century. | Reconstruction
(U.S. history, 1865–1877)—Georgia. | United States—History—
Civil War, 1861–1865—Influence.
Classification: LCC E628 .M35 2019 | DDC 973.7082–dc23
LC record available at https://lccn.loc.gov/2018045331

For Saoirse

Contents

Preface

In May of this year I went back to Belfast, the place where I was born and grew up, and which I left in 1972 in the midst of "the Troubles," as Irish people call the civil war that broke out in the late 1960s over the legitimacy of British rule. Northern Ireland is now formally at peace, and the British Army is mostly withdrawn, but the scars are everywhere. Belfast is a tense, traumatized, still divided place.

I felt this acutely that day in May when I went on a tour of West Belfast. The other thing I felt was how connected I remain to that place and the dilemmas it bequeathed me. The tour of Catholic and Protestant neighborhoods was led, consecutively, by two former political prisoners, one from each side of the conflict. The Irish Republican Army (IRA) guide talked of the community's desire to heal and of his hopes in the peace process. But as he led us from one memorial to another honoring the IRA dead, it became clear that the cityscape kept the conflict alive.

Standing in front of one memorial, I scanned the names of the "Volunteers" who had given their lives in the cause of "Irish freedom," a column of names chiseled in bronze on black stone. And sure enough

I found what I was looking for. There they were: Dorothy Maguire, nineteen years old; Maura Meehan, thirty-one; Anne Parker, eighteen; Eileen Mackin, fourteen; Annemarie Petticrew, nineteen; Cathy McGartland, twelve. These were IRA volunteers who had fought and died in the Troubles. This was part of the war I remembered and still carried with me.

I have always felt a particular shame in conceding to be taught a history with no women in it, as if women never lived or mattered in the making of that history. To me women are an indispensable part of wars and their consequences, one half of the human race divided by such wars and experiencing their violence and devastation. It is the exclusion of women from histories of military conflicts that is the artificial construct. I came to this perspective from my own personal and scholarly experiences.

I grew up in a war zone and came of age and into political awareness under British occupation. Every day there were paratroopers patrolling my street, Saracen tanks with rotating sniper turrets covering foot soldiers' progress through my Falls Road neighborhood, security checkpoints everywhere. Political conviction came easily in such a place. I entered adolescence obsessively preoccupied with matters of violence and political legitimacy. Mine was a nationalist community dominated by men but in which the sense of injustice was felt by all kinds of people, moving men, women, and children to resist the occupiers and the colonial claim. Everyone who lived there knew that. If there was any doubt about women's involvement, we had the example of Bernadette Devlin, a charismatic figure who began by organizing civil rights marches, got herself elected to the Westminster Parliament (at age twenty-two), and was radicalized by the failure of conventional political means of protest and the violence with which they were met in Northern Ireland. Women are passionate parties to their people's struggles. I learned that lesson when I was young, and I never forgot it. Newspaper coverage of ongoing conflicts provides frequent reminders, if any are needed. I cannot recognize histories of war that leave women out. Certainly, I would never write one.

My life moved me far away from Belfast, and by a long, unpredictable path, into the writing of American history, first of the slave South and then of the Civil War. There is definitely a connection between my Belfast youth and my scholarly focus, although it took me years to grasp it. The big ethical questions of power and moral legitimacy that African slavery posed to the United States, the world's leading democracy in the nineteenth century, won my attention as an undergraduate and never let go their grip. An immigrant's fascination, perhaps, with an American culture so aggressive in its exportation of new truths and yet so obviously defined by darker, formative forces. The fact that slaveholders' power was enacted bodily and directly, and that violence was the main strategy of domination, made such a society legible to me. As I became a historian I struggled to articulate the connection between the relations of power of men and women in families and communities like the one in which I had grown up, and the big public political decisions about which history is usually written. Eventually I found a way to think about gender and politics, and to integrate my feminist and scholarly selves.

In writing my two previous books, I saw the significance of women and gender relations to the central issues of the American Civil War era: southern secession, slave emancipation, and Confederate defeat. I wrote about how slaveholding elites pulled off the secession of the southern states from the Union by embracing non-slaveholding men in a coalition of free men and masters that cast secession as a defense of the Christian family; how poor white women and enslaved men and women, though entirely disenfranchised and discounted, thwarted

Confederates' proslavery national ambitions, ensured their political failure, and contributed to military defeat; how enslaved women emerged as rebels and leaders on Confederate plantations; and showed how the destruction of slavery was the work of men and women alike, highlighting women's role in the wartime process of slave emancipation. In each book, I treated women as fully as I could. But I was never finished with that part of the story. Indeed, I became increasingly convinced that I had only begun to plumb the depths of it. I continued to follow the many lines of analysis women's history offered into other questions about war and its meanings in the era of the American Civil War. I began to learn more about other civil and international wars, and to recognize the daunting scope of women's role in military conflicts in the modern period.

As I wrote this book, I slowly recognized how much of my past I had carried with me and why it mattered so much to write it—to tackle fictions about women and war, to challenge the writing out of women, and to insist on the value of women's perspective on wars and their aftermaths. The kind of history that is chiseled into that memorial in West Belfast shaped the persistent questions of my intellectual life. It brought me, finally, to write this history of women and the American Civil War. It is a very small part of a much larger history.

Women's War

Prologue

In the beginning of her book *The Unwomanly Face of War,* Svetlana Alexievich asks about Russian women who fought in combat roles in World War II: "But why? . . . Why having stood up for and held their place in a once absolutely male world, have women not stood up for their history?"[1] It is a profound question, and one with broad application, including to the history of the American Civil War.

There are few ideas more powerful in western culture than the idea that women are outside of war. Like Antigone, women belong to the realm of the family and peace, not the state and war. It is a belief belied by a long history, but one that is mostly still unrecognized and unwritten. It would take an army of historians to gather the evidence and assemble the pieces into a coherent picture, even just for the modern period.

When it comes to the American Civil War, the fiction is a powerful one that shaped the conflict itself and the way we write about it. It showed in many different ways during the war, including in Union soldiers' belief that they did not make war on women and children. Women, one soldier said, were entitled to protection, even if they were the wives and daughters of rebels. There is a great deal at stake in the idea of women's innocence, of women as parties to be protected in war. It represents an investment in the (hierarchical) gender order itself and the desire to limit the destructiveness of war. It helps to explain the deep reluctance of US soldiers to confront the role of women as participants in the war when it was ongoing, and the need to forget or deny women's actions, including as enemies, partisans, and combatants, once it was over. But women mattered in the making of that history. Their imprint is all over it.

Women are never just witnesses to war. When wars break out, they are swept into the same raging currents of history as the men in their families and communities. Wars force everyone to fight, if only to survive. But some women are also invested in the causes of war. Across the sweep of modern history, we have had plenty of evidence of that, of women's political commitments and willingness to fight for them in civil wars, world wars, and wars for national independence.

In the American Civil War, which divided communities as well as a nation, there was no place of refuge and little neutrality. War came to everyone's door. Wealthy women in New York City could no more escape the terrible new reality than poor white farm women in rural Tennessee or African American women enslaved on plantations in the Mississippi Valley. In the Union border states and Confederate states, white southern women faced an army of invasion just as the men did, and endured a war on their home territory that nurtured murderous loyalties and divisions. African American women enslaved in those states faced a battle for survival and liberation that involved as much danger and promise for them as for the men in their families and communities. And when Confederates were finally defeated at the end of that bloodbath, and elite white southerners lost all the property they had once claimed in those human beings, women were among the most bitter and vengeful of ex-slaveholders. The Civil War was not confined to the battlefield. It was not just the history of men. Nobody could escape it. And when it was over, nobody was the same.

Women are not just witnesses to history but actors and makers of it. In the American Civil War, the issue of women's stakes and roles in the military conflict bears on all the defining elements of it: the new "American" way of waging war, the process of slave emancipation, and the challenges of building a postwar order in its aftermath. Women are indispensable subjects in the story of the Civil War—as indeed they have been, and continue to be, in all wars.

What follows are three dramatic examples of women's war, each of which played a critical part in defining the stakes of the American Civil War. The first looks at the Union Army's encounters with enemy women and their lasting consequences for the idea of innocence and civilian immunity in war. The second examines the challenges black women fugitives posed to a Union emancipation policy aimed only at enslaved men, and the limits of a conventional emancipation narrative focused on black soldiers and military service. The third focuses on one former Confederate woman's efforts at reconstructing a life amid the ruins of the slave South, a process so daunting, elemental, and protracted it marks Reconstruction as a fundamental break with the prewar slaveholding past.

These stories introduce a new or previously marginal cast of characters to the larger Civil War story and set out to show the transformative role women played in it, including in conventionally male realms of military and political history. Each chapter takes up a different moment and pressing issue in the conflict. They proceed chronologically and cover the entire period of the war and Reconstruction. Taken together, they demonstrate the power of women's perspective to transform our vision of war, even of one already so exhaustively dissected as the American Civil War.

When Union soldiers marched into the southern states in the late spring of 1861, they thought they knew who they were fighting. They certainly did not expect to make war on women and children. But the soldiers' encounters with Confederate women in the path of their armies were a profoundly unsettling experience, not just for the soldiers themselves but for the international laws of war that governed the conflict. The military threat posed by enemy women bore directly on the assumption of women's innocence in war—the core belief on which the identity of the civilian, or noncombatant, was, and is, premised. By late 1862, when the Lincoln administration sponsored a new code of law to govern the conduct of its armies, the war with women assumed new importance and scope. "Lieber's Code" as it was known, after Francis Lieber, the man who authored it, became a template for all subsequent codes, including the Hague and Geneva Conventions in the twentieth century. The question of gender and innocence posed by Confederate women identified as enemies had a far-reaching impact that extended long past the American Civil War.

The challenge of fighting a "peoples' war" that mobilized invaded populations along with official military forces had been evident throughout the nineteenth century, at least since the invasion of Spain in the Napoleonic Wars. When Francisco de Goya's images of that war, *Los Desastres de la Guerra*, were published in 1863, they included more than a few representations of militant women ("mujeres de valor") manning cannon in defense of their cities and engaged in hand-to-hand combat in the streets. Little of that history was recognized when the American Civil War began. Some officers like Henry Halleck,

Francisco de Goya, *Que Valor!* in *Los Desastres de la Guerra,* 1863 Goya Lucientes, Francisco de. *Los desastres de la guerra: colección de ochenta láminas inventadas y grabadas al agua fuerte por . . .* Publícala la Rl. Academia de Nobles Artes de San Fernando. Madrid, Real Academia de Nobles Artes de San Fernando, 1863 (Lit. J. Aragón). Real Biblioteca, Inf / 6133.

who had studied modern warfare and served in the army of occupation in the Mexican War, had a vague idea that women would fight to protect their homeland. But nothing prepared Union soldiers for the furious resistance of Confederate civilians, among whom women figured prominently. For about two years, the Union adopted a policy of conciliation, attempting to win citizens back to loyalty to the Union and extending protections to women. But in the face of relentless evidence of women's participation in guerilla warfare, including as saboteurs, spies, smugglers, and informants, Union officers, soldiers, and policymakers reluctantly came to recognize Confederate women as enemies who counted and to treat them as a military threat.

This was an unacknowledged part of the turn to "hard war," as General William Tecumseh Sherman called the decision to take the war to Confederate civilians. Unlike emancipation—the other signature of hard war—it had a lasting impact on the laws of war.

One woman appears to have played an outsized role in this development: Clara Judd. A Confederate widow, Judd was arrested and charged as a spy in December 1862, at precisely the moment officers in Tennessee were demanding a harsher policy toward civilians. The problem enemy women like Judd posed for Union armies prompted a harsh response on the ground but also a set of military orders that were immediately incorporated into the ambitious legal code the Columbia law professor Francis Lieber was writing for the Union government.

Lieber's code is widely recognized as a landmark in the history of international law precisely because it rewrote the distinction between combatant and civilian on which the whole body of law is founded. With Lieber, the protections accorded civilians in war were eroded, even eviscerated, and the balance between immunity and accountability shifted radically. What that had to do with enemy women, or women of any sort for that matter, has never been part of the story. But it is. The actions of Clara Judd and other women like her impinged directly on the writing of Lieber's code. The erosion of civilian immunity, and the disjoining of women and innocence that undergirded it, is part of a particular Civil War history—a women's history and a gender history with material effect on the modern laws of war.

Confederate women were not the only ones whose pursuit of their own objectives in the war posed a daunting challenge to the Union Army and government. The same was true of the countless enslaved women who fought for survival and for their freedom amid the turmoil of the Civil War. Like the many black men now celebrated as heroes of the war, women seized the dangerous opportunity the war presented to secure their liberty in the orbit of the Union Army. Flooding into Union lines by the thousands and attaching themselves to the rear of columns on the move, these women faced a different and more forbidding landscape than the men.

Since the first days of the war, the army recognized the military value of male fugitives and hammered out policies to justify holding them as the confiscated property of Confederate traitors. But by the middle of the war, even as the Lincoln administration officially embraced emancipation and the enlistment of black soldiers, the government still had no military use for women and children. Enslaved women and children seeking refuge constituted a military and humanitarian crisis of massive proportions. They further posed a problem of governance that confounded and shaped Union emancipation policy for the entirety of the war.

The solutions the government and army reached at critical junctures revealed deeply held beliefs about marriage, the family, and the proper place of women in American society, beliefs officials were determined to apply to newly free black women. When the first fugitive slaves arrived at Fortress Monroe on the Virginia peninsula in May 1861, Union officer Benjamin Butler immediately construed every female refugee or "contraband" as some particular man's wife, regardless of their actual status. As Union policies took shape, it became clear that, as far as the government was concerned, enslaved men were to take the martial path to freedom and enslaved women the marital one.

From the earliest moments of the war, Union officers conceived of the slaves in rebellion as male and the women fugitives, however improbably, as their wives. No matter that marriage was illegal for slaves, or that many of the women who made it to Union lines had no husbands with them when they arrived or were heads of households themselves. It is a pattern evident in all of the key elements of emancipation policy starting in 1861. This points to a crucial and unacknowledged pattern in the long history of slave emancipation across the hemisphere: how governments administering the transition from slavery to freedom repeatedly reached for the paradigm of marriage to usher men into headship of households and women into legal dependence. In the American Civil War, the administration of slave women as wives was the solution federal policymakers most often reached for to address the problem of fugitive women and dependency. Emancipation was inconceivable without the prior and anchoring order of patriarchal marriage. Every enslaved woman had to be a soldier's wife.

This policy fiction had powerful consequences for the women themselves. It shaped what women were up against in their attempt to destroy slaveholders' claims on them and their children, as well as the difficult terrain they had to navigate to survive and achieve their freedom. It also tells us a lot about the conditions of that freedom for those who lived to claim it, and about their status as women citizens after the war. The story of black soldiers' wives speaks directly to the indispensability of marriage and the gender order as a tool of politics and policymaking, state-building and citizenship.

The ends of wars are always dangerous moments, ripe with possibilities of every sort. Civil wars leave particularly dangerous legacies, not least because after the enemy is defeated, he does not withdraw but remains in place. It is never easy to enforce the peace after military conflicts or to construct a viable postwar social and political order.

Everywhere after wars, women live those histories in ways peculiar to their sex.

In the spring of 1865, the people of the Confederate States of America arrived at that juncture. On a plantation outside of Augusta, Georgia, one woman, Gertrude Thomas, lived through it all: destruction, defeat, occupation, emancipation, political uncertainty, and, for her, a long, grinding descent into poverty. Along with occupation by Union victors, Thomas and the rest of the slaveholding elite faced the additional penalty of emancipation. In the American Civil War, where the enslaved had been crucial allies of the Union military, conquered and liberated alike lived through the process of reconstruction in conditions of dreadful proximity. Thomas left a forty-year record of her life that captured this historical passage and illuminated it in new ways. Among other things her diary includes disturbing revelations about her father that show how the sexual violence of slavery set a deep explosive charge beneath every negotiation over the terms of freedom in postwar American society.

What Gertrude Thomas offers is a woman's perspective on history, which is precisely what makes it valuable. Thomas's effort at reconstructing a living and a life was exquisitely syncopated with the chaotic process of experimentation in politics, labor, and family forms that emancipation unleashed. Yet she looked out on it all from a domestic—which is not to say private, but rather familial—space. Her view necessarily took in the impact of social collapse and postwar reconstruction in personal as well as political realms. When slavery was ripped up, virtually everything was uprooted with it, not just the relationship between master and slave that constituted capital wealth, governed labor, gave value to land, grounded white supremacy, and shaped local and national politics. In dismantling slavery, emancipation showed how deep slavery's roots had gone, penetrating and organizing every element of life and requiring their reconstruction as well. Thomas's perspective allows us to see how the huge structural changes in land, capital, and racial ideology that form the usual subjects of Reconstruction history were inextricably wound up with highly intimate matters of marriage and family, sexuality and love. In the postwar American South, reconstruction involved a revolution on the level of every household and every family. Gertrude Thomas provides an intimate accounting of that juncture in history, a way to gauge the real extent of the break emancipation and Reconstruction represented in public and private lives and the fundamental nature of the reordering underway.

Women don't usually tell war stories. Almost everything we know about war we know from men. But women's perspective transforms our vision of war because they lived through that history in a different way. They see things that men do not. When we view war through women's eyes we learn things we did not already know. Women's accounts of military conflicts are not easily confined to the battlefield, the war room, or the treaty table but range onto unfamiliar ground. Their views necessarily include the impact of war, social collapse, and postwar reconstruction in personal as well as military and political realms. Women pull into the record allegedly "private" but highly consequential matters of marriage and the family, revealing the way war disorders even these fundamental relations of social and political life. The consequences can be traced in individual human lives lived in the maelstrom of war, and then in the strategies and policies governments and armies were forced to adopt to contend with the military, humanitarian, and political consequences of such massive social disruption. Wars are transformative events for everyone who lives through them.

The task of governing continues in the midst of war. Indeed, the need only becomes more urgent as social conditions grow more desperate and people more radical in response. In this context, women of all races and social classes pose challenges of governance that shape the history of war as profoundly as men in uniform and armies on the field, whether by participating directly in military conflicts, seizing the opportunities of war to change their status, or taking measures in a bid to survive. Women also shape the peace, as we more readily acknowledge, or the lack of it, as is so often the case in postwar societies.

One striking element of governance runs through and connects these three very different stories of women's war: marriage. The centrality of the institution of marriage to the events of the American Civil War serves as a potent reminder that the family itself is a realm of governance, a polity in fact, and one of great significance to states. Political theorists in earlier centuries routinely acknowledged this, but modern theorists and historians for the most part have forgotten. It was a tenet of nineteenth-century liberalism, as Francis Lieber wrote, that "property and marriage" were the "two first elements of all progress and civilization." The family, he said, is crucial to the "essential order of things [and it] cannot exist without marriage."[2] Marriage played a particularly crucial role in slaveholding societies like the United States, because wherever the institution of slavery existed, it required the relegation of considerable personal authority to the owner to control his property. Usually cast as the right of the household head to govern his dependents unimpeded, slavery established those households as domains of private power outside of state control, and in the process linked marriage and slavery as the twin "domestic" relations on which the social and political order rested. It certainly explains why proslavery ideologues relied so heavily on the analogy between marriage and slavery in the antebellum United States, an analogy that was useful, in part, because it worked to tie non-slaveholders into a political coalition of "free men" and masters of households and dependents. From this perspective, as proslavery ideologues argued, what fanatical abolitionists threatened to destroy was not just slavery but marriage and the Christian family. It was an argument, not incidentally, that gave non-slaveholders a potential stake in the defense of slavery, secession, and Civil War. In the slave South and the slaveholders' new nation, the Confederate States of America, marriage joined slavery as a realm of governance contained within the household, a form of civil government for those—women and slaves—not fit to govern themselves. When slavery was destroyed, men's power over women looked much less secure.

The family and the polity; the family *as* a polity. In ways we have not always recognized, marriage was a foundational institution of political life, structuring both the domestic polity and the rules governing the international order. Certainly, that was the case in the Civil War as the perspective of women's war makes abundantly clear. It was evident alike in Union soldiers' reluctance to hold wives accountable for treason; in Union policymakers' insistence on African American marriage as the essential condition of emancipation; and in the extensive work involved in the reconstruction of the family that came with the destruction of slavery and creation of free families and free homes in the post-emancipation South.

In an era of radical change, marriage was one institution of governance carefully carried over into the new postwar order. It was needed to ground the system of gender—of power between men and women—which no society, apparently, can do without. It is a truism to say that gender is a central relation of power in human history; indeed, that it is the one most consistently evident across time and space. It is also the relation of power most easily and fully naturalized. As such, it provides a reliable foundation of other hierarchies allegedly based on natural and bodily difference. It is surely telling that even as the US government abandoned one of the relations of domestic dependency that had undergirded the republic since the founding, it clung resolutely to the other. In that sense, the stories of women's war told here point directly to the indispensability of marriage—and the patriarchal gender order—not just as a tool of politics and policymaking but of state-building and citizenship in the United States.

In the end *Women's War* raises a larger, more difficult issue: why, given all the potent evidence of their significance, have women been rendered invisible in histories of war? That is a profound question, the answer to which is embedded deep in the histories themselves. It owes a great debt to the loyalty men felt, and continue to feel, to the idea of women as outside war, meaning both men who waged wars and men who write about them. The idea of women's innocence—the principle that we do not make war on women and children—was, and is, at odds with the direction of modern peoples' war and, more lethally, of total wars. It has been openly contradicted by the actions women took and take as direct participants in all of those military conflicts, as partisans invested in their peoples' cause—manning a cannon, luring soldiers into an ambush, gathering intelligence, penetrating enemy lines, conducting sabotage, planting bombs, fighting in a militia, joining the military—or as human beings caught up in the devastating effects of war, fighting to survive. The fact that women are perpetrators and active participants in war is a disturbing truth acknowledged only reluctantly and under duress in the midst of conflicts. It places great strain on the idea of civilized warfare and civilized armies.

One of the most striking aspects of the American Civil War, like so much about women's participation in war in the modern period, is how much of that history was acknowledged in time and place but promptly and purposely forgotten—literally written out—as soon as the war was over. That was true of the American Revolutionary War, when women's capacity for treason was explicitly acknowledged in constitutional law. And it was true of the Civil War, when the lesson about enemy women and military treason had to be learned all over again. After it was over, even men like Francis Lieber, who knew better, returned quickly to comforting fictions about the role women had played in the war as beloved wives, mothers, and daughters. In such reassuring post-conflict fictions, the United States is hardly alone.

Women's history *is* the history of war, of politics, and of statehood. That all of it was denied in the postwar period, the knowledge suppressed, is part of the larger story *Women's War* tells. The challenges that issued from women's participation in war, in the destruction of slavery, and in the struggle to shape the postwar peace were fundamental, not incidental, parts of the history of the Civil War and Reconstruction. This is the history we need to write, the kind with women still in it.

1

Enemy Women and the Laws of War

"We do not make war on women and children."
—Illinois Private, 1862

One of the most important legacies of the American Civil War, not just in the re-United States of America but in the nineteenth- and twentieth-century world, was the new laws of war the conflict introduced. "Lieber's Code," named after the man who authored it for the Lincoln administration, was a set of instructions written and issued in April 1863 to govern the conduct of "the armies of the United States in the field." It became a template for all subsequent codes, including the Hague and Geneva Conventions.[1] Widely understood as a radical revision of the laws of war and a complete break with the Enlightenment tradition, the code, like the war that gave rise to it, reflected the new, post-Napoleonic age of "people's wars." As such it pointed forward, if not as the expression of the first total war then of the first modern one, with its characteristic blurring of boundaries.[2]

In no area was Lieber's code more significant than its meaning for the distinction between combatants and civilians. "The distinction" has constituted the foundational concept in the laws of war since at least the sixteenth century. "Upon the distinction between the civilian and combatant . . . the whole idea of the law of war depends,"

15

Francis Lieber, c. 1855–1865   *Frances [sic] Lieber,* Brady-Handy Photograph Collection, Library of Congress, Prints and Photographs Division, Washington, D.C. [LC-DIG-cwpbh-01400].

Geoffrey Best wrote in his classic study *Humanity in Warfare.*[3] In rewriting "the distinction," as it is shorthanded in international law, Lieber broke down the wall between soldiers and noncombatants—including the assumption of women's innocence on which the identity of the civilian was (and is) premised.[4] Among other things, Lieber's code—and the laws of war—responded to the challenge posed by enemy women in the American Civil War.

Although overlooked historically, the Union military's experience with women in the path of their armies was an entirely unexpected and deeply unsettling element of the war. It subverted longstanding assumptions about women's political identity and status, and provoked a profound reassessment of the protections accorded to noncombatants. The problem of enemy women emerged as a critical issue in the conduct of the Civil War and its aftermath, through new laws of war that long outlived the conflict itself. Far from a matter of significance only to women's history, the issue bears directly on the matter of humanity in war.

This argument differs from the one recently offered by John Fabian Witt in his book on Lieber's code, titled, revealingly, *Lincoln's Code: The Laws of War in American History*. Witt brilliantly locates Lieber's code at a crucial moment in the prosecution of the war (January 1863), with Lincoln's adoption of the "hard war" policy of uncompensated slave emancipation. He points to the articles on slavery as the "most original" of Lieber's entire code in that they constituted a total reversal of all previous US policy on the protection of property (that is, chattel property or slaves) in war, as was now required by the new role of the Union Army as an army of liberation.[5] Viewed in the tradition of the *American* law of war, Witt is undoubtedly right. But something important is lost in the alignment of the code's hard-war logic so fully with Lincoln's emancipation policy. For in the *international* law tradition, the most radical innovation of the code was not the parts on slavery, which were quickly dated, but those on irregular war and especially civil war—section X—and their authorization of an awesome use of force unconstrained by any limits aside from "military necessity." It was also the most immediately relevant part of the code, as European states in the mid-1860s and 1870s increasingly confronted the problem of people's war and irregular soldiers, who posed the most difficult questions for jurists engaged in debates over the laws of war. In terms of law and its relationship to power, Lieber's code forged a new path. Indeed, the question of what an army can legitimately do to noncombatants or civilians in war, and the broad scope for violence thereby established, was fundamental to the origins, drafting, and revision of Lieber's code in 1863, and to its enduring significance in the international laws of war. Best calls it the "arch-occupiers'" code.[6]

What this has to do with enemy women—or with women of any sort—does not figure in the historical literature on Lieber's code, the laws of war, or the American Civil War. For political theorist Helen M. Kinsella, it is impossible to grasp the "the distinction" between combatants and civilians without grappling with the matter of women and gender. Her book brilliantly lays out the fundamental merging of the concept of woman and civilian (or noncombatant) and the discourse of gender, innocence, and civilization that underwrote the category. And yet, even as Kinsella fully appreciates the significance of Lieber's code in redefining civilians—and weakening the protections accorded them—she misses the particular gender history behind the introduction of the new terms. The two sections of the code she identifies as crucial—sections 155 and 156—were not only added by Lieber at general-in-chief Henry Halleck's insistence; they were lifted virtually verbatim from a set of field instructions Halleck issued in March 1863 urging harsh measures against women insurgents in Tennessee. Thus, Kinsella concludes, the "principle of distinction held for the great majority of the American Civil War," even with respect to the protection of white women and children in guerilla warfare.[7] But it did not. The disjoining of women and innocence, and the subsequent erosion of civilian immunity represented by Lieber's code, has a particular Civil War history—a women's history and a gender history that has had material effect on the modern laws of war.

The idea that women "were outside war" is at least as old as *Antigone* in western civilization. The heroine of Sophocles's fifth century B.C. play, Antigone was a powerful representation of women's primal commitment to the family. They belonged to the realm of kinship, not citizenship; household, not polity; family, not state. The idea of women as the essential noncombatants has a long history. It goes back to Francisco de Vitoria in the sixteenth century, to Hugo Grotius in the seventeenth century, to Emer de Vattel in the eighteenth, and to Lieber in the nineteenth. Grotius delineated the principle clearly in his book *The Laws of War and Peace.* "One must take care, so far as possible, to prevent the death of innocent persons, even by accident," he wrote, specifying women and children as those who should be spared. Emer de Vattel's *Laws of Nations* distinguished between those enemies who composed the state's human means of making war, and those beyond the power of arms-bearing, namely, "women and children," who did not. Women were enemies, he acknowledged, but they were not to be treated "like men who bear arms, or are capable of bearing them."[8] The definition of noncombatant starts with those (women) who do not bear arms—and moves outward to encompass children, feeble old men, sick persons, and all unarmed people. It is a concept widely acknowledged yet rarely analyzed by scholars. Assumptions about women that undergird the pairing of "gender and innocence" in war, as Best calls it, are taken as facts of nature, stable over time, or inviolably engrained in culture.[9]

But there is nothing self-evident about these assumptions. Although central to international law, "'the distinction' has always been frail," Kinsella insists, largely because of the instability of the gender categories and discourses on which it rests. Certainly, it is not safe to assume that women's inviolability follows from their physical weakness and incapacity to wage war. As early as the fifteenth century, Christine de Pizan reminded her readers that women not only waged war but possessed attributes (above all, intelligence) that made them worth "ten soldiers." The rationale for "the distinction" and the logic of sex difference that underlies it has changed over time. Vitoria, for example, credited women's blamelessness to their lack of reason. Nevertheless, the distinction always owed a great deal to the institution of marriage, and the idea that women did not "devise wars," subject as they were to the guardianship of husbands. Women and children were innocents because they were "outside war."[10]

The distinction at the time of the American Civil War was deeply tied to an understanding of women's normative status as wives and, under the law of coverture, as persons subject to the guardianship of their husbands. Coverture was a legal arrangement of great antiquity—the law of Baron and Feme (or Lord and Woman), as it was called—inherited from English common law that survived the Revolutionary War intact. It was one with profound implications for women's political status and identity as citizens.[11] The law put women under their husbands' authority in the interests of marital unity. In marriage, the husband and wife became one, and that one was the husband. Matrimony established a domestic relationship of power and dependency between husband and wife, not least of all by awarding him exclusive control of her body and ownership of any property she brought into the marriage.[12] After marriage a wife did not own her body, its labor, the wages she earned, the children she produced, or any property in her own name. Indeed, marriage was itself a form of governance—and one in which the state was greatly invested.[13] It established husbands as household heads for purposes of taxation and political representation, while relegating women to the realm of virtual representation. After marriage, a woman's husband became her legal and political representative. The "transformation of woman into wife made 'citizenship'—a public identity as a participant in public life—something close to a contradiction in terms for a married woman," the legal historian Hendrik Hartog argues.[14] Citizenship has been gendered since its origin, differently shaping rights and obligations for men and women. Adult white women were citizens in a constitutional sense, but nobody thought of them as such. They possessed few of the political rights that increasingly defined their male counterparts' standing in the new republic as free men and voters, and they assumed few of the attendant obligations of citizens, including military service in defense of the state.

There was one notable exception to women's submersion in the political identity of their husbands: as citizens, even married women had an individual obligation to refrain from treason. The conflict between this principle and every other tenet of the law of marriage was not often put to the test. In 1861, on the eve of the Civil War, the issue stood very much where it had been left by the key post-revolutionary case of *Martin v. Commonwealth of Massachusetts*, which concerned the state's confiscation of the dower property of a loyalist wife. The case, which was heard in 1805, tested whether Anna Martin's adherence to England in the Revolutionary War was an act of treason punishable by confiscation of her dower property, since Martin's husband was an officer in the British Army. Her son wanted her property returned. The case, and verdict, revealed vividly the divergent priorities of societies in war and in peace. In a strictly legal sense the case should have been straightforward: the Massachusetts treason statute had been carefully written to include women, and the radical lawyer James Sullivan believed it should be enforced. "Cannot a feme-covert levy war?" he asked. To him the answer was clearly yes. Women were sovereign beings, accountable to their government for their own political choices, including that of loyalty and treason. But the plaintiff's lawyer, George Blake, found that claim preposterous. "What aid can they give to the enemy," he asked contemptuously. Married women may be citizens but not citizens whose loyalty mattered. As a *feme covert*, a woman "had no political relation to the state any more than an alien." Anna Martin was a married woman and, as such, her paramount obligation was to her husband. If he "commanded it, she was duty bound to obey him, by a law paramount to all other laws—the law of God." Blake's proved the winning argument, repeated virtually verbatim in the decision for Martin. Are we to believe that the government really intended to encourage a woman "in violation of her marriage vows, to rebel against the will of her husband?" Judge Theodore Sedgwick wrote. In 1805, with the din of war safely behind them, the answer to the question of whether a married woman could levy war in *Martin v. Commonwealth* was a firm, thermidorean no.[15] At the dawn of the American republic, John Adams had justified women's exclusion from political life on these same grounds. The government, he said, was indifferent to the matter of loyalty and treason in women.[16]

In ways we have not always appreciated, marriage was a foundational institution of political life, structuring both the domestic polity and the rules governing the international order. Vitoria and Grotius both reasoned from that basis and so too, much later, would Francis Lieber. It was a tenet of Lieber's liberal faith that "property and marriage" were the "first two elements of all progress and civilization," as he once explained to John C. Calhoun. The family is crucial to the "essential order of things," and it "cannot exist without marriage." In 1838, already spooked by the emancipationist claims of Mary Wollstonecraft and Angelina Grimké, Lieber laid out his views about the difference of the sexes and marital unity in *Manual of Political Ethics*. Woman's "true sphere is the family," he declared, in her role as wife and mother; by the "laws of nature" she is "excluded from political life." The "woman cannot defend the state," as he put it in an echo of Adams.[17]

In the nineteenth century, as the feminist legal scholar Reva B. Siegel has noted, the common law "established the family as a kind of gendered jurisdiction." Certainly, this law of coverture was not static. In the antebellum period legal reformers pushed through married women's property rights in a few states and the right of divorce in others. A small minority of women's rights activists advocated for more radical political change, including women's right to vote. Nevertheless, as Siegel has observed, statutes such as married women's property rights did not so much destroy coverture as modernize it. After all, marriage fulfilled crucial public functions, especially the "privatiz[ation]" of women's economic dependency," which thus relieved the government of the burden of public welfare. In that respect, its importance only increased with the emancipation of 4 million enslaved men, women, and children in the Civil War. Throughout the first republic and beyond, the parameters of female citizenship were established by the perceived necessity of marriage and its gender asymmetries between man and wife, and by the state's commitment to upholding marriage, the law of coverture, and husbands' authority over their wives. Women had a particular kind of citizenship and a secondhand relationship to the state.[18]

At the beginning of the American Civil War, such views governed military policy. Union soldiers were committed to the powerfully resilient historical idea of women as "outside war." "We do not make war on women and children," an Illinois soldier assured his wife in 1862. At the outset of the conflict this assumption was evident in military policy, the conduct of the war, and the laws of war; as much as slave emancipation, its abandonment marked the turn to hard war. Women were inscribed by law and custom as victims of war, not perpetrators of it, and thereby figured as subjects to be protected from the war's destructiveness. In the Civil War, as in other wars, that assumption was about imposing limits on war's destructiveness. Given the human capacity for violence, the need was urgently felt. "It is the men with arms in their hands upon whom we make war. The women are entitled to protection even if they are the wives and daughters of rebels," the Illinois soldier elaborated.[19]

But the limits of that deeply customary respect for coverture and women's distance from the state were severely challenged as the demands on citizens intensified and both states, Union and Confederate, geared up for a war that tested the loyalty of every man, woman, and child, enslaved and free.[20] As it turned out, the tension between marriage and citizenship, between women as dependents (or innocents) requiring protection and women as the enemy accountable for treason, would run like a leitmotif through Union military policy and the new laws of war written to guide it.

Women's immunity from war had never been seen as absolute. It was always conceded to be contingent. As part of the population with whom the state was at war, women were recognized as the enemy, as Grotius wrote in the seventeenth century, because "injury may be feared from such persons also." To preserve immunity, they had to be "enemies who make no resistance." "If the women wish to be spared altogether," Vattel wrote in the eighteenth century, "they must confine themselves to the occupations peculiar to their own sex, and not meddle with those of men by taking up arms." The possibility that they would—and indeed already had—hovered always in the background as a condition at once marked and obscured in the written codes of war. Each publicist advanced the general principle of women's immunity or "inviolability" as noncombatants, while acknowledging women's other identity as potentially dangerous enemies, up to and including Lieber. As a Prussian émigré and survivor of the Battle of Waterloo and Greek wars of independence, Lieber was no naïf. He knew there were exceptions to the rule: the women of Zaragoza, Spain, who in the resistance to the Napoleonic invasion, "abide[d] by their fighting husbands unto death," and the many other women who "in periods of extremity . . . could suddenly step upon the wall and look into the enemy's face." It was a startlingly vivid image, especially for 1838. But these women, Lieber insisted, acted simply as wives. Anything else would have been a transgression of nature itself.[21]

Women's other identity as dangerous enemies quickly became apparent in the Civil War. The Union armies' battle with enemy women started early. Commanders in places such as Missouri, New Orleans, and the Shenandoah Valley found it difficult to confront such fundamental challenges to the gender order. Confederate women quickly earned a reputation for violent secessionism. And yet at the beginning, and even as prominent women spies were arrested and imprisoned, the right of white women to protection was still observed as a fundamental element of the social compact.[22] Confederate women in the path of Union armies routinely applied for and received official "orders of protection," which instructed guards to protect their persons and property. At least two women, Mary Greenhow Lee and Cornelia Peake McDonald, who were later expelled for treasonous activities, received these protections in Winchester, Virginia, in early 1862.[23] One soldier called the women's "brazen secessionism . . . intense, bitter and unbearable."[24] The pattern of restraint and forbearance was evident all over the occupied South in 1861 and 1862. The treatment of southern white women was striking, especially in contrast to that meted out to other women by Union armies: the indiscriminate slaughter of Cheyenne and Arapaho women at Sand Creek, Colorado, in late 1864, for example, the complete lack of regard for human life regularly displayed toward the columns of African American refugee women and children—who were not enemies but allies—following the armies.[25] Clearly, southern white women were given the benefit of the doubt, their innocence and status as civilians assumed even as evidence to the contrary mounted.

Like the obligation to return slave property, this commitment to protect the persons and property of Confederate civilians was a key element of the Lincoln administration's initial soft-war policy, designed to restore southerners' loyalty to the Union. In February 1862, that policy was reiterated to the troops in the Department of the Missouri, about to move south into Tennessee. "Let us show to our fellow-citizens of these States that we come merely to crush out rebellion and to restore them to peace," the orders read. "They have been told that we come to oppress and plunder. By our acts we will undeceive them." There was to be no pillaging or destruction of private property, no concealment or stealing of slaves, and no admission of fugitive slaves into Union lines or camps except when ordered by the commanding general. And then, directly invoking the laws of war, the orders reiterated the principle that "women and children, merchants, farmers, mechanics, and all persons not in arms are regarded as non-combatants and are not to be molested either in their persons or property." The usual condition was appended: "If, however, they aid and assist the enemy they become belligerents and will be treated as such. If they violate the laws of war, they will be made to suffer the penalties."[26]

It is one of those fantastic coincidences of history that the man under whose command the orders were issued, Major General Henry Halleck, was himself a main authority on the referenced law of war and widely recognized as such at the beginning of the war. Halleck's text, *International Law; or, Rules Regulating the Intercourse of States in Peace and War,* had just been published in 1861, and as such stands as an important statement of the antebellum status quo in international law. In his 1861 text, Halleck hewed pretty closely to the conventional position of Grotius and Vattel that women constitute the quintessential noncombatants, people "exempt from military duty" because they are "incapable of handling arms or supporting the fatigues of military service." Especially now, Halleck wrote, when wars are conducted by regular troops, noncombatants—"persons who take no part in the war and make no resistance to our arms"—had nothing to fear from the enemy's sword. For women and children especially, he emphasized, the presumption of innocence was strong, and commanders violated it at their peril.[27]

But Halleck was different from his predecessors, and prescient, in one respect. Far more than Vattel, he was alert to the dangers noncombatants could pose to armies of occupation: "It *often* happens," he wrote, "in cases of invasions," that all kinds of people, even women and children, "take up arms and render good service in the common defense." Indeed, Halleck anticipated many of the circumstances that would attend a war of rebellion or civil war, including the necessarily expanded scope of martial law. In this way he contested Vattel's claim that each party to civil war was equally entitled to the protections of international law. He saw that as "a direct violation of the rights of sovereignty and independence."[28] In these comments, Halleck's text registered the weighty lessons of the Napoleonic Wars, and especially the Peninsular War, famously depicted in Francisco de Goya's *Los Desastres* (finally printed in 1863), with its riveting images of Madrileñas and peasant women rising in armed defense of their country. It also registered his own experience in the Mexican War.[29] Halleck knew that in cases of invasion women could be expected to step upon the wall and look the enemy in the face. Commanders would respond, and there would be no immunity.

When his book was published, Halleck was serving as commander of the Department of the Missouri, an arena of war that was deeply challenging in its irregularity and further tested "the distinction." He was disturbed by the nature of warfare in the border states, and especially the difficulties in distinguishing guerillas from the surrounding civilian population. He came to believe that he was operating in a hostile country, no less so than when he had been in Mexico. Faced with hundreds, perhaps thousands, of guerilla fighters, tired of being shot at and harassed from the woods, of wasting energy and men in fruitless pursuit of a phantom enemy and of the drain on troops to guard railroad bridges and lines, Halleck abandoned any pretense of conciliation and hit back hard against irregulars and their support networks. For Halleck had learned that guerillas' ability to operate depended crucially on the support of the local population: To fight guerillas you had to go after the people—often networks of kinfolk—who aided and abetted them. When you did, you ended up fighting not just the men but the women as well.

The added weight of these experiences in Missouri would be relevant when in 1863, serving as general-in-chief of the Union armies, Halleck would collaborate with Lieber in the writing of a radical new code.

By the spring of 1862, a cordon of federal power rimmed the Confederacy, and the belligerent population to be controlled was growing fast. In the Union border states and occupied parts of the Confederate states, officers and soldiers rapidly accrued bitter experiences, not just as anticipated with the Confederate Army but also with enemy civilians. These experiences would crucially influence policy and law. Confederate women posed an especially difficult challenge, and events in 1862 drove commanders to question foundational principles, including the previously strict gender distinction between combatants and noncombatants, men and women, that set limits on the destructiveness of war.

The struggle played out in many places simultaneously, and most famously in New Orleans, where Major General Benjamin Butler's attempt to defuse the threat facing his troops by forcing elite women off the streets using municipal prostitution laws incited a transatlantic fracas about the protection of women in war. Butler famously vowed to treat offenders as he would any "woman of the town plying her avocation."[30] But if New Orleans garnered all the press, the situation was not so different in Winchester, Virginia, a town that changed hands more than seventy times during the war. There, Union commanders

Nathaniel Banks and Robert H. Milroy faced similar challenges from women such as Mary Greenhow Lee, whose "soldier work," as she called it, included stockpiling weapons and conveying military intelligence to rebel officers in the Shenandoah Valley, Stonewall Jackson among them. All over the occupied South, Union officers were confronted with the evidence of women's treasonous activities. The soldiers stepped up surveillance and gradually abandoned chivalrous notions of protection.[31]

After Butler's infamous order in New Orleans, Jefferson Davis wrote Robert E. Lee that this was becoming "a savage war" in which "no quarter is to be given and no sex to be spared."[32] Davis exaggerated, but by the summer of 1862, a landmark of sorts had been reached. Union occupying authorities in New Orleans, Winchester, and elsewhere required that women ("heretofore citizens of the United States"), like men, swear a formal oath of allegiance to claim the protection of the US government and the privilege to reside, work, travel, or trade in Union territory. It was an effort to identify and expel those intent on "rebellious or traitorous acts."[33] It was also a way to force them to acknowledge defeat. By August, oaths had been administered to more than eleven thousand citizens.[34] By the time the provost marshal general in Louisiana issued General Orders No. 76 in September 1862, women were explicitly identified as among those "enemies of the state" required to register and take the oath.

John Adams was wrong. The government was not indifferent to the matter of loyalty and treason in women after all. Requiring women to take the oath was an important shift in Union war policy and an entirely new estimation of women's political significance and standing in relation to the state.[35] For officers and men in the occupied South, one thing was clear: it was not just "the whole manhood of a nation" that was mobilizing against them.[36] The presumption of women's innocence was becoming increasingly difficult to sustain.

Policy changes emerged from the particulars of military operations all over the battlefield. But the key developments in noncombatant protections in the laws of war came in response to guerilla warfare in the border states of Missouri, Kentucky, Tennessee, and Arkansas. By mid-1862, women there were routinely surfacing in Union military reports on Confederate guerillas.[37] Conditions of warfare in these regions were so murky, relentless, and challenging, and distinctions between enemy soldiers and hostile civilians so impossibly ambiguous, that officers demanded a policy statement to guide the Union response. It is deeply relevant that the request went to General Halleck, who knew the border state conditions so intimately. In fact, as early as December 1861, Halleck had authorized the use of military commissions to try treasonous activity by civilians in Missouri. But there was a great deal of confusion about military tribunals that troubled Halleck, including the legality and practicality of using them to punish treason.

Union military men faced a particular challenge in fighting treasonous activity whether by men or women: they had no way to punish it. In the United States, treason was a very particular crime purposely defined in the Constitution in such a way as to restrict its application. Treason against the United States consisted "only in levying war against them, or in adhering to their enemies, giving them aid and comfort." It purposely excluded any treasonous speech or plans that were not manifest in explicit acts. It set a high bar for proof requiring the testimony of two witnesses in open court to secure conviction. And it was a capital offense to be tried only in federal court in the original jurisdiction of the criminal act. Only forty such cases have been prosecuted over the entire course of US history. At the beginning of the Civil War, indictments were brought regularly but very few went to trial. Convictions were difficult to secure. For Union Army officers in the border states or occupied South, it was not merely difficult but functionally impossible to punish treason. The variety of treasonable activity they faced did not all rise to the level required by the Constitution. But the bigger problem was one of jurisdiction: either the civil courts were not functioning (as in areas governed under military law), or, where they remained open, the cases would go to trial before juries of southern, often openly pro-Confederate men. It was precisely because treason could not be punished under military law that officers like Halleck gradually built up a parallel body of law to try a wide variety of "military offenses" they deemed to be of "a treasonable character."[38] Under the circumstances it is hardly surprising that Halleck, a devotee of the law, sought something more than an *ad hoc* solution. In July 1862, he turned for the first time to Francis Lieber, a professor of law at Columbia College and a known expert on the laws of war. Halleck had known Lieber since early 1862, when Lieber wrote him about the series of lectures on the law of war he was delivering at Columbia College Law School. They became personally acquainted in difficult circumstances soon thereafter, when Lieber sought Halleck's help in finding his son, Hamilton, wounded at the Battle of Fort Donelson while serving under Halleck's command.

Halleck explained the immediate problem to Lieber, that the "rebel authorities claim the right to send men in the garb of peaceful citizens, to waylay and attack our troops, to burn bridges and houses, and to destroy property and persons within our lines," while insisting that they be accorded the same protections of prisoners of war as "ordinary belligerents."[39] He wanted Lieber to establish clear rules on the matter.

In setting Union policy, Halleck's experience in Missouri in the winter of 1861–1862 proved crucial. Among other things it had challenged his antebellum belief in the distinction between guerillas and civilians. When Halleck solicited the memorandum from Lieber,

Union officers under his command were arresting and imprisoning women for their participation in guerilla war.[40] But if this was already a known and troubling element of irregular war, none of it was evident in the document Lieber produced. In August 1862, conventional gender assumptions held. The laws of war lagged perilously behind conditions on the ground in the Civil War.

Lieber's response to Halleck's request, his guerilla paper, did break new ground in the laws of war. It deployed a functional distinction between those who fought like regular soldiers and those who did not, regardless of their official standing and the wearing of uniforms. Unlike Halleck in *International Law*, Lieber distinguished between partisans and guerillas. Authorized partisans were *always* to be extended the protections of the laws of war, he insisted, and treated as prisoners of war when captured. In addition, people who rose up to repel invasion were also entitled to the full benefits of the laws of war, so long as the defenders did so in respectable numbers "and in the yet uninvaded or unconquered portions of the hostile country"—a crucial distinction, it is worth noting, in reference to the border states of the Upper South, which were already under Union military occupation.[41]

But guerillas were a more complicated case because they moved between "occasional fighting and peaceful habits" and used the absence of uniforms to disguise their aims. Thus, Lieber recommended that the "rule be laid down" that guerillas came under the protections of the laws of war when "captured in a fair fight and open warfare." Lieber knew the significance of guerilla war in the border states, where rebel bands worked separately *and* in cooperation with regular Confederate troops. He was willing to extend the protection of law to guerillas who fought openly, but he was merciless when it came to "the spy, the rebel and the conspirator," people particularly dangerous, he said, because they made hostile use of the protections afforded by the modern law of war. These "renewers of war in occupied territory," people who cut telegraph lines, burned bridges, engaged in secret communication across the lines, conveyed military intelligence to the enemy, or supported brigands—all routine activities for women rebels—would find no mercy. Even as Lieber introduced new categories to the laws of war, he was confident he knew who he was dealing with: "The war rebel, as we might term *him*."[42] In August 1862, in the law but not in the war on the ground, enemy women were still irrelevant, a protected class perhaps, but certainly outside war.

There is another striking thing about Lieber's first revision of the laws of war: his guerilla paper purported only to summarize the law with respect to *international* war, that is to say, war between sovereign states. "I do not enter upon a consideration of their application to the civil war in which we are engaged," he wrote. "The application of the laws of war and usages of wars to wars of insurrection or rebellion is always undefined," he insisted stubbornly, and it was not for him to define it.[43] That reluctance to confront the issue directly in front of him would persist in the writing of his famous code four months later, and require the decisive intervention of Henry Halleck, who was by then general-in-chief of the Union armies.

In the six months following the publication of Lieber's memorandum, the challenge of guerilla warfare and the associated problem of enemy women in the occupied South escalated dangerously. Radical innovations on the ground to counter guerilla operations made their way into Union policy and, almost immediately, into Lieber's code. The mode of transmission was a particular order Halleck issued on March 5, 1863, which Lieber, under pressure, would "weave" into the new code of laws.[44] The consequences were enormous for the erosion of the distinction, beginning with its presumption of female innocence.

Halleck's instructions of March 5, 1863 introduced pregnant new terms to the laws of war by insisting on distinctions *among* enemy civilians on the basis of loyalty. Whereas in 1861 he had talked loosely of "treasonous activity," now he talked specifically of "military treason," a new crime punishable under military law. In Halleck's instructions, Union policy was responding first and foremost to local conditions. The March orders encapsulated a host of particular recommendations issued by commanders in the theater of war.

In Missouri, Kentucky, and Tennessee, the pressing issue was "the reign of terror" that Confederate guerillas visited on loyal people and Confederates' deadly coordination of regular and guerilla military campaigns. By November 1862, Halleck rejected the soft "milk and water" policy against rebels in Kentucky and urged "an iron hand" against "domestic traitors." In February 1863, with the Emancipation Proclamation allegedly destroying Union sentiment in Kentucky, and parties of guerillas burning bridges and tearing up railroad lines in support of a Confederate invasion, the fear of cooperation between regular and irregular troops peaked. Then Major General Horatio Wright, he of the "milk and water" approach, adopted a hard line, abandoning the "regular system of warfare" to meet rebel guerilla parties "with their own tactics."[45]

Things were bad in Kentucky and Missouri, but Halleck's instructions emanated most directly from conditions in the area around Murfreesborough, Tennessee, which had been under military occupation since December 1862. There, officers in General William

S. Rosecrans's command of the Army of the Cumberland, men like Major General J. J. Reynolds of the 14th Army Corps, 5th Division, operated with Confederate cavalry officer John Hunt Morgan raiding supply lines in their rear and amid the constant danger of coordinated attacks by rebel guerillas. In February 1863, Reynolds filed a report describing a typical expedition of his troops through a patchwork of territory, Union and Confederate. His men were in great danger, as were the loyal people of Tennessee who tried to attach themselves to his columns for protection. Reynolds had had enough. Conditions, he said, called for the opening of a two-front war against the Confederate military *and* rebel civilians: "The only effectual mode of suppressing the rebellion must be such a one as will conquer the rebellious individuals now at home as well as defeat their armies in the field; either accomplished without the other leaves the rebellion unsubdued." Talk of rebel "inhabitants" and "rebellious individuals" involved Union officers and men in struggles not just with enemy men but with women as well, as the new orders would confirm.[46]

In contrast to Lieber's guerilla paper, Reynolds's call for harsher treatment of rebel civilians generated a policy response notably explicit in its gender terms. The officer who forwarded it up the chain of command was clear: "The conciliatory [approach] has failed," he told General Rosecrans, and a far more rigid policy was called for. "However much we may regret the necessity, we shall be compelled to send disloyal people of *all ages and sexes* to the South, or beyond our lines." Rosecrans added his endorsement and sent the report to the War Department. Two weeks later Halleck issued a lengthy response that would prove decisive in the new laws of war that Francis Lieber was already drafting.[47] In places such as Tennessee it had become a matter of survival for soldiers to make distinctions *between* civilians—

between those who posed a danger and those who did not. Women, they had learned, could pose a clear military danger.

Whatever Union soldiers had once thought, Confederate women left no room for doubt that this was their war. By March 1863, the evidence, and danger, had accumulated. In the Department of the Missouri alone, large numbers of women had been arrested for war crimes, most commonly for disloyal speech, forging permits, sewing rebel flags and uniforms, and running illegal Confederate mail networks. In St. Louis on March 5, one officer reported his discovery of "a large number of women . . . actively concerned in both secret correspondence and in carrying on the business of collecting and distribution of rebel letters." They were the wives and daughters of officers in the rebel service, he emphasized, "avowed and abusive enemies of the government."[48] Amid the steady drip of covert activity behind the lines, women's resistance veered ominously into military espionage. Women smugglers and spies were particularly dangerous. Significant numbers were arrested for passing contraband military goods to the enemy: fifty thousand percussion caps, enough opium allegedly to treat the diarrhea of half of the Confederate Army, two hundred yards of uniform cloth bound for use by rebel officers, and on and on.[49] So many smugglers were arrested that at the beginning of 1863, the Union started to employ female detectives as informants and to search the bodies of women at checkpoints.

Women were also dangerous because of their role in conveying military intelligence. They were caught running rebel spy networks all over the district, including inside Union refugee camps. Several were arrested for clandestinely collecting and reporting information on military installations. One, Anna Johnson, claimed not implausibly to have official rank and pay as a colonel in the Confederate Army for her services as a spy. Another, Jane Ferguson, was also arrested as a spy, accused of conducting a mission for a rebel captain scouting troop numbers at three different Union camps. When apprehended she was still wearing her disguise of a Union soldier's uniform, a particular war crime already outlined by Lieber in his guerilla code.[50] Indeed, it appears that the frequency of the arrest of women smugglers and spies, and the confusion over how to handle such treasonous acts in areas under military occupation (the usual penalty for spies would be execution), was one proximate cause of Halleck's harsh new instructions.

In the kind of people's war waged in the border states, assumptions of women's innocence could prove deadly. It did not take many examples to make the point. In the border states, Union officers routinely targeted women who played essential roles in rebel guerilla networks. There is no evidence that the Union used torture to extract intelligence, as the Confederate Army did, but they did take increasingly harsh measures, subjecting women to trial by military commissions and lengthy terms of imprisonment for harboring guerillas and deserters. In August 1863, after a summer of closely monitoring and making arrests among the mostly female households of guerilla fighters around Independence, Missouri, General Thomas Ewing ordered the forced removal of the entire (and mostly female) population of three counties. Many commanding officers concluded, as did Ewing before his harsh expulsion order, that "one of the greatest difficulties" the military faced was "the constant and correct information which the families of bushwhackers give of every movement the troops make." ("Bushwhackers" was another term for rebel guerillas.) Women were filling a crucial, even systemic role in guerilla action, not just by providing the domestic supply line but also by acting as scouts and spies, turning their households into key outposts in the war.[51]

Union officers arrested women who had gone beyond the provision of logistical support and engaged in direct acts of sabotage. More than a few women were caught cutting telegraph wires, an activity that had plagued the Union war effort since the outset of the war and that was usually conducted in conjunction with the operations of regular Confederate troops. Sarah Jane Smith, a nineteen-year-old, was caught, arrested, and released twice for cutting telegraph wires in the area around Rolla, Missouri. The third time she was sentenced to hang. Her sentence was commuted by order of General Rosecrans to imprisonment for the duration of the war. For the entire length of her imprisonment Smith refused to divulge the names of her collaborators. As in other wars, those kinds of dangerous military activities tended to be the preserve of young women. In Missouri, Union men were forced to conduct a manhunt for Kate Beattie, who launched a raid to free a Confederate officer from a St. Louis prison. Beattie was held in leg irons in solitary confinement before trial. Women also acted routinely as decoys, deploying their gender as a disguise. Three men in Captain James A. Ewing's cavalry troop were killed when they were lured into an ambush by a woman working with a Confederate guerilla band. And yet other women simply rode out with guerillas as full-fledged members. One such woman, a member of William Callahan's notorious band, dressed in male attire and, disguised as "a negro man," participated in armed robberies of Union soldiers and attacks on Union families.[52]

By March 1863, in areas under military occupation and defined by people's war, assumptions of women's innocence virtually collapsed. Neither womanhood nor whiteness was sufficient protection, and that policy crumbled in the face of women's ongoing military activity. By 1863, even racial privilege had reached its limits as Union commanders confronted white Confederate women's systemic role in the conflict and attempted to meet the challenge of people's war.[53]

The abandonment of women's inviolability marked the turn to hard war, just as surely as the emancipation of slaves.[54] As war reached shocking proportions, parties to the conflict on both sides had retained, and only partially surrendered, their deeply held assumptions about women's innocence and their human reluctance to see women as parties to war. The turn to hard war encoded the palpable danger posed by enemy civilians, and soldiers now routinely included women in this category. Union headquarters and field offices responded in increasingly harsh terms. Union prisons filled up with rebels, among them a growing number of women. By the time the war was over, almost 200 women had been subjected to military commission trials for violations of the laws of war; 120 were convicted, and several sentenced to death.[55] Many more faced justice in the provost marshal system, the Union occupation's military police. Most of those women were never tried or imprisoned (thus generally eluding the archival net) but simply arrested, held, and then ordered out of Union-held territory. There is no definitive count or study. But 360 women were arrested and imprisoned by the provost marshal in the St. Louis area alone.[56] The number of women arrested, tried, or imprisoned for treason during the war was not large in the scheme of things.[57] But the steady encounter with women who operated in a military capacity was enough to undermine confidence in their irrelevance or innocence. As Halleck had warned, in the Civil War as in other cases of invasion, all kinds of people took up arms and rendered service in the common defense—even women.

The idea that men make history, mostly by making war, is generally accepted and retaught with each generation. "Warfare," the military historian John Keegan says, "is the one human activity from which women, with the most insignificant exceptions, have always and everywhere stood apart." Women, he says categorically "do not fight."[58] In that erroneous assumption, the Civil War, like the scholarship about war, was no different. Ideas about women's innocence ran deep in military culture and were difficult to revise or renounce. Lingering ambivalence materially shaped events. As civilized soldiers bound by the laws of war, men in the Union Army proved anxiously vulnerable to the charge that they were "making war on women." Nor were they alone in that, evincing a pattern that cuts across wars in the modern period. "The embarrassment is knowing what to do with them," one Union officer bluntly confessed. Women spies were banished repeatedly beyond the lines, only to be picked up again engaged in the same act; prison sentences were commuted, and dangerous women released. In the people's war of the border states, many fit Lieber's definition of the "war rebel," renewers of war in occupied territory. Yet the ultimate penalty for treason was never exacted during the war. Death sentences were handed down to women spies and saboteurs but never executed.[59] Among those who escaped was Clara Judd.

The case of Clara Judd is buried in the voluminous official records of the Civil War, and like so much else that involves women, relegated to the margins, if noticed at all.[60] And yet there is reason to believe it was "one of the little pivots on which the fortunes of a campaign or fate of an army turn," as the arresting officer said.[61] The file of Judd's particularly troubling case landed on General Rosecrans's desk at precisely the moment he turned to Henry Halleck for a tougher policy against disloyal civilians of both sexes, so there is also reason to believe that it materially informed the policy change requested in early February 1863. Rosecrans was personally troubled by the case. Judd was remanded to prison by his orders, and after she was released in August 1863 (without his consent), he continued to track her for the duration of the war, convinced that she was "a spy of the worst description."[62] The Judd case is thus a small but critical historical convergence of the problem of enemy women and the laws of war in the Civil War.

Judd was arrested by army police fifty miles outside Gallatin, Tennessee, on the Monday before Christmas in 1862 on charges of being "a spy as well as a smuggler." She was believed to be working for John Hunt Morgan, a charge seemingly confirmed by the suspicious coordination of their movements. Her arrival in Gallatin coincided precisely with Morgan's strike on Union railroad communications above the town. Judd had aroused suspicion by passing frequently through the lines between Confederate and Union territory. In fact, she was arrested in part on the testimony of a Union informant assigned to follow her, to whom she had positively identified herself as a spy. After Judd's arrest, her case was remanded to the provost judge of the 14th Army Corps.[63]

In the counter insurgency waged by Rosecrans's command, Judd's was not an isolated case. Other women were later sent to prison by his orders. But the Judd case acquired outsize significance. It "created not a little excitement in army circles," Provost Judge John Fitch noted in his memoirs, and was "personally examined by the general commanding and his staff." "The crime was the highest known to military law," Fitch observed, and "the only adequate punishment was death." But, he continued, "the person implicit was a woman and the reverence for the sex which brave men ever feel" meant that it could not be executed. Still, "cases of this kind being of frequent occurrence by females," Fitch said, examples had to be made.[64] On January 13, 1863, Judd was sent to the military prison at Alton, Illinois, "by command of Major-General Rosecrans" to be confined "during the present war or until tried." Judd deployed gender assumptions in her proclamations of innocence, a common strategy evident in the many testimonies women gave when they were court martialed. "I never had anything to do with political affairs, neither do I wish to have," she said—but her words were belied by her movements after she left prison and by her rearrest in November 1863 on direct orders of Rosecrans.[65] Judd seems a classic case of what Lieber had warned about in his definition of the war rebel: noncombatants who employ their protection under the law of war as a dangerous disguise. But this time, the noncombatant was a woman.

The call for a harsh policy in response to the military danger posed by disloyal civilians arose from a convergence of events. But the explicit inclusion of women—and its challenge to "the distinction"—seems to have been entangled specifically with the arrest and imprisonment of Clara Judd. Certainly, her case was the escalation point, the moment between January and March 1863 when local conditions in Tennessee materially informed the new laws of war on which Lieber was beginning to work. On February 18, 1863, General Rosecrans sent the reports of his subordinates to General-in-Chief Henry Halleck. Two weeks later came the response.

Halleck's March 5 orders took direct aim at the distinction and its predicate assumptions of gender and innocence. Throughout Halleck spoke explicitly in terms of the "laws and usages of war," amending them radically even as he claimed only to deploy their extant forms. In those instructions Halleck not only approved the "more rigid treatment of all disloyal persons within the lines"; he further urged the adoption of strict distinctions between noncombatants on the basis of loyalty, thus winnowing the "truly loyal . . . who favor or assist the Union forces . . . [and] should receive the protection of our arms," from the "class known in military law as non-combatants," who in "a civil war like that now waged" should be assumed "to sympathize with the rebellion rather than with the Government." Having thus jettisoned the assumption of innocence, Halleck moved decisively against the co-requisite entitlement of noncombatant protection. Here he broke new ground in the laws of war, instructing officers in the army of the United States to pursue as "war rebels"—a term introduced by Lieber in the guerilla code—and "military traitors"—an entirely new category—those noncombatants in occupied territory caught rising in arms or giving information to the enemy. Such people, Halleck said, incur the penalty of death. He left no doubt that he meant to include women. Parties found to be engaged in "military treason," he instructed, "not only forfeits all claim to protection, but subjects *himself or herself* to be punished either as a spy or military traitor, according to the character of the particular offense." The particular dangers posed by enemy women had, finally, become manifest and explicit. When it came to military treason there would be no distinction of sex. In explicitly gendered language, the ominous category of military treason or "war traitor" was introduced. Appearing first in field orders, the concept would almost immediately be woven into the new, official laws of war the Union government adopted.[66]

It was a momentous development. The idea that noncombatant protections were never absolute, that even women could surrender immunities, had been part of the laws of war for centuries. But Halleck's instructions of March 5, 1863, radically amended the law by introducing troubling new categories that eroded the crucial distinction between combatant and civilian and the associations of gender and innocence on which the laws of war rested. It is surely worth noting, given how explicit Halleck was about women's accountability for treason, that he did so based on precisely the idea of "war treason" that historians and theorists have long assumed to be the creation of Lieber and his famous code.[67] The turn to hard war and the new laws of war that came with it encoded a particular history with enemy women.[68] Even as Lieber was writing his code, gender had proven an unreliable material basis for the distinction, and the scope of allowable violence had expanded dangerously.

On December 17, 1862, Lieber had received official orders that appointed him to a board to write a new code of war.[69] The code was published on April 24, 1863, and widely distributed quickly thereafter, including in a pocket-sized version. It entered history as General Orders No. 100, "Instructions for the Government of Armies of the United States in the Field." It was a code perfectly expressing the new Union resolve to wage hard war, the decision to take the war directly to slaveholders by the emancipation and military enlistment of their slaves, and to civilians by revoking the immunity of those whose treason sustained the Confederate cause. It was a philosophy succinctly expressed in article 29, "The more vigorously wars are pursued, the better it is for humanity. Sharp wars are brief." And in articles 14 and 15, which offered a definition of "military necessity" so permissive it authorized virtually any action "indispensable for securing the ends of the war," including those against traditionally protected parties. This was the first definition of military necessity ever offered in the laws of war. Hence, while the code embraced the principle of noncombatant protection "in modern regular wars," and accepted and even extended the conventional idea of women as a specially protected class in war—most famously in article 37, which prohibited rape—it also gave wide latitude to commanders about the extent and kind of violence allowable in pursuit of military advantage. Generations of international lawyers have seen it as a great humanitarian document, but, as John Witt has argued, "Its warrant for violence was daunting."[70]

And indeed, there is little quarrel among historians either about the historical significance of the code or its most radical features.

General Order No. 100—Adjutant-General's Office.

INSTRUCTIONS

FOR THE

GOVERNMENT OF ARMIES

OF THE

UNITED STATES,

IN THE

FIELD.

PREPARED BY

FRANCIS LIEBER, LL.D.,

AND REVISED BY A BOARD OF OFFICERS.

NEW YORK:

D. VAN NOSTRAND, 192 BROADWAY.

1863.

General Orders No. 100, *Instructions for the Government of Armies of the United States, in the Field*, 1863 *Instructions for the Government of Armies of the United States, in the Field* (New York: D. Van Nostrand, 1863). Digitized by the Internet Archive in 2007 with funding from Microsoft Corporation, contributed by University of California Libraries, https://archive.org/details/governarmies00unitrich.

Lieber's code is widely recognized as a landmark in the history of international law precisely because it fundamentally redefined the distinction between combatant and civilian on which the whole body of law is founded. Lieber's code proved such a radical historical break because it responded to the conditions of modern war. Lieber was an advocate of hard war. "The shorter war is, the better; and the more intensively it is carried on, the shorter it will be," he wrote as early as 1861. "It must never be forgotten that the whole country is always at war with the enemy ... and there is in the case of war—especially in a free country where no 'cabinet wars' are carried on—by no means that distinction between soldiers and citizens which many people either believe to exist or desire to."[71] In advance of the total wars of the twentieth century, his code confronted the obvious difficulty of observing the distinction between combatants and civilians in an era in which women were part of "the people"—the population—waging war. With Lieber, the protections accorded civilians in war were eroded, even eviscerated, and the balance between immunity and accountability shifted radically. Geoffrey Best says Lieber's code introduced the idea of "the Civilian as Enemy." Witt says it "tore down the wall between soldiers and non-combatants that Enlightenment jurists had tried to build." By way of illustration, historians point consistently to the definition of military necessity offered in section V, and especially to section X, "Insurrection—Civil War—Rebellion," which introduced a fundamental distinction between loyal and disloyal civilians, and instructed commanders to throw the full burden of war on the disloyal. In section X, the idea of "war treason"—a new concept in the laws of war—is fully articulated and expressed: "Armed or unarmed resistance by citizens of the United States against the lawful movement of their troops is levying war against the United States, and is therefore treason." Helen Kinsella points specifically to articles 155 and 156 of section X, in which the condition of the noncombatant's loyalty appears, as key to the code's radical erosion of civilian immunity. "General Orders 100 invokes gender and civilization to serve the distinction in ways familiar from the past," she concludes, but "the referents of *innocence* now also include loyalty as well as inoffensiveness or ignorance evident in prior uses."[72]

The various drafts of Lieber's code are available in his personal papers. And if, as these scholars argue, section X and articles 155 and 156 bear the weight of historical significance more than any other in the code, it is surely relevant that the document as originally written by him included neither of those articles—indeed contained no section on civil war at all.

The idea for the code originated with Lieber himself. He lobbied Halleck about the need for a "set of rules and definitions, providing for the most urgent cases, occurring under the law and Usages of War and on which Articles of War are silent." Even as Halleck secured Lieber's appointment, their underlying policy motives were never the same. Lieber tried to address Halleck "the jurist, no less than the soldier" about the need for a code on matters as diverse as the "Spy, Paroling, Capitulation, Prisoners of War etc." Lieber was ambitious, and his concerns were largely professional and focused on rules governing war between sovereign states, as was conventional in international law. He was determined to challenge the dominance of Vattel and also the American Henry Wheaten, so often cited as an expert on international law. But Halleck responded less as a jurist than as a soldier, or rather the general-in-chief, far more concerned with the particular civil war he was fighting than with generic international warfare. In tapping Lieber to write the code, Halleck's main concern was to get a legal structure that legitimized the use of military courts and martial law in the occupied South. He wanted to force Congress to recognize that there was a "common law of war" so that he could get "tribunals" and punish offenses, including treason, under it. That "is all we want," he wrote his friend. As it turned out, he got much more—and much less—than he asked for.[73]

Lieber started on the document around the end of December 1862. By February 20, 1863, he had completed a first draft, which he printed and sent to a number of people including Halleck. "Nothing of the kind exists in any language," he wrote the general. "I had no guide, no ground work, no text book," but was "laying down, for the first time such a code, where nearly everything was floating."[74] But if all was amorphous and free-floating, Lieber nonetheless brought to the task some fundamental beliefs, none more passionately held than the unity and sovereignty of the nation. It was one of Lieber's core principles that "the National type is the *normal* type of Government of our race in modern times." It was a statement he made virtually verbatim throughout his long life. It goes some way toward explaining why the first draft of his code treated only international war: for Lieber, international law governed war only between sovereign states. Indeed, to him, sovereignty had meaning exclusively in the international sense. "The United States are sovereign with reference to other independent or sovereign States, and that is all," he once explained. There could be no such thing as sovereignty of individual US states (South Carolina, for example), as was claimed by secessionists and ensconced in the Confederate Constitution. The very idea of it he denounced as a species of "hyper-Calhounistic remarks" and a relic of the barbarism of slavery.[75]

There was a great deal that was new in Lieber's first draft of the code. It already included the expansive definition of military necessity mandated by hard war. And it included many crucial articles on emancipation and black soldiers.[76] But, strikingly, as with the guerilla pamphlet six months before, Lieber avoided entirely the issue immediately in front of him: the code as first drafted contained no section X on Civil War. "I have said nothing on Rebellion and Invasion of our country with reference to the Treatment of our own citizens by the commanding General," he told Halleck in the letter accompanying the first draft. It fell, he said, outside the charge of "our board."[77]

Halleck was not amused. The general-in-chief's response is preserved in Lieber's papers, and his notes and emendations were decisive in shaping the final form of the code, and its historical significance for the distinction as now understood. Across draft article 19 (what became article 37), which accorded amplified protections for noncombatants and "especially women," Halleck wrote, "I think it would be well to point out the military status of different classes, *vide my letter to General Rosecrans, March 5.*" The damage to the distinction was done right there. The reference to Halleck's orders embedded war as it was waged against enemy civilians and enemy women in Tennessee in the laws of war thereafter. The location of Halleck's marginal note on the text is weighted with meaning. It indicates beyond a doubt that he understood his orders, and the condition of loyalty they introduced, as an explicit limit on noncombatant protections and a rejection of the *a priori* conjunction of women and innocence on which they were usually based. Halleck's dissatisfaction with the draft code was evident. On the back cover of the printed draft he wrote this preemptory note: "The Code, to be complete and to be more useful at the present time should embrace civil war as well as war between states or distinct sovereignties. The attention of Dr. Lieber & the Board is particularly called to this subject." Just in case there was any confusion, he added, "I would respectfully suggest that the question of risings en masse be more fully discussed. Risings en masse not authorized by the law of the land, or by special military authority are not deemed lawful by European juris consults." In seeking a code for the war that they were actually fighting, the practical needs of the military man informed those of the scholar of international law. Witt says that Lieber sought to write a new code for the age of democracy, mass armies, and people's wars. To the extent that he did, it is clear he was forced to the task by Halleck.[78]

Francis Lieber would eventually write a code of war for civil wars as well as international ones, but he was never comfortable with the task. The prolix version he ultimately drafted—cut to the nub in the final document—included a preamble full of disclaimers about shoehorning civil war into the law of nations. Still, after he received Halleck's response, he immediately got a copy of Halleck's orders of March 5, 1863, and incorporated them into the revised code, including the radically new idea of war treason. "The contents of your letter to Genl Rosecrans came in much better at the end where I, now, speak of Civil War, than where you point to it by marginal note," he informed Halleck as he was rewriting. On March 23, he sent Halleck a new draft explicitly acknowledging his debt: "I have added some sections to the portion of the Code which treats of insurrection, Rebellions etc—sections in which I have been motivé by your letter to Gen Rosecrans." Halleck whittled that draft back considerably, but the crucial articles remained, concrete, material traces of his original orders in the new laws of war.[79]

In the end, Halleck's orders of March 5, 1863—its terms of loyalty as a condition of civilian immunity and the crime of military treason on which they were based—became permanent in General Orders No. 100. But even as the debt of the first document to the second was noted, the original unity of its key concepts and their historical context were lost, including the particular challenge of enemy women that was so evident in Halleck's formulation. That is because, in the final version of the code, Lieber split the orders into two parts, embedding the definition of war treason in section V and the distinction between civilians on the basis of loyalty at the end of section X. Thus section V, articles 90, 91, and 92, defined the war traitor and specified the punishment: "If the citizen or subject of a country... invaded or conquered gives information to his own government... or to the army of his government, he is a war traitor and death is the penalty of his offense." And section X, articles 155 and 156, set the new terms of the distinction, at least as it applied in civil wars. Article 155 repeated the conventional distinction between combatants and noncombatants ("unarmed citizens of the hostile country") and then proceeded, per Halleck, to eviscerate it: The military commander of the legitimate government in a war of rebellion distinguished "between the loyal citizen... and the disloyal citizen," and further subdivided the disloyal between those who simply sympathize and those who "without taking up arms," give "aid and comfort" to the enemy. Article 156 codified the protection of the persons and property of those known to be loyal while instructing the commander to "throw the burden of the war... on the disloyal citizens," and to subject "noncombatant enemies" to a "stricter police" than they have "to suffer in regular war." What remains of the distinction after article 157 is difficult to discern: "Armed or unarmed resistance by citizens of the United States against the lawful movement of their troops is levying war against the United States, and is therefore treason." The sentence in Halleck's orders that explicitly included enemy women in the scope of the law—the pointed use of the male and female pronouns "himself and herself"—was dropped. Substantively, women's accountability as war traitors was already provided for: section V, article 102, stated that "the law of war like the criminal law regarding other offenses, makes no difference on account of the difference of sexes, concerning the spy, the war-traitor or the war-rebel." But what that had to do with the Civil War or new conditions of loyalty or innocence imposed on civilians was no longer discernible from the text. In splitting the orders and excising the particular reference to women, Lieber changed our reading of the code.[80]

The problem of defining military necessity runs through the law of war from the sixteenth to the early twenty-first century. And as is so often the case, in Lieber's code the conduct of the army toward women is seen to epitomize the problem. In reference to them the code defines the scope of violence the law allows and the imperative of restraint it must enact. In 1863, in the context of the American Civil War, we see in the code Lieber wrote the pull of the same two forces evident in Union policy on the ground: are women innocent parties to be protected in war or are they the enemy? To put it another way, who are to be recognized as noncombatants and what protections must be accorded them? What Lieber added to the laws of war is not in doubt. With Lieber's code the protections accorded civilians in war were eroded, even eviscerated, and the balance between immunity and accountability shifted radically. His code changed the answer to the question about what armies can legitimately do to noncombatants in war and the broad scope of violence thereby established. Behind his reformulation lay the experience of the Civil War and the bitter lessons it taught, including that women are not simply victims of war or prize booty in it. In any rising en masse, they are part of the people who militarily resist. Women do fight, especially (but not only) when their country is invaded. In the Spanish Peninsular War (the touchstone of all thinking about modern people's war), in the American Civil War, in the Italian wars of unification, in the Spanish Civil War, in the Algerian War—the same lessons are taught, reluctantly learned, and promptly forgotten.[81] Women are not outside war. They are not passive witnesses to their people's struggles.

This focus on enemy women is, admittedly, counterintuitive. The great preponderance of feminist scholarship on women and war, international law, and human rights reflects a deep commitment to the principle of protection and, as such, mostly focuses on the adoption and enforcement of protective measures and resolutions, particularly with respect to sexual violence. Lieber's code figures centrally in this literature as well, usually with a focus on article 37, the "first 'modern' effort to prohibit rape in war." The way women participate in conflicts as active combatants, fighters, or members of military resistance movements figures far less prominently, although it is a critical historical dimension, particularly because of its implications for "the distinction."[82]

By 1863, it was impossible to distinguish between combatants and civilians on the basis of gender alone. Loyalty was now a key condition, for men and women alike. The damage to the distinction—the disruption of the pairing of women and innocence and the related erosion of civilian immunity—had roots in the struggle of the Union Army with enemy women. The collapse of the gender assumption that had long undergirded the category of the civilian thus was a cause, and not just a consequence, of the weakening of the distinction in Lieber's code. It was a gendered history, obscured but manifest in the laws of war.

The publication of General Orders No. 100 was only the beginning of the controversy over it. The code had a long life at home and abroad. In the Civil War, the Union Army faced a situation that would be common in the wars of the twentieth century, in which it was impossible to distinguish between combatants and civilians on the basis of gender alone. The Union's harsh measures against enemy women suggest that the recognition of women as enemy combatants or resistance fighters, which eventually rendered the distinction "immaterial," did not await the world wars of the twentieth century or the post-1945 wars of national liberation such as the Algerian War. In the long arc of war, the blurring of civilian and combatant was already a crucial feature of the American Civil War in the mid-nineteenth century.[83]

The code's harsh formulations on war rebels and military traitors were used by US Army officers against Filipino resistance fighters in the Spanish-American War. It was not replaced as the standard set of instructions for the US Army until 1914.[84] Lieber's influence on the international law of war was even more long-lasting, not least because his code was adapted by European jurists such as Johann Bluntschli and the Russian Fedor Frederick Martens. General Orders No. 100 became the template for resolutions adopted by the Brussels Conference in 1874, and the Hague Conventions of 1899 and 1907.[85] International lawyers might continue to celebrate the code as a great humanitarian document. But that view has taken hold in places far removed in time and place from its original field of operation. Indeed, in 1870, when one of Lieber's French correspondents, the political theorist Édouard Laboulaye, wrote an introduction to a French edition of Lieber's code, it was the powerful new scope of state power he celebrated, not its humanitarianism. "These instructions are a masterpiece," he wrote. "It is no small accomplishment to have established right within the empire of force by placing the uses and even the excesses of war under yoke of the law." Laboulaye had watched with great interest as Lieber hammered out the code, convinced of its importance to France's *nouveaux liberaux* (new liberals). What it offered, Laboulaye thought, was a project of democratic imperium so new that it served as a model of modern governance for liberal European colonial powers such as the French in Algeria: by marrying national sovereignty to the advancement of individual liberty and rights, it gave France all the moral authority of the republic *and* the power necessary to govern its colonies.[86]

Lieber's code was at once a testament to the American political tradition of using law to constrain state power and to expand it. The code, after all, was a set of instructions written to govern the operations of armies in the midst of a brutal civil war for the nation's existence. But if that was one posited relationship between law and power, the code's transnational and enduring utility and relevance followed from another, equally important part of the American political tradition: the tendency to make law a means of claiming new powers. For the strong states of Europe waging their own wars of occupation in the 1870s, Lieber's code was a brilliant model because of how he used law not to constrain power but to *create* it—to make unprecedented claims of military power lawful for the states who chose to use them. Section X, with its harsh occupiers' code, was especially salient.[87]

In the United States and the Confederate States of America, the damage to the distinction was recognized immediately. Questions of what humanity was owed in war and what the laws of war required of armies emerged immediately upon the code's adoption, and focused precisely, and predictably, on the protection of women and children. That issue was the substance of the Confederate response to the code itself, and it erupted again repeatedly over the legality of General William Tecumseh Sherman's actions in his military campaign in Georgia and South Carolina in 1864 and 1865.[88]

The official Confederate response to the adoption of General Orders No. 100 conveyed shock at its assault on time-worn and honored practices. Confronted with the code in June 1863, an outraged

James A. Seddon, the Confederate secretary of war, honed in immediately on the main issue: the meaning of the code for "the distinction between the private individual belonging to a hostile country
and . . . its men in arms." Indeed, Seddon charged the Union with
adopting "a barbarous system of warfare on the pretext of a military
necessity," authorizing acts of atrocity and violence that shocked the
moral sense of civilized nations. And while his iteration of that list
included the "Union's employment of a servile insurrection as an in-
strument of war," his denunciation of the code as uncivilized and
immoral was first and foremost about the way it authorized acts of
violence against "non-combatants, and especially the women and
children," not excluding even, he emphasized, bombardment. Seddon
took particular aim at the idea of war treason, attributing its un-
American views to the foreign-born Lieber. "The words war-traitor,
war rebel are not words of an American vocabulary," he said. The use
of martial law to punish treason could be embraced only by one "alien
by nativity to the Constitution, laws and institutions of the United
States," a man like "the German professor" far more familiar with the
ways of "imperial or military despots on the continent of Europe."
Seddon thus repudiated outright any claim to humanitarianism on
the part of the Union, seizing that mantle for the CSA, whose army,
he insisted, continued to abide by international conventions on the
protection of women and children designed to mitigate the destruction or "calamities" of war. The Confederate response was partisan
but not inaccurate. General Orders No. 100 was indeed, as Seddon
charged, a radical departure in the law of war tradition. In pursuing
emancipation as an end of war, and hard war—including against
enemy civilians—as the means, it "reorganized the relationship between justice and humanitarianism," and exposed the Union to charges
of barbarism. Jefferson Davis, the Confederate president, predictably

exploited the propaganda value, denouncing the code as turning "the savage ferocity" of the army against "helpless women and children."[89] Notwithstanding its own violent struggle with enemy women—which included the use of torture—the Confederacy officially embraced the traditional principle of women's innocence.[90] There was little confusion about what was new in the code.

With General Sherman the issue immediately became concrete. More than anyone else it was Sherman who posed the issue of what the new code in fact authorized, both because of his actions and his propensity to defend the legitimacy of his hard-war ways. Sherman had long made his views clear. As he once explained to General Halleck, "We are not only fighting hostile armies but a hostile people" and must make them "feel the hard hand of war, as well as their organized armies." As early as 1862, he was convinced that "the entire South, man, woman and child is against us, armed and determined." Sherman also believed that civil war and rebellion required different rules than regular war; the Union, he said more than once, was fully within its rights to treat the South to the same brutal treatment England had adopted in the occupation of Ireland when that colony was "in a state of revolt." Sherman had studied section X. For the "persistent secessionist," male or female, he advised, "death or banishment" was the answer. Like Halleck, he had no illusions left about the innocence of women.[91] These were the views he brought to his last campaign. It was not just Confederate officials who leveled charges. Lieber kept a very nervous eye on General Sherman and his army as it headed into South Carolina in early 1865. And well he might. God only knows, Lieber wrote Halleck, that South Carolina had earned the deep and bitter hatred the Union Army expressed against it. But Lieber implored everyone who had any say on the matter "to stay the hand of mere ruthless revenge": "no ruthless burning, killing, violating women by the soldiery."[92] What Lieber could not know was that Sherman had the explicit backing of his superiors, including for his decision to force the evacuation of the civilian population of Atlanta. "The conduct of the enemy, and especially of non-combatants and women of the territory which we have heretofore conquered and occupied," justified any policy, however harsh, Halleck had assured Sherman when advised of his intentions.[93] Sherman was fully aware that his actions would "raise a howl against my barbarity & cruelty."[94] He relished the fight.

Lieber's code was Sherman's law, and as Sherman said, he knew "the books." Amid the battle over Atlanta, he and his Confederate counterpart, John Bell Hood, engaged in a vitriolic exchange of letters across the lines about whether the forced evacuation of the city was authorized by the law of war. It was an extraordinary exchange that went to the heart of the matter about what armies are allowed to do to enemy noncombatants in war. Predictably enough, the entire exchange turned on the obligation of armies to protect innocent women and children. The mayor of Atlanta had already attempted to stem the evacuation by pleading the suffering of "poor women." Hood, a West Point man, made the same argument but with repeated references to the international law of war, denouncing the evacuation order as utterly "unprecedented." Sherman's orders, he charged, transcended in "cruelty . . . all acts . . . in the dark history of war— expelling from their homes and firesides the wives and children of a brave people." He denounced Sherman for his "barbarous cruelty" in firing on the city and its inhabitants without prior notice as is "usual in war among civilized nations." Sherman, he said, would answer to the civilized world for his abuse of the common laws of war and the abandonment of his obligation to protect innocent women and children.[95]

The central issue, of course, as all knew, was the distinction, and on the legal matter Sherman gave no quarter: the Union had both "right and law on our side," he insisted, defending his particular actions not just by necessity, as Hood would have liked, but in reference to the new laws of war. "See the books," Sherman told Hood. Indeed, Sherman made a show of his lack of interest in "the humanities of the case." General Hood has "raised the question of humanity," Sherman told General Ulysses S. Grant, but "I am not to be moved by such tricks." Nonetheless, Sherman also, revealingly, defended the reputation of his army in the language of civilization that had long governed the law of war, which is to say in relation to its obligation to protect innocent women and children: "I say it is kindness to these families of Atlanta to remove them now at once from scenes that women and children should not be exposed to." In Atlanta he claimed the right: "God will judge us in good time, and he will pronounce whether it be more humane to fight with a town full of women and children or to remove them in time to places of safety among their own friends and people."[96] It was an extraordinary exchange and a substantive airing of the meaning of Lieber's new code. And indeed, for Sherman and Hood alike, the central question throughout was the extent of allowable violence against civilians, and then and ever since, that was argued first and foremost as a matter of the conduct of the army toward women and children.[97] That, all acknowledged, is how the world would draw the line.

In the American Civil War, as in other regular wars and rebellions of the nineteenth and twentieth centuries, women could and did make war, and armies had to deal with them. In 1863, amid a brutal people's war that started to show the scope of modern warfare, the Lincoln administration rewrote the laws of war in accordance with that new reality. But even so, the cultural power of "the distinction" and its gendered conjunction of women and innocence were not easily abandoned. For parties on both sides of the conflict, the protection of women continued to set the standard of a civilized army and a civilized cause. However fragile, the distinction was always rehabilitated.[98]

There is a great deal at stake in the idea of women's innocence and of noncombatant protection in war. It represents an investment in the gender order itself (in marriage and its hierarchies) as a necessary basis of the public order and in the desire to limit the destructiveness of war. It helps explain the deep reluctance to confront the role of women as participants in war, and the need to forget once the war is over. When it comes to women, the lessons of war, once taught, are promptly and officially forgotten. As was the case after the American Revolution, so after the Civil War, on matters of gender, Thermidor set in.

Frances Lieber himself, ironically, illustrated this pattern of a rush back to orthodoxy. Notwithstanding all he knew about war in the nineteenth century—about the Spanish women fighters celebrated by their nation and forever associated with the Peninsular War; about the women partisans and guerillas in European wars of national liberation and unification; and, not least, about the women guerillas, soldiers, spies, rebels, and war traitors targeted by the Union and his own code of war—Lieber obscured as much as he revealed in the code itself. And in the postwar period, appalled at the demand for women's suffrage in his own state of New York, he stuck willfully to the view that women had played no part in the war except as patriotic "mothers and sisters and daughters." That "there are exceptions" in moments of national emergency, he was willing to admit. But by nature, he insisted still, women belonged to the realm of marriage and the family, not politics or the state.[99]

Neither Lieber nor anyone else could restore entirely the antebellum gender order. Battles over the legal and political status of women intensified in the postbellum years. With a women's rights movement behind them, activists led by Elizabeth Cady Stanton and Susan B. Anthony harbored real hope that they could convert a new public rationale of service and sacrifice into the vote, or some concretely expanded set of women's rights. They failed, but it was not an entirely unreasonable thought. Slave emancipation provoked a process of constitutional revision so fundamental it was difficult to constrain its meanings for marriage.[100] Yet, as so often before, in the Civil War era, radical political change ran aground on the shoals of gender. If anything, the emancipation of 4 million men, women, and children only intensified the value of marriage as a tool of public policy. How else could the federal government absolve itself of responsibility for the welfare of all those dependents? War breathed new life into the old republican paradigm of the citizen-soldier. African American men, so it was said, earned freedom, citizenship, and the right to vote by virtue of their military service to the nation. Among the freedmen's new rights were the right to a wife and the powers of a husband and a father. The American Civil War did not just advance the struggle for women's rights: it erected powerful new impediments to any serious reconceptualization of women's political identity and standing in the nation.

In the end, then, the case of enemy women and the laws of war in the Civil War compels us to contend with the larger historical problem of women and war: about how much of that past is disowned—or rendered exceptional—when it is in fact foundational. In the face of all the evidence, Lieber reconstructed the liberal idea of women as passive witnesses to a history made by men. That makes it all the more important to insist on the other history of women, the one he would not own up to but which materially shaped the laws of war by his hand into the twenty-first century.

2

The Story of the Black Soldier's Wife

A little more than a year into the war, as Abraham Lincoln actively contemplated emancipation and members of the 37th US Congress fought over the wisdom of freeing enslaved men and enlisting them as soldiers, a strange debate developed in the Capitol about the existence and claims of the "slave wife." An unlikely subject for US senators, but there it was: a New York senator had introduced a provision that "when any man or boy of African descent" renders military service to the US government, "he, his mother, his wife and children, shall forever thereafter be free."[1] No sooner had the black soldier been imagined than the black soldier's wife materialized in Congress. The subjects emerged into history together, produced at the same revolutionary juncture.

The debate might seem an unremarkable development in the rapidly unfolding history of the Civil War, except that, legally, there was no such thing as an enslaved man's "wife."[2] Since the passage of laws of maternal descent in the 1660s, enslaved couples had been denied the right of marriage, and their families constituted on a different legal footing. That Congress created such a figure was at once testimony to the transformative properties of people's war and the centrality of marriage to the domestic political order—including, and perhaps especially, in a moment of crisis.[3] Indeed, the necessity of recognizing enslaved women as wives was the outcome of a fraught and consequential encounter between the Union Army and enslaved African American women, both fugitives and refugees, who were attempting to seize their freedom in the chaos of war. Flooding into Union lines and camps by the thousands and attaching themselves to the rear of armies as they moved, the women posed a critical logistical challenge to the armies in the field. If Union officers and soldiers came to see the utility of African American men as laborers and soldiers, the same could not be said of the masses of women and children who also sought refuge with the army.

The debate over the Second Confiscation Act and the Militia Act is but one moment when the matter of enslaved women's status—and, more broadly, gender and emancipation—erupted unwittingly in a process pursued in the context of war. The sudden materialization of the black soldier's wife in June 1862 points to one crucial but little noticed pattern in the history of nineteenth-century slavery, not just in the United States but across the western hemisphere: the repeated recourse to marriage as an organizing principle of state-sponsored emancipations.

In the United States, emancipation came with war and the competition for black soldiers, and marriage was woven deeply into emancipation policy, although historians have largely overlooked it. As they contemplated the emancipation of 4 million enslaved people, military men and politicians turned again and again to the institution of marriage and the heterosexual, patriarchal family to impose order on a massive, chaotic process. From the earliest moments of the war, when Union officers construed the slaves in rebellion as male and the women fugitives as their wives, marriage was part of the basic template of federal emancipation policy wherever it appeared. Nor did that emphasis ever wane. From the earliest glimmer of possibility in coastal Virginia in May 1861 to the formal constitutional codification in the Thirteenth Amendment, federal policymakers relied centrally on marriage to shape the terms of slave emancipation. Looking toward the postwar world, the act establishing the Bureau of Refugees, Freedmen, and Abandoned Lands adopted marriage as the indispensable form for the new population to be governed when it referred to "destitute and suffering refugees and freedmen and their wives and children."[4] During the Civil War, the significance of the marital regime, and the normative dependency of wives, for the political life of the nation became very clear.[5]

The attempt to govern African American refugees and freedwomen within marriage, as wives, was a highly consequential solution, especially for the women themselves. It was also an impractical one, undermined by history itself. The register of marriages that Union chaplains kept at Vicksburg, Mississippi, with its long, heartbreaking list of previous relationships ended by "Force," conveys the trauma of slavery and violence that shaped African American families over generations, when enslaved people lacked the civil right of marriage. There were black soldiers' wives during the Civil War: women married by law or custom to enlisted men. Against great odds and with limited success, they fought to secure recognition of those relationships and lay claim to their ostensible benefits. But there were many other enslaved women flooding into Union lines who did not fit the description: women who were not married to soldiers; women who had no partner and came with their children or other family members, or in groups of fugitives from one plantation or neighborhood; and others who had once been married but had lost their husbands to the slave trade, the war, or the diseases that ravaged refugee and army camps.

Indeed, whether married or not, enslaved women occupied a singular position in the history of the Civil War and emancipation, all forced to pursue their own struggle—for survival itself; for destruction of their masters' claims; and for recognition, status, and rights as free people—despite a military emancipation policy indifferent, and even hostile, to their efforts.[6] Their struggle was only ever partly and poorly aligned with state purposes and goals.

The idea that every enslaved woman was a particular soldier's wife was an elaborate and powerful fiction embedded in the Union government's evolving approach to emancipation. But it is also an idea stubbornly embedded in the historiography, an example of the baking-in of official categories that characterizes literatures dependent on state archives.[7] If the dominant national narrative used to be that President Abraham Lincoln freed the slaves, decades of painstaking social historical work have restored the slaves themselves to the center of that narrative.[8] The idea that slaves earned emancipation and citizenship by military service now occupies the center of Civil War and Reconstruction literature, with the black soldier elevated as the emblematic figure in the process. Perhaps no group of historians has made this case more powerfully than the editors of the Freedmen and Southern Society Project, who have published multiple volumes of documentary evidence on which such a case can be made. "Throughout the slave states," they argue, "black enlistment and slave emancipation advanced together and, indeed, became inseparable. . . . Fighting and dying for the Union advanced the claims of black men and women to the rights and privileges of full citizenship." It is a powerful narrative, but one that obscures many questions about gender and emancipation. Who can fight and die for the Union? The implications are clear: slave women were liberated by their men. Sometimes the argument is explicit, as in the chronology of men's flight to Union lines, their enlistment in the army or navy, and their daring raids back into Confederate territory to "liberate their wives and children." More often it is grammatically implicit in the heroic narrative of slaves (who could only be men) who fled to Union lines, demonstrated the value of their military labor or service, and made emancipation a matter of military necessity.[9] In that now standard account, slave men took the martial route to emancipation, and slave women the marital one. In other words, women got freedom secondhand, by way of marriage and in relation to their husbands' rights.[10]

Whatever the merits of the new narrative, and they are considerable, its simplifications distort. And it is surely worth noting that they distort precisely along the lines of Union military emancipation policies themselves. These policies attempted to govern enslaved women as wives, overlooking the extent to which both men *and* women fought to destroy slaveholders' claims on them as property and to establish themselves as free, self-possessing people. The now-extensive body of feminist literature on enslaved women and emancipation in the United States tells that history, as does the broader literature on gender and emancipation in the hemisphere. Although it has not yet made much of a dent in the prevailing political narrative, this body of work definitively establishes that women played central roles in plantation insurgencies during the Civil War; that women and men both worked to destroy slavery and the Confederacy, and to advance the Union cause; that women were recognized as rebels and leaders on plantations and as the "heads" of slave rebel gangs murderously pursued by Confederate scouts; and that planters, Confederate guerillas, and the military did not spare women from their retributive violence.[11] All of this we now know. Nonetheless, by the time any of the women made it to Union lines, the inexorable logic of the military state—its relentless focus on men of military age—had prefigured and constrained women's identity, just as it would shape the subsequent Civil War archive and history. If slave men were potential soldiers, then women were a burden and a problem, in military policy and elsewhere.

Slave emancipation was finally embraced as "a military necessity" as the Emancipation Proclamation declared.[12] It thus evolved as a specifically *military* policy, designed in response to an incrementally escalating war. Crucially, in the United States, as in many other places across the Americas in the nineteenth century, the process of emancipation unfolded in war. From the American War of Independence to which the "first" US emancipation was tied, to the last, Brazilian surrender of slavery (1888) in the aftermath of the Paraguayan War, to virtually everything in between—Saint-Domingue, the Spanish-American Wars of Independence, the American Civil War, and the Ten Years' War in Cuba—in every single major case, except for the British colonies, slaves fought for and won their independence in the context of war.[13] It was in this context that slave men became particular objects of state interest, and "able bodied men of military age" the focus of intense competition between warring states for political loyalty and military service. In this respect, the American Civil War was hardly unique. In the United States, military service and emancipation were temporally and causally linked, just as manhood and citizenship would be in the war's aftermath.

Now that we so commonly think of "slaves" as earning emancipation by military service, it is all the more urgent and important that we ask about the implications for women of an emancipation accomplished in war. US historians see emancipation as something secured not by "great documents that announced the end of chattel bondage" but by a protracted, highly contingent process in which the enslaved themselves "became the prime movers in securing their own liberty."[14] But this process over four years of war was not just contingent on administrative reluctance, regional particularities, proximity to Union troops, or any number of random circumstances, as the literature currently emphasizes, but everywhere contingent on gender itself. Where military service emerged as a path to emancipation, enslaved men's and women's opportunities to claim the status of free people differed fundamentally, to such an extent that we might think of them as taking distinct routes altogether. The relationship between military service and the gender patterns of emancipation was fundamental— emphatically not incidental—to the way the process unfolded in the United States.

The story of the black soldier's wife highlights the association of marriage and emancipation, and newly illuminates the gender logic undergirding wartime policies already exhaustively described in the literature in the United States. But it also focuses attention on a population—enslaved women—written into those policies as dependent parties, irrelevant to the making of history, but whose existential struggle to define a new future in fact forced an expansion of the cramped perimeters of military emancipation at every turn. Marriage and the administration of slave women as wives was the solution to the problem of fugitive women and dependency most often reached for in federal policy. It is striking how little scholarly attention this has inspired outside feminist circles, especially in a field that subjects the most minute elements of policy to exhaustive study. But the significance of the gender history can hardly be denied, either for the women who had to navigate the narrow terrain of freedom that it opened, or for the history of emancipation that we are still writing.

The story of the black soldier's wife does not start in in the American Civil War. To tell it you have to begin with the French colony of

Saint-Domingue, in the late eighteenth century. For more than fifteen years, war consumed the island and the whole of the Caribbean. This was a multifaceted struggle—among free colored men, insurgent slaves, planters, and, after 1793, when Britain declared war, among France, Spain, and Britain, in a war of imperial competition.[15]

Much of the subsequent history of gender and emancipation, and the foundational case of emancipation in war, emerged here. As early as 1790, some parties in the revolutionary struggle in Saint-Domingue moved to arm and train their own slaves, most notably, the free colored colonists (*gens de couleur*). Events in Paris, and especially decrees of the Constitutional Assembly in 1791 that extended voting rights to qualified mulattoes, had emboldened them in their demands for equal citizenship.[16] A much greater number of slaves, however, armed themselves in the north of the island in 1791, in the historic revolt of enslaved men and women against planters, slavery, and the French republican state intent on preserving it. By the end of 1791, after this slave revolt, black leaders had built substantial slave armies that allied with already existing bands of fugitive slaves (called maroons). From this position of strength, self-proclaimed black generals negotiated the terms of their service with contending European powers, including the Spanish (invading from the other half of the island), the French republican forces scrambling to hold the colony, and, after 1793, the English.

In early negotiations with French republican civil commissioners in late 1791, black generals demanded freedom for themselves and four hundred of their followers.[17] The deal would have obligated them to force the remainder of their own insurgents—presumably both men and women—back into plantation labor. Even that limited deal was refused. By late 1792, facing French republican forces allied with *gens de couleur* in the project of restoring slavery on the island, leaders of the biggest slave armies in the North cut deals with the Spanish in exchange for supplies and official recognition of black soldiers' freedom. If they negotiated any terms for women and other members of their families and kin groups, historians have not noted them.

In these early years of the Haitian Revolution, as it is now called, universal emancipation was an unthinkable goal, liberty at issue only in the most militarily delimited way and available only to men directly under arms—and not even to all of them.[18] Two years after the slave insurrection, insurgent leaders had massive numbers of enslaved men under arms (Georges Biassou had at least six thousand and Jean-François almost as many).[19] But many more men and women still lived on plantations, in maroon bands in the hills, or in the British-occupied zone, and the only new route to emancipation—military service— was open solely to men.

In June 1793, Léger-Félicité Sonthonax, one of the civil commissioners sent by the French Republic, was facing a coup by the governor-general of the colony. He made a desperate bid for the loyalty and military service of the mass of slave men. He offered liberty to all slave insurgents who would fight for the republic. The timely arrival of reinforcements under the control of two black generals and the sack of Le Cap turned the tide, emboldening Sonthonax to extend the offer. He issued a proclamation in Creole and French that promised freedom "to the womenfolk of black warriors as long as they were prepared to go through a Republican marriage ceremony."[20] These were the terms, in a highly militarized context, by which slave women, including insurgents, could negotiate freedom.

Marriage and patriarchal authority were central to the French republican emancipation policy, as they would be fifty years later in the American Civil War. Historian Elizabeth Colwill notes that because the state compensated owners for slave soldiers freed, the emancipation of women "took the form of a purchase (indemnity) that transferred women slaves from the hands of their masters to those of their husbands through the intervention of the Republic." The difficulties of access to that provision—not least because slave women did not possess the right to enter contracts, and notaries often refused to register their marriages—was only one of its limitations, although one that would recur in the United States. More broadly, whites and colored men across the political spectrum were constructing the slaves in insurrection as male and forging a new model of the republican citizen-soldier that would long constrain the meanings of freedom for women.[21]

For French radicals, especially Sonthonax, emancipation was a principled act but one shaped irreducibly by war. As such, it touched men directly and women only indirectly, by virtue of their marriage to the republic's soldiers. When Toussaint Louverture took his army over to the French following the decree, he preceded it with a call to his "brothers" to unite with him in the fight for liberty and equality in Saint-Domingue.[22] Born in war, it could seem sometimes as if the nation itself was male.[23] Even after Sonthonax, backed up by legislators in Paris, declared *all* slaves free, the reach of that administrative decree depended entirely (as would the Emancipation Proclamation in the United States) on military victory. For years women in the British-occupied zone had no route (not even marriage) to emancipation, and women in the North would struggle to document their own and their children's freedom through marriage and baptismal records, so tenuous was their hold on that status.[24]

Notwithstanding the great document—the first universal emancipation decree in history—there was nothing final about slave emancipation in Saint-Domingue in 1794. Until 1803, when Saint-Domingue's black armies defeated Napoleon and the French, slavery was still a threat (and indeed restored on other French islands), emancipation was still not secured, and military service of men was still required as part of the extended process by which Saint-Domingue's enslaved people finally could call themselves free. In Louverture's long struggle to prevent the restoration of slavery and move the island toward independence, this element of "martial masculinity" never disappeared. Writes Colwill, "his promotion of marriage, Christianity and militarism was not just a discursive strategy: it served as the foundation of citizenship, social order, and morality," a key to his "practice of state building—and even nation-building—within the French empire."[25]

As with other places where emancipation was secured in war—which is to say, most places in the late 1700s and 1800s—emancipation in Saint-Domingue came in stages and was extended first to those willing to perform military service in defense of the republic. The gendered dimensions of freedom for women were concrete and real, even if in Saint-Domingue, as in the United States, historical narratives scarcely recognize this.[26] In Saint-Domingue and Haiti, the militarization of society meant that for years, men were siphoned off to the army and women forcibly returned to the plantations as part of the colonial and national project of resurrecting the plantation sector of the export economy. It comes then as a sharp reminder of women's alternate conception of citizenship that in 1796, women workers went on strike during the harvests until promised equal pay.[27] This suggests the limits of a state view of enslaved women as recipients of freedom through marriage, as dependent parties, or as minors in the historic project of slave emancipation.

More than half a century later, American slaves made their bid for emancipation in the context of a war close in scale to that which had convulsed the Caribbean in the 1790s—and with similar conceptions of republican freedom and emancipation. In the United States, as in Saint-Domingue, despite the "apparent certitude and finality of the Great Document," the enslaved claimed a status as free people through a dangerous, protracted, and eminently reversible process. In the American Civil War, southern slaves' insurrection against both slavery and the Confederate state alerted the Union military to the potential utility of their labor, loyalty, and military service, and put emancipation on the agenda. In that respect the text of the Emancipation Proclamation instrumentalized what Lincoln described in his economical style as a "fit and necessary war measure."[28]

The slave insurgency began on the plantations in the Confederate South, and planters readily acknowledged that it was the work of men and women both.[29] But, as in Saint-Domingue, the Union government's interest in military-age men immediately construed the "slaves of persons . . . engaged in rebellion" as if they were all male.[30] This *de facto* definition of insurgents as male reverberates today even in the most progressive accounts of slave emancipation.

The gender patterns came directly to the fore in key moments in the tangled course of emancipation in the Civil War. It materialized in the contraband policy at Fortress Monroe, Virginia, in May 1861, by which slaves were first confiscated from their owners; in the congressional debate extending that policy and authorizing the enlistment of black soldiers in 1862; in the process that evolved in the Union-occupied Mississippi Valley after the Emancipation Proclamation; and in the belated 1865 arrangement to recruit and emancipate slaves in the Union border states, especially Kentucky, that were exempt from the proclamation. Military emancipation policy in every case seized on the "soldier's wife" as the privileged identity for enslaved women. That the Confederate government adopted a similar view in its desperate move to enlist slaves in the last year of the war only confirms the undergirding logic.[31]

Union general Benjamin Butler took command of Fortress Monroe, a federal fort in coastal Virginia, in May 1861, shortly after Virginia's secession. He was charged with holding the fort and preventing the erection of Confederate batteries anywhere in its vicinity within a half day's march. No sooner had Butler arrived than slaves began to "deliver themselves up" to his picket guards—first three men, then three days later a "squad" of men "bringing with them," Butler said, "their women and children." It is stunning how quickly the problem of fugitive slaves emerged in the Civil War, which testifies first and foremost to enslaved peoples' sense of historical possibility. The first group of three men belonged to Colonel C. K. Mallory, of the 115th Virginia Militia, the unit involved in holding and fortifying the village of Hampton Roads across the causeway from the fort. At a conference under flag of truce, Butler refused to return Mallory's slaves, claiming they were "contraband of war."[32] Within twenty-four hours of his arrival, Butler had not only confronted the problem of fugitive slaves that would steer the emancipation process throughout the war; he had also reached for a solution that would prove formative of all subsequent policy.

General Butler sensed the enormity of his decision. Within hours he detailed his course regarding Mallory's slaves to his superior, General-in-Chief Winfield Scott, because "this is but an individual instance in a course of policy which may be required to be pursued with regard to this species of property." Butler immediately sought the authorization of the War Department. Within a week of his first report, the "contraband" question had risen to a cabinet-level discussion and elicited President Lincoln's personal attention. The president thinks it "a very important subject," Postmaster Montgomery Blair informed Butler, "requiring some thought in view of the numbers of negroes we were likely to have on hand in virtue of this new doctrine." Cabinet members were already calling it "Butler's fugitive slave law."[33]

Butler's ad hoc "contraband policy," as first explained to Scott and Secretary of War Simon Cameron, justified holding fugitive slaves on the grounds that it deprived the Confederate government of the military use of their labor in support of the rebellion. "I am credibly informed that negroes in this neighborhood are employed in erection of batteries and other works by the rebels," Butler told Scott, "which it would be nearly or quite impossible to construct without their labor. Shall they be allowed the use of this property against the United States, and we not be allowed its use in aid of the United States?" They were a "species of property" confiscated from the enemy—and thus legitimate contraband of war according to the international law of war—and "very serviceable" to him in light of the great labor shortage in his quartermaster's department. He immediately put the fugitives to work digging entrenchments. From the very start, Union justifications focused on precisely those military-age male slaves impressed from their owners by Confederate authorities to build batteries and other fortifications. As one Massachusetts private under Butler's command, Edward Pierce, put it a few months later, slavery would be forced to yield to "the logic of military law."[34]

There was a certain genius to Butler's rationale for holding fugitive slaves. But the gender implications and conundrum were immediately apparent. Butler acknowledged that he had no legal rationale for holding women and children. Despite the obvious value of their labor, Confederate authorities never impressed women slaves. When able-bodied, "these negroes are of the last importance," Butler noted. "As a military question it would seem to be a measure of necessity to deprive the masters of their services." But how, Butler asked his superiors, "can this be done? As a political question and a question of humanity can I receive the services of the Father and the Mother and not take the children?" At first, as his comments suggest, he thought he could make it work by employing the men *and* women at the fort and charging the support of dependents to the "men laborers" and "able-bodied persons" in the family group. Butler appeared confident that he was dealing with nuclear families, "men and women with their children—entire families, each family belonging to the same owner." And perhaps in the first instance he was. But within a week, as knowledge of the "freedom fort" spread, the numbers of fugitives increased, and with them the social complexity of the contraband problem.[35]

Edward Pierce, the young volunteer assigned by Butler to supervise the labor of contraband on the trenches, commented on the diverse structures of fugitives' families. He mentioned fugitives who were as white as their owners, like the "young woman who had been three times a mother without ever having been a wife," and families destroyed by the slave trade, leaving husbands without wives and wives without husbands. The slave trade had ravaged families in Virginia, a state known nationally as a "slave-breeding country" and net exporter of slaves. Pierce and Butler saw clearly the imprint of slavery and sexual violence on the Virginia fugitives who made it to Fortress Monroe.[36]

The gender complications of Butler's contraband solution grew inexorably as the number of fugitives increased. Butler was desperate for instructions, especially as officers in other departments passed harsh orders that forbade any fugitives from coming within their lines. By the end of July 1861, 900 "negroes" within Butler's lines had sought "protection and support ... 300 of whom are able bodied men, 175 women, 225 children under 10 years, 179 aged 10–18 and many more coming in." Butler wrote to Cameron that the population posed very embarrassing questions: "First, what shall be done with them? And, Second, what is their state and condition." Butler frankly admitted the limits of his contraband idea when it came to women and children and sought guidance from the War Department. Was General Irvin Mc-Dowell's order "to be enforced in all military departments?" he asked with obvious distress, referring to an order that permitted slaveholders access to camp to reclaim fugitive slaves. "Is anyone more or less a fugitive slave because he has labored upon the rebel intrenchments?" If he so labored, "if I understand it, he is to be harbored." But the ones who had not—women and children—"cannot be treated on that basis," and thus must "be considered the incumbrance rather than the auxiliary of an army, and, of course, in no possible legal relation could be treated as contraband." Butler recoiled at the implications. Left to his own devices, he said, he would take a different course. But the contraband policy and its narrow logic prevailed, not least because, as Pierce noted in an influential November 1861 article in *Atlantic Monthly*, it assuaged widespread revulsion at the confiscation of private property.[37]

As Butler was well aware, a humanitarian crisis of considerable proportions was already unfolding in areas under Union occupation in the first summer of the war. By November 1861, that would extend to the rich rice and sea island cotton plantation region of lowcountry South Carolina and Georgia, where the population was more than 80 percent enslaved. From the start, Butler had seen the contraband problem as a humanitarian as well as a military issue. He felt a deep obligation to the women fugitives who worked at the fort—"women who had served us," as he put it—and he cast around desperately for a means to justify holding them and their children. Butler readily acknowledged the value of the women's labor. But the instructions he received from the War Department, and orders issued by other military commanders in 1861, made it abundantly clear that the Lincoln administration was prepared to abandon them. On May 29, Montgomery Blair, a member of President Lincoln's cabinet, wrote Butler to endorse his decision to declare "secession niggers contraband of war," but advised him to take only the "working people," leaving "nonworking classes of these people" to the secessionists. Secretary of War Cameron likewise approved Butler's move in respect to the "negroes who came within your lines from the service of the rebels," authorizing him to hold slave men "employed in hostility to the United States," and even to receive "into the service of the U.S." fugitives belonging to loyal men with a provision of future compensation. On the subject of women and children, Cameron had nothing to say.[38]

This was no oversight or omission. By the time Cameron gave Butler those instructions, that inhuman disregard had already been codified in the First Confiscation Act, approved by Congress on August 6, 1861. The act provided access to freedom only for slaves of rebel owners who had been forced to take up arms against the United States or, as was more likely, employed at work on any "fort, navy yard, dock, armory, ship, entrenchment, or in any military or naval service whatsover." In many ways that act simply formalized into law Butler's first steps in May. But as the first *official* military emancipation policy, it deepened the gender trouble and hostile environment for women fugitives, because as the contraband approach lost its ad hoc quality, it also narrowed to exclude the humanitarian issue that concerned Butler. From its earliest formulations in coastal Virginia, Union policy touching slave property took shape as a competition with the Confederate States of America for the bodies of slave men—first for military labor and, later, military service. As historians have noted, that narrow calculation about whose labor counted meant that the First Confiscation Act provided "slight access to freedom" for any slaves—and virtually none, I would add, for women.[39]

The problem Butler faced did not abate. Unwanted, still the women and children came. The flood of refugees to Union lines steadily increased, as did the scale of the humanitarian crisis involved in the slow, vicious wartime destruction of slavery. Commanders continued to complain about the thousands of "useless negroes" within their command, "two thirds to three fourths of whom are women and children incapable of army labor, a weight and incumbrance," as one later put it. Indeed, by the summer of 1862, there were at least ten thousand people in refugee camps in eastern North Carolina; between ten and eighteen thousand in the Department of the South (which included Union-occupied parts of South Carolina, Georgia, and Florida); and by November, when General Ulysses S. Grant put Chaplain John Eaton in charge of contraband in the Mississippi Valley, about another four to six thousand people there. The proportion of the refugee population comprising women and children only increased over time. One census of "contraband" within Union lines at Yorktown and in Elizabeth City and Warwick Counties, Virginia, in August 1863 reported 24,000 black men and women, 15,000 of them slaves of Confederate owners, 11,949 of whom were women. Women's determined pursuit of their own liberation turned military posts into refugee camps, confronted commanders like Butler, Henry Halleck, and Grant with a humanitarian crisis, and perpetually challenged the limited parameters of the government's military emancipation policy.[40]

But if the problem of women in contraband policy emerged first at Fortress Monroe, so too did the outlines of the solution resorted to throughout the war: to transform women fugitives into contrabands' wives. General Butler was fully aware of the limits of contraband policy and, perhaps for that reason, insisted on treating all fugitive women as if they were members of nuclear, male-headed families. In this way he could stretch the narrow military logic to cover women and children.

Fugitive African Americans fleeing to Union lines, 1862 Timothy O'Sullivan,
Rappahannock River, Va. Fugitive African Americans Fording the Rappahannock, August 1862, Civil War Photographs, 1861–1865,
Library of Congress, Prints and Photographs Division, Washington, D.C. [LC-B8171-518].

In his 1861 correspondence with his superiors, Butler talked of them quite specifically as "the women and children of the men who had fled . . . within my lines for protection" and were now employed on entrenchments. Most of the women earned their own subsistence, he added, providing domestic service for soldiers, while the children were supported by rations issued to their fathers. And, as Edward Pierce confirmed, "the contrabands" who worked on the entrenchments were issued rations as pay, a soldier's full allotment for each military laborer and half a ration additionally for each dependent wife or child. Pierce was fully aware of the single women and mothers among the fugitives, but like Butler, he embraced the fiction that they belonged to intact families with a claim on the protection of specific husbands and fathers. Thus, when Pierce took it on himself to publicly vindicate his commanding officer's haphazardly crafted policy, in his *Atlantic Monthly* article, he explained that the Union public ought to embrace contrabands as part of the American people. Each black man who served the cause of Union, he wrote, "had vindicated beyond all future question, for *himself, his* wife, and their issue, a title to citizenship, and become heir to all the immunities of the Magna Charta, the Declaration of Independence, and the Constitution of the United States."[41]

From the earliest moments of the war, advocates of slave emancipation in the United States imagined the contraband as male and the women as their wives, and proposed that male slaves would earn citizenship with military service to the Union and transmit its benefits to their wives and children. No matter that marriage was illegal for slaves or, more immediately, that many of the women who made it to Union lines or contraband camps had come on their own or as heads of families themselves. The "woman [who] came through 200 miles in Men's clothes" to Fortress Monroe had no husband, or at least none with her when she arrived.[42]

The recourse to marriage in military emancipation policy reflected deep-seated beliefs about adult women's dependency and normative position as wives. Assumptions about patriarchal order threaded seamlessly through and connected military and welfare policies in the crisis of the Civil War: Republican political makers simply assumed that each enslaved woman was, or was to be, the wife of a formerly enslaved man. In this, politicians and commanders were animated by a host of pressing concerns, chief among them male responsibility for dependents. The government was hardly equipped to meet the needs of the refugee population. The army and the Lincoln administration were entirely overwhelmed by the scale of the humanitarian crisis unfolding around them, not least how to house, feed, and clothe the thousands of refugees from slavery and war flooding into Union lines. A network of philanthropic and missionary societies developed over the course of the war, and by 1865 the federal government had formed the Bureau of Freedmen, Refugees, and Abandoned Lands to administer the transition of enslaved people to freedom. But it was the advance of the Union Army that established the terrain of freedom, making the army on the move and its multiplying and shifting encampments a magnet for fugitive slaves. That never changed. The task of relief and administration of refugees thus fell first and most heavily on military commanders. Ill-equipped as it was for the job, the army was the relief agency of first resort in the American Civil War.[43] Worries about self-support and the specter of massive public welfare hung over all of the discussions about how to administer the growing population of fugitive slaves under Union control.

Policymakers and military men turned repeatedly to marriage to exert order on the process and avert greater crisis. Would slave men assume responsibility for the support of their dependents? The very question unleashed the problem of marriage—of *slaves' marriages*—from Pandora's box. The idea of male "self-possession" and of slave marriage as a *condition* of emancipation—as evidence of male slaves' willingness to follow the patriarchal ethos—had been central to British emancipation schemes in their earliest eighteenth-century versions. And it had a significant place in republican emancipation plans in late eighteenth-century Saint-Domingue. In the mid-nineteenth-century United States, enslaved men's willingness to embrace marriage and its attendant responsibilities was always part of the assessment of their fitness for freedom and citizenship. In envisioning a future, Union policymakers imagined nuclear families in which freedmen could be relied on to support all freedwomen and children. The idea that each woman was, or would be, the wife of a man who would support her was a critical element of every emancipation plan. This explains why slaves' sense of the marriage relation was of such public interest. It was one of the first questions asked at the hearings conducted by the congressional committee appointed by Secretary of War Edwin Stanton in 1863 to investigate the condition of former slaves and make recommendations about their employment and welfare.[44] And it was why regularizing slave marriages was an episodic preoccupation of Union occupying forces, commanders of contraband camps, missionary teachers, and army chaplains.

Politicians' inability to envision freedwomen as anything other than the "wives" of freedmen had a direct impact. Wherever contraband camps sprung up in 1861 and 1862, the army was tasked to promote marriage. At Fortress Monroe, Reverend Lewis C. Lockwood, the first relief agent to work with the army, began officiating at marriages of former slaves starting in September 1861, with the support of Butler's successor, General John E. Wool. Marriage, Lockwood said, was his first goal. Similar initiatives were pursued in Roanoke and Alexandria, Virginia; in Port Royal, South Carolina; and in Camp Fiske, Tennessee, where couples living together were required to marry legally "under the flag." General Grant adopted the same policy over the contraband camps in his jurisdiction in Tennessee and northern Mississippi. Tera W. Hunter notes that agents encouraged and coerced refugees to marry or resanctify their marriages under the government's authority. Given that only free people could legally marry in slave states, there was a lot to be said for getting your name into a "government book." It was an insurance policy of sorts if the terrain of war and freedom shifted, putting you back on Confederate-held, slaveholding ground, and a common strategy of enslaved women elsewhere.[45]

The Union occupied the South Carolina and Georgia Sea Islands beginning in November 1861, and the massive flight of planters left thousands of slaves under federal jurisdiction. Here, enslaved people's coupling and marital practices, and their attitudes toward marriage, troubled and confounded white observers. Indeed, for people enslaved on the Sea Islands, the Civil War was only the latest turn in a long cycle of forced disruptions and reconstitutions of marriage and family life. Under those circumstances, Hunter emphasizes, marriage among slaves had evolved to "encompass committed conjugal relationships, whether legal or not, monogamous, bigamous, polygamous, or serial," and black heterosexual intimacy included a range of domestic arrangements, not all of which were thought of as marriages. Edward Pierce, who had been reassigned to the Sea Islands, conducted the first marriages only days after disembarkation. His successor, chaplain Mansfield French, when confronted with the alternative marital and family regime at Port Royal, took it as one of his chief tasks to get enslaved people to marry "under the flag." An order of General Rufus Saxton, issued in the summer of 1862, supported French's efforts by requiring that "Negroes having more than one 'wife' were now obliged to make a choice." Marriage, monogamy, and the Christian family were official Union policy.[46]

Whatever the complications—and there were many, as the quotation marks around "wife" suggest—federal policy most often gravitated to marriage and the administration of slave women as wives to solve the problem of contraband women and dependency. That instinct, so socially ingrained as to appear natural, even to historians, resurfaced virtually everywhere that the Union Army came into control of large populations of slaves of rebel owners. From the earliest moments of the war, when "contraband" first emerged as a population under Union governance, policymakers immediately sought to render male slaves to the jurisdiction of the state and army, and women slaves to the jurisdiction of marriage.

That much was clear in the summer of 1862, when the black soldier's wife became an officially recognized figure in Union policy. As the Union moved to embrace hard-war tactics, and President Lincoln floated the idea of a Preliminary Emancipation Proclamation to his cabinet, US senators debated a much tougher confiscation bill that would ultimately declare "forever free of their servitude" *all* slaves of rebel owners now under the control of the US government.[47] That same bill also empowered the president to use persons of African descent in any way he saw fit to suppress the rebellion. The Militia Act passed the same day gave him explicit authority to enlist men of African descent in the US Army.[48] Congress took up the issue largely in response to military field orders, including General David Hunter's early and defeated attempt to arm slaves after the occupation of the South Carolina lowcountry.[49] Slaveholders' property rights, first undermined by the Confiscation Act of July 1861, were further eroded in March 1862 when Congress directed the armies of the United States to stop enforcing the Fugitive Slave Act. By June a new confiscation bill landed in the Senate, which amended the law wholesale and radically, to provide not only for freeing slaves but arming them to fight. A ferocious, wide-ranging, and highly unpredictable debate ensued, and this is how senators found themselves engaged in strange exchanges about the existence and claims of the slave wife.

Debates over the Second Confiscation Act and the Militia Act made visible the military logic of confiscation, its gendered terms, and its implications for enslaved women. Senators fought over the reach of the bills: Should they authorize the confiscation of slaves of loyal or only of rebel owners? Should they permit the enlistment of black soldiers? Should they award freedom only to the soldiers themselves or to their families and dependents—their wives and children—as well? These questions may seem surprising, but this was not the only or last time that congressional debate over emancipation policy would wind through concerns about women and gender.[50] Even so, it is surely noteworthy that senators first invoked the figure of the slave wife at precisely the moment they first focused on the slave soldier. In this debate, congressmen *created* the political category of the black soldier's wife, opening up a route to emancipation some women could try to take. But the debate also sent up plenty of warning flares about how difficult this path would be, as senators flagged every problem and difficulty involved in implementing such a policy. Among them: where slave marriage was not legal, the bond of husband and wife had no power to dissolve the master's property right in his female slaves. Was there such a thing as a slave wife? And, if there was, did Congress have the authority to free her as well as her soldier husband?

The entire debate was highly contentious and polarized, dividing Democrats from Republicans, with border state Democrats making the staunchest arguments against. But it also divided Republican advocates of hard war, such as John Sherman of Ohio, who proposed the crucial amendment limiting the law's reach to the slaves of rebels, and Preston King of New York, who advocated for the most expansive terms. Border state Democrats, supported by the handful of Senate Unionists, bitterly opposed confiscation of any kind, regardless of enlistment. Senator Willard Saulsbury, Democrat of Delaware, raged about "the elevation of the nigger . . . not only to political rights but to put him in your army, and to put him in your navy." He cast that as putting "arms in the hands of the southern slaves to murder their masters." Senator Garrett Davis, a Unionist from Kentucky, said border state people would never stand such "atrocities," and took up floor time with a stock account of the horrors of "negro insurrection," including, predictably, in Saint-Domingue. He also went on a tirade against Massachusetts senators whose state had profited handsomely from the slave trade and who now proposed to put arms in the hands of men who would take revenge on their masters: "Men who feel so much for the slaves feel nothing for the white women and children of the South who faced immolation at their hands."[51]

Given the ferocity of the debate, it must have come as a shock when, quite early on, Senator King proposed the additional provision—one version of which survived into the final act—"That when any man or boy of African descent" shall render military service to the US government, "he, his mother, his wife and children shall forever thereafter be free, any law usage or custom to the contrary notwithstanding." Saulsbury denounced the proposal as a "wholesale scene of emancipation," not only freeing those persons but "everyone dependent upon them."[52] But the extension stuck. With the slave soldier had to come the soldier's wife. But that wife was a slave, as was her husband, chattel property by state law and incapable of entering a civil contract, including the bond of marriage. If the slave soldier was a problem for Democrats, the slave soldier's wife raised the murkiest issues of legal rights and congressional power.

The problem was obvious and soon pointed out by a sympathetic Republican. "I am constrained to say, whether it is to the honor or dishonor of my country," Senator Jacob Collamer of Vermont offered, "that, in the land of slavery, no male slave has a child . . . no slave has a wife, marriage being repudiated in the slave system." He knew that the practice of slave life was in "violation of theory," but legally speaking marriage was a thing "unknown, unrealized, incapable of being understood by four million of our people." He thought it wrong, and unchristian, but nonetheless true: "I have simply to say that these people have no wives, they have no children, and this provision . . . of the amendment is, to all practical purposes, a dead letter." Collamer's point haunted and loomed over the subsequent debate, and indeed over the history of emancipation. Slave women owned by *loyal* men only complicated the already complex issue. Republican senators divided bitterly over whether they had any right to confiscate the slaves of men who were loyal to their country. John Sherman wanted slave soldiers. "They are our natural friends," he insisted. He also believed quite stunningly that black men owed "military service just as much as the white man. . . . The fact that he is held to service does not relieve him," a point even Confederates denied. But in light of opposition from border state men and fellow Republicans who worried that the proposed act violated the international laws of war, Sherman proposed a crucial amendment to allow enlistment but "to confine the emancipation clause to the slaves of rebels." "It is a burning and an eternal shame" to let a man defend your life and country at arms and then return him to slavery, the Republican senator from Michigan objected. But in the final vote, Sherman's column beat back by one vote Preston King's more progressive proposal.[53]

As the bill narrowed to embrace only slaves owned by rebels, senators turned to the implications for slave men's "dependents." What if black soldiers' wives (unlike their husbands) were the property of loyal men? "This is a paper law," Senator Orville Browning of Illinois stormed. "It is the army that will free them and not Congress. The government has no right to legislate in regard to them at all." Browning worried aloud about the implications of such a move; if we have the power to do this, we could "go boldly to work and pass a law for the emancipation of all the slaves in the country." But black soldiers had their champions, not least among them Senator James Henry Lane of

Kansas. "What would freedom be worth to you if your mother, your wife and your children were slaves," he demanded to know of Browning, offering an impassioned image of a scarred warrior in Washington after the war and a government determined to force his loved ones back into slavery. How could they restore to slavery the "mother, wife, and children" after "that father and husband has been covered with wounds in defense of the country," Lane stormed. God would turn his face against such a country. A loyal man could be compensated "for the loss of his slave, just as the Senator and I could for the loss of our horses, or mules or wagons," he insisted. Senators Lane and King thus fought hard for the recognition of all black soldiers' wives and their share of the soldiers' bounty of freedom. But the strangely cacophonous mix of terms—of humanity and endearment, property and value—rang ominously. Slave women were beloved wives and children, but also property like mules. To some senators it was all highly improper, nowhere more so than the discussion of compensation for slave men and women confiscated from loyal owners. The Senate should not engage in this "traffic," Senator Samuel C. Pomeroy of Kansas declared. "I do not propose to embark this Government in the enterprise of buying up slaves." Anyway, he added, "we cannot afford it."[54]

As the debate dragged on and amendments voted on, the bill's purview narrowed with powerful consequences for the enslaved themselves. In the end, the Second Confiscation Act declared "forever free of their servitude" all slaves of rebel owners under the control of the government of the United States. It also empowered the president to employ "as many persons of African descent as he shall deem necessary" in any capacity to suppress the rebellion. The military logic of confiscation, its gendered terms, and the implications for women were all spelled out the same day in the Militia Act. That act authorized the enlistment and emancipation *only* of slave men owned by rebels. But it retained the provision that extended to soldiers' wives, *provided* they too were owned by rebel owners. Lest there be any confusion, Congress spelled it out: "Provided, that the mother, wife and children of any such man or boy of African descent shall not be made free by operation of this act except where such mother, wife and children owe service or labor to some person who during the present rebellion had borne arms against the U.S. or adhered to its enemies."[55] That clause would have brutal implications for the enslaved wives of black soldiers owned by loyal men, some of whom were left until 1865 at the mercy of their owners, with no route to legal freedom.

Congressional action in the summer of 1862 was clearly rife with possibility and danger for slave women who might try the only official route to emancipation open to them—marriage. The contraband wives of Butler's ad hoc order had found no recognition in the First Confiscation Act. But women's actions over the course of a gruesome year of war had an impact on the second version of that act. Nonetheless, Browning's point about the Second Confiscation Act remains: with respect to soldiers' wives, was it a paper law as charged? Much of what the authors of these acts meant or intended about family emancipation remains obscure. There was something unreal about the images of women that the senators invoked in debate. Historians' lack of interest has not helped clarify matters. It is not clear, for example, with respect to the Militia Act or any other similar federal policy, whether marriage was *required* as a condition of slave women's freedom, or what would constitute evidence of marriage to a black soldier in the absence of a legal certificate. What was clear, however, is that at least as Union politicians and military officials saw it, women's freedom (although which women no one quite specified) followed from their men's military service. If slaves put themselves on the wartime political agenda as historians now commonly acknowledge, then women slaves who continued to pour into Union lines unbidden, unwelcome, and unmarried did so in direct contravention of a federal policy that construed them as a problem and a burden, at best as dependents of the slave men whose labor and military service the army coveted.[56]

The military route to emancipation has carried tremendous political and interpretive weight in the estimation of contemporaries and historians alike. Its significance for real men and women was profound. The Militia Act opened up that possibility. But the Lincoln administration fully committed to the recruitment of black soldiers only after passage of the Emancipation Proclamation in January 1863. Abraham Lincoln called the proclamation an "act of justice," and that it was. But the authority to declare it derived specifically from the president's power as commander-in-chief of the army and navy of the United States. It was undertaken as a "fit and necessary war measure," and as such it tied emancipation to military service. The proclamation applied to all enslaved people in the states in rebellion—excepting the parts already returned to loyalty—without regard to gender or ability to serve.[57] But its power to emancipate reached only where the army did, which not only meant that emancipation was tenuous and reversible according to fortunes on the battlefield, but also that newly emancipated people would be governed under military authority of one kind or another. In January, when Lincoln issued the proclamation, he still envisioned the use of black soldiers for garrison duty only. But by March, when his administration was forced to adopt a highly unpopular policy of national conscription, manpower needs were such that the War Department began the systematic and coordinated recruitment of black troops, including for combat duty. By May, the War Department had formed the Bureau of Colored Troops to oversee the effort. Acknowledging the attendant issues of mass emancipation, Secretary of War Stanton also convened a committee, the American Freedmen's Inquiry Commission, to investigate the condition of refugee slaves and consider how best "they may defend and support themselves."[58] After the passage of the Emancipation Proclamation, the US Army was officially an army of liberation, charged with recruiting black soldiers at the same time that its movements announced emancipation.

Nowhere did this policy work to greater effect than in the Mississippi Valley, which was entirely in Union hands after the fall of Vicksburg in the summer of 1863. As the Union Army moved into the region in 1862, the densest concentration of slaveholding in the United States, the man in charge of the offensive, General Ulysses S. Grant, mourned how little Congress had yet done to handle "the military complications arising out of the conditions of slavery in the midst of which our armies are moving." His first concerns were military, but, like his counterpart in the East, Benjamin Butler, he could not "ignore the dictates of mere humanity."[59]

Even before the fall of Vicksburg, Grant staggered under the task of dealing with the thousands of fugitive slaves who attached themselves to his army. In late 1862, he turned to John Eaton, army chaplain in the 27th Ohio Infantry, appointing him to take charge of all contraband within his command. Eaton offered an unforgettable description of the scene in his memoirs. With every advance of Grant's massive 45,000-man army, slaveholders abandoned their plantations, and the "negroes flocked in vast numbers—an army in themselves—to the camps of the Yankees." To Eaton it was an exodus of biblical proportions: a slave population rising up and leaving its ancient bondage, coming barefoot and shod, "individually or in families and larger groups—an army of slaves and fugitives, pushing its way irresistibly

toward an army of fighting men, perpetually on the defensive and perpetually [exposed] to attack. The arrival among us of these hordes was
like the oncoming of cities," he recalled. There were 22,000 "contraband" (as he still called them) in Eaton's department by the spring of
1863. But the fall of Vicksburg brought an additional flood of destitute people into Union lines—Eaton estimated 30,000 more—
overwhelming his fragile arrangements for food, shelter, and medical
care. Emancipation was a huge experiment conducted in the maelstrom
of war. The suffering was so great that forty years later, Eaton was still
defensive about Union efforts to alleviate it. By the summer of 1864,
Eaton administered a network of camps stretching from Cairo, Illinois,
in the North to Davis Bend, Mississippi, in the South, and was responsible for the wellbeing of about 114,000 souls. By 1864, of course, the
fugitives were all legally free people, but they were all also, in one way
or another, under the government's guardianship.[60]

The scale of the humanitarian crisis that followed wartime emancipation in the Mississippi Valley continually outpaced any solution
by the army or War Department. The enormity of the task came
through clearly in the congressional hearings held by the American
Freedmen's Inquiry Commission in the spring of 1863 to gauge the
impact of the Emancipation Proclamation. Commissioners referred
to the task facing the United States as "one of the gravest social problems ever presented to a government." In that they did not exaggerate.
They were palpably anxious to present proof that the newly freed
people would not be "any burden whatever on the government for relief." The commissioners were equally preoccupied, and for the same
reason, with slaves' "false ideas touching chastity," and insistent that
freed people could (and must) be taught "the obligations of the married state in civilized life." To that end, commissioners encouraged
marriage as the determined policy in Union refugee camps, so as to

"impose upon the husband and father the legal obligation to support his family." The officials recommended that arrangements be made not only to encourage marriage but to ensure that each married laborer or soldier cede a part of his pay for the support of his family in all cases where they were dependent on the government.[61] Clearly marriage was the solution to the massive problem of dependency and social disorder they faced. But that was not all: to abolitionists and liberal reformers, marriage was also a moral issue, and the foundation of the civilizing mission. In fact, the commissioners' report evinced precisely the logic of colonial commissions of inquiry that anthropologist Ann Laura Stoler has identified as one of the technologies of new liberal states. It betrayed the same preoccupation with the intimate lives of its subjects, and the same phenomenon she identifies of information "out of place," for it is hard to know what else to call commissioners' obsessive questions about sex in a government report.[62] Universal emancipation was unthinkable without the preexisting disciplinary structure of the monogamous patriarchal family.

Unsurprisingly, then, Eaton, an army chaplain, reached immediately for the model of Christian marriage to organize the huge population of newly freed people under his care in the Mississippi Valley. Eaton's sense of Christian mission toward the freed people was clear, but so was the burden of proof they faced about their entitlement to freedom: "The hordes that swept down upon our armies in the Mississippi Valley were to all intents and purposes barbarians," Eaton wrote. His account of emancipation is distinctly orientalist—and also heavily relied on by historians. Like so many other Union officials in the flux of historical transformation, he was preoccupied—even obsessed—with the "promiscuous intermingling" of the freed people and evidence of marital nonconformity in refugee camps. Even the most well-intentioned abolitionist seemed unable to grasp the moral codes of community developed over generations of enslavement. Eaton's comments show what freed people had to contend with, even from their government friends. He acknowledged the brutal history of slavery, but his account clearly still attached moral stigma to its victims. So Eaton could at once acknowledge how many husbands and wives had been "forcibly and hopelessly separated by the direct operation of the system of slavery," and observe that a moral "licentiousness" inculcated by slavery "had taken deep root in the Negro character." For putative racial progressives such as Eaton, who believed in the "capacity of these people to develop themselves as a race, into the self-supporting, self-respecting, and moral type of human being," matters of welfare and marriage merged inextricably; indeed, they were part of the same moral question. That was why the Freedmen's Department exerted itself "to enforce and maintain the marriage relation by every means in its power."[63]

The "strict enforcement of marriage regulations" was the policy adopted for all of the freed people under Eaton's guardianship in the Mississippi Valley. Eaton began by adopting "the essential features" of Butler's contraband policy, as he readily admitted, including the idea that black men were responsible for their dependents. His main goal, he said, was to make "the Negro a self-supporting unit in the society in which he found himself [and] start him on the way to self-respecting citizenship." The male pronouns went on for a paragraph, grammatical confirmation of the lasting epistemological construction of the "contraband" as male. "There was to be no promiscuous intermingling" among freed people in the camps. "Families were established by themselves. Every man took care of his own wife and children." He proudly listed the number of marriages performed—119 in one hour at one service, in one instance—and lauded fugitives' embrace of the sacrament and obligations of marriage, even as he commented on the case of the black minister living with a woman not his wife, who could not be persuaded to marry her or to give her up. Eaton could not comprehend the coexistence of devout religious faith with marital nonconformity. Clearly there was resistance, but Eaton was unflagging in his efforts to impose the forms of the patriarchal family on enslaved people as the terms of emancipation.[64]

The promotion of marriage remained official Union policy, even as the government launched a wholescale campaign of black enlistment that further threatened fragile families. That initiative siphoned off a significant portion of the military age men in refugee camps, separated couples who had only recently gained their freedom, and skewed the remaining camp populations even more heavily female. The proportion of women and children grew over time. In the spring of 1863, Brigadier General Lorenzo Thomas was dispatched from Washington to head up a major campaign among the now freed slaves to recruit black soldiers and reorganize the constantly growing number of plantations in occupied territory. Plans proceeded in tandem, with Thomas and his men aggressively routing (or impressing) black men of military age into the army while assigning women, children, and elderly or unfit men to plantation labor under northern lessees.[65] Disturbingly, this federal policy resembled that of Sonthonax, Louverture, and Jean-Jacques Dessalines (the first ruler of independent Haiti) more than fifty years earlier.

The scale of the recruitment was huge, and freedmen's consent often irrelevant. At first Thomas recruited among the freedmen gathered in Mississippi Valley contraband camps. Eaton accompanied Thomas on one of his first recruitment missions in May 1863, visiting all of the principal camps in his jurisdiction. After that Eaton noted how quickly men were pushed to enlist, oftentimes at the very moment they made it to Union lines. But Thomas did not simply wait for men to come to him. Once the government entered into the "definite and acknowledged policy of making soldiers of the ex-slaves," every army foray became a recruitment mission. The army brought on black leaders as recruiters, men such as Martin Delaney and John Mercer Langston, and began to pay recruitment bounties for every man enlisted. Major George Stearns, the commissioner for recruitment of black troops, who pressed the secretary of war to adopt this policy, insisted that it would encourage men to "venture within the enemy's lines" to recruit slaves.[66] And indeed, by the summer of 1863, the Union Army was recruiting men directly off of liberated Confederate plantations. Thomas and his men would visit abandoned plantations, announcing the Emancipation Proclamation and ordering all young men, eighteen to forty-five, to march out with the army. The military sent out raiding parties into Confederate-held territory and returned with all of the male slaves they could get their hands on. Historian Erik Mathisen said of Thomas's methods, "Though many African Americans voluntarily signed up to serve, in places like Mississippi, Lorenzo Thomas's military recruitment was really forced conscription." His men swept up so many unfit for military service that they were dismissed on medical examination. Indeed, his methods were so "unsavory" that other officers complained about the "oppression of the poor black by officers" who gathered up "the unwilling or willing, sick or well negroes apparently but with one object," namely, the bounty.[67]

The women liberated on Confederate plantations had little more immediate control over their fates, as they too fell under military authority. General Thomas's orders for the Mississippi Valley charged him not just with recruitment but also with the management of abandoned plantations—valuable resources that the government planned to use to provide for the massive nonmilitary age population of ex-slaves. From the outset, Thomas had a clear idea of how to handle those he could not enlist. "I shall take the women and children, and the men who cannot go into our army organization," he explained, and put them to work on abandoned plantations in the occupied South. Various other departments widely applied Thomas's solution until the end of the war.[68] Whatever the circumstances, slaves were all subject to the same military process of "sorting": men of military age were siphoned off to the army, while women, children, the elderly, and unfit men were remanded back to labor on seized plantations.

Mary Jane Clear described how she stuck close to her husband when Union troops recruited him off their Washington County, Mississippi, plantation. But she did not get far. "All the women were put off the boat at Hawes Harris' landing," an army friend of her husband later recalled, "and the men were carried off to Lake Providence to enlist." Clear was immediately hired out to a lessee and remanded to a plantation to labor at a wage fixed by the government—seven dollars per month for the women, ten dollars for the men.[69] Thavolia Glymph's deeply researched account of the experience of refugee women and children in the Mississippi Valley confirms just how common this experience was. She follows Louisa and Israel Smith, a married couple, who started their journey to freedom from the plantation in Washington County where they too had been slaves. They left together on a Union gunboat, but then their lives diverged. When the boat reached Goodrich's Landing, Louisiana, Louisa and the other women, children, and men deemed unfit for military service were ordered ashore. The boat carried her husband, Israel, and the other able-bodied men fifteen to twenty miles farther to Lake Providence, where they enlisted in the army in May 1863. About 100 people a day were arriving at Goodrich's Landing, a refugee camp, and Lake Providence, a military recruitment camp, in early 1863, and more than 1,250 daily by the first two weeks of February 1863. Lake Providence and Goodrich's Landing were important as military staging sites and to "the ancillary mission of turning abandoned plantations into profit-making enterprises that could simultaneously take care of the refugee problem." The register of marriages kept at Vicksburg records the gendered geography, as it lists the "place of residence" of many new soldier husbands as their army unit, and new wives at camps such as Goodrich's Landing, Davis Bend, or Vicksburg.[70]

By the spring of 1863, with military recruitment in full swing, the population of the refugee and plantation labor camps of the Mississippi Valley was primarily women and children. Indeed, in June that year, when the commissioners of the American Freedmen's Inquiry Commission issued their preliminary report, one of their main recommendations was that all "'contraband camps' . . . be regarded as places of reception and distribution only," and superintendents informed that it was "the policy of the government . . . to dispose of the women and children as laborers on plantations where they could be 'self-supporting.'" In one three-month period in 1864, the superintendent of freedmen sent 12,700 freed people, the majority of them women, more than a few of them black soldiers' wives, from contraband camps and shantytowns around Vicksburg to work on plantations. The women and children forced onto those plantations faced innumerable dangers. Many of the plantations taken up by northern lessees as money-making propositions were in locations highly vulnerable to raids by the Confederate military, a point Eaton and others complained about repeatedly to the War Department. In June 1863, shortly after Louisa Smith was remanded to Goodrich's Landing, the camps there came under attack, twenty plantations went up in flames, and many women and children were slaughtered—either roasted alive or shot down in the cane break. Some 1,200 survivors were captured and reenslaved by Confederate soldiers. Louisa Smith mercifully survived. Of the situation in the Mississippi Valley, Glymph writes, there were too few "places of safe refuge, too few Union commanders willing or able to help, and too much silence from Washington." It fell to the women to turn those inhospitable camps into places capable of sustaining life. Indeed, as Glymph sees it, what African American women did in those places helped to make a new world of freedom no less than what their husbands did by military service. Developments in the region underscore the essential point that, whether married or not, black men and women were forced to pursue very different paths, all wending through war, to emancipation.[71]

It was not a good sign that, notwithstanding passage of the Emancipation Proclamation, President Lincoln and his secretary of war, Edwin Stanton, persisted in referring to the freed people as "contrabands" and in making rigid distinctions between those capable of military labor or service and those of no use to the state, who presented a massive problem of dependency. Advising Secretary Stanton on how to respond to General Stephen A. Hurlbut's dilemma in the Mississippi Valley— Hurlbut had complained about women and children "incapable of army labor" as a "weight and encumbrance" on his army—Lincoln put it bluntly: "The able bodied male contraband are already in the army. But the rest are in confusion and destitution. They had better be set to digging their subsistence out of the ground."[72] And so they were.

The Mississippi Valley confronted on a massive scale the problem of contraband women, first glimpsed at Fortress Monroe. But with military recruitment came new and more obdurate gender distinctions between fugitive slave men and women who wanted to lay claim to freedom by sticking close to the US Army. As in Saint-Domingue, women did not simply submit to the official gender division of labor. In the South Carolina and Georgia Sea Islands, where the same policy was underway, women fieldworkers on one plantation resisted men's forcible drafting, attacking "the black soldiers [sent to take them] with

Group in contraband camp, Virginia, 1862 James F. Gibson, *Cumberland Landing, Va. Group of "Contrabands" at Foller's House*, May 14, 1862, Civil War Photographs, 1861–1865, Library of Congress, Prints and Photographs Division, Washington, D.C. [LC-DIG-cwpb-01005].

their hoes." Soldiers opened fire on the women. In the Mississippi Valley, women remanded to plantations often refused to work on the cotton crops, or simply got up and left, following husbands and other family members to Union Army camps, contraband camps, or the freedmen's villages that cropped up wherever the army and its growing numbers of black soldiers made camp. Military records document the struggle to control these women, as well as the inhuman disregard for life evidenced by some officers and enlisted men. Some officers continued to refuse women access to their lines. Others issued orders that columns on the march should abandon the women and children who tried to keep up, "the useless negroes" who impeded the march and consumed supplies.[73]

In the Mississippi Valley, after the Emancipation Proclamation, the gender delimitations of the Union military's emancipation policy were abundantly clear. All told, the Union enlisted 178,000 black soldiers and sailors, most of them former slaves. More than 17,000 black soldiers were recruited in Mississippi between 1862 and the end of the war, fully 20 percent of the military-age black male population and 18 percent of the black men recruited in the Confederate states. Only Louisiana and Tennessee raised more troops. There were almost 42,000 from Mississippi and Louisiana alone (about a quarter of the military age population), and another 50,000 from Arkansas, Tennessee, and Kentucky in the upper part of the valley. Escaped slaves did indeed prove to be the "great reserved force" that the governor of Massachusetts had predicted early in the war.[74]

But there were many more freed people than that within Union lines by the end of the war; estimates range widely, between 500,000 and 1 million. This means that most of the freed people—and all of the women—made the transition to freedom not as soldiers in the army of the republic but as laborers on Union-held plantations, or unwelcome dependents in contraband camps and freedmen's villages, clinging desperately to the authority and protection of the Union Army.[75] Even when slave women had the same access to legal emancipation as men by virtue of the Emancipation Proclamation, federal policies, especially the focus on the military recruitment of black men, established fundamentally distinct possibilities and conditions on men's and women's attempts to lay claim to and preserve their status as free people.

Lorenzo Thomas cast the Union's Civil War as a black revolution in the Haitian mold to draw attention to the obvious comparison: the federal government's willingness to link emancipation and enlistment as a way to secure black men's loyalty and military service. In invoking Louverture and Haiti, he hardly meant to invoke the other comparison: the consignment of freedwomen to enforced plantation labor and the reliance on marriage to structure federal policies governing black men's and women's transition to freedom and citizenship. Yet as in coastal Virginia, North Carolina, and South Carolina in 1861, federal officials in the Mississippi Valley turned to marriage time and again to regulate the government's relations and obligations to this massive new population of freed people. When General Thomas went down to Goodrich's Landing in October 1863 and addressed the new "negro troops and the contrabands generally" on the "duties and responsibilities of freedom," welfare and the specter of dependency were foremost on his mind. *Harper's Weekly* published a sketch of the scene. Like so many others confronted with the same population—Benjamin Butler, Abraham Lincoln, the War Department, the American Freedmen's Inquiry Commission, Chaplain John Eaton—Thomas urged marriage on freed people as an integral part of the social contract they were making with the Union government.[76]

The promotion of marriage remained the firm policy of the US government for the remainder of the war.[77] After recruitment began, federal officials in the Mississippi Valley issued intermittent injunctions to black soldiers to legalize their marriages, and a blizzard of directives and orders extending access, rights, and benefits to particular women as the wives of black soldiers.[78]

The opening of the right to marriage to people recently enslaved was no small matter. It gave couples the right to sanctify and legalize their unions, both longstanding and new, and to confer legitimacy on the children they had together. Even in the coercive context of Union military orders, couples who chose to marry were still claiming a dignity and respect long and purposefully denied them.[79] But the new possibilities of marriage were matched by women's difficulties in securing them. Women without soldier husbands obviously suffered under this policy, but it was difficult even for black soldiers' wives who fit the policy's stipulations and descriptions to secure recognition and respect for their marriages. Special orders could be issued, marriage certificates written, and those certificates recorded in a government book, but that did not mean Union officers and government officials would recognize a black soldier's wife when she presented herself to them. The identity of the "soldier's wife" had been conjured into being by the Militia Act, and then given substance by the Emancipation Proclamation and the enlistment of black men into the Union Army, but women had to fight to make that identity real and secure the protections and benefits to which the law and their husbands' service allegedly entitled them.

These women had their advocates, especially among chaplains of black regiments, men such as C. W. Buckley of the 47th United States Colored Troops, stationed in Vicksburg, Mississippi, who championed the rights of those he had married in camp. Buckley was confident that marriage certificates would eliminate "any difficulty . . . experienced in identifying such wives," and armed with the documents, he pressed his superior to pay the death benefits owed to the widows of soldiers in his regiment. To Buckley it was a clear-cut matter: the men "upon leaving their homes have been assured that their families should be provided for in their absence, and in case they never returned, a grateful country and a beneficent government would watch, with paternal care, over their orphaned children." And indeed, in recruiting black troops, the War Department had committed to protect and support the men's families, specifically through the payment of bounties, advance pay, and rations to dependents. In this sense it was simply extending to black women the protection and support previously promised by both governments (Union and Confederacy) to white soldiers' wives. In 1863, General Butler, stationed once again at Fortress Monroe, acknowledged the obligation to women and children, observing that such support was particularly crucial because "colored soldiers have none of the machinery of 'State aid' . . . so liberally provided to the white soldiers." By the provisions of the *Dred Scott* decision, which still held, black men were not citizens of the United States or of individual states. Nonetheless, black men who enlisted had entered into the social contract and expected it to be honored. Ann Summer, a black soldier's wife, referred to Butler's order promising rations "to all the soljurs wives of color" when she claimed her entitlement from the Quartermaster Department. Like poor white women in the Confederacy, black women grasped the lever provided by wartime policy to press their claims on their government and enforce a debt owed to the wives and children of black soldiers.[80]

But there was nothing straightforward about these wives' identities or their ability to make claims on the government. The first struggle, as the original debate over the Militia Act forecasted, was for recognition or, put another way, for the legitimacy of their marriages. Not everyone had a marriage certificate, although even that was not always sufficient. The contradictions of slavery flagged in congressional debate—is there such a thing as a slave wife and how would we know her?—were no mere abstraction.

As far as black soldiers were concerned, the quid pro quo of military service and family liberation was personal, direct, and immediate. Once enlisted, they attempted to trigger the provisions of the Emancipation Proclamation, corralling white officers to help them gather up their wives and children, and their brothers' wives and children, as

Black soldier, his wife, and daughters, c. 1863–1865 *Unidentified African American Soldier in Union Uniform with Wife and Two Daughters*, Liljenquist Family Collection of Civil War Photographs, Library of Congress, Prints and Photographs Division, Washington, D.C. [LC-DIG-ppmsca-36454].

their units marched. The archival record is full of poignant examples, including that of Joseph Harris, who begged General Daniel Ullman to make a brief detour across the Mississippi River at Bayou Sarah, Louisiana, "and take a way my Farther and mother and my brothers wife with all their Childern." It would not be more than three or four hours' trouble he assured the general. Harris had been trying to free his family for the entire three years he had "bin in the servis . . . and Could never get no one to do for me." Many other soldiers showed up themselves, backed up by the power of the Union Army and government, as Spotswood Rice, another formerly enslaved black soldier, described it.

Sometimes they were accompanied by sympathetic white officers, but not always. Five "negro soldiers" visited the plantation of a Mr. Villarie in St. Bernard Parish, Louisiana, in August 1863, and Captain George Davis, the provost marshal, reported to his commanding officer that they "loaded their muskets in front of his door and demanded some colored women whom they called their wives."[81] The qualifying quotation marks around "soldier's wife" were still there, either literally or in phrases such as "whom they called their wives" or who they "claimed as their wives," which appear throughout the military record.

That kind of contempt for women's claims was commonplace in the Union Army, and it dogged black soldiers' wives at every turn during and after the war, as did the complexities of their marital and family relations as slaves. Women not recognized as wives but trying to reach male family members were repeatedly driven out of Union camps, denied rations and benefits, and left in destitution. Commanders threw them out of camp as prostitutes when they showed up on payday to get their husband's wages. It is "just within the bounds of possibility," one officer acknowledged, "that some virtuous wives may have been amongst the number so excluded from camp, but I gravely doubt it." Officers removed them from camp "as lazy vagrants" or designated them as people "having no visible means of support" when they claimed rations due them from the men "who claim them as wives," as the officers put it.[82]

Thus, even as the Union urged black soldiers to marry, white officers blocked or undermined the legitimacy of those marriages, often contemptuously. Some officers lodged complaints, as did one overseeing the "colored troops," about the morality of the enlisted men of his command, who were "much in the habit of marrying Common place women of the town." That officer demanded that all marriage certificates issued at his camp be approved by headquarters, and that no soldier be allowed to bring "his wife" into camp without the approval of his company commander. Such charges of immorality were impossible to escape because they were fundamental to the web of racist assumptions these men brought to the task of disciplining black soldiers. In barring women from camp as prostitutes, one explained, he was trying to "prevent the camp of the said regiment from becoming a brothel on a gigantic scale. The marital relationship is but little understood by the colored race, and, if possible still less respected." The officer claimed that he had tried to ascertain how many men were legitimately married "by any process known to civilization, or even those who by long cohabitation might be looked on as possessing some faint notions of constancy and decency." But even by this lax standard, he insisted, "not more than one in four who claim to have wives can support that claim." White officers assumed the right to judge the legitimacy of black soldiers' marriages and women's right to the identity of soldier's wife. But with every marriage cast as an illicit sexual relationship, it is little wonder that black women were more recognizable to white officers as vagrants or prostitutes than as soldiers' wives.[83]

This had dire consequences for black soldiers' wives. Women who had successfully resisted efforts to remove them to plantations and were living in camps close to their husbands' units were threatened with removal. Open conflicts erupted in both Natchez and Vicksburg over the right of soldiers' wives to reside within city limits. White officers' efforts to force "unemployed and vagrant Negroes" out of the camps in Natchez to "some place of labor" (meaning to plantations or "home farms") swept up soldiers' wives indiscriminately with other refugees and indigent people. A year after the first attempt to clear the area, an assistant surgeon reported on the increasingly dangerous sanitary conditions of the portion of the city known as "Under the Hill" and ordered the removal of residents. "A large majority of these claim to be Soldier's Families," he acknowledged, "and have no other visible means of support." Showing little concern for the health of the people living there, he condemned the "shanties" as "the very best places conceivable for engendering disease" and demanded their removal as a matter of public health. In Vicksburg, indigent people, most of them the wives of black troops quartered in town, had been allowed to occupy vacant land and erect dwellings. About three hundred acres in the suburbs of the city were assigned to the 50th US Colored Troops (USCT) for the use of "the families of the soldiers" who are living there, many of them "in destitute circumstance." The unit chaplain reported the soldiers' efforts to build dwellings and lay out gardens for their families on the assigned land, and also recorded the legalization of thirty-three marriages in his regiment in one month. But despite their husbands' efforts, black women were in the most precarious condition as at once soldiers' wives and indigent people. Thus, in another case in Mississippi, when the provost marshal of freedmen ordered that "a large number of the colored people of the city . . . that were living in idleness and vagrancy in & about the camps of the soldiers be removed," he included the women resident in the "shanties near the 52nd USCT." He recommended it as "a sanitary precaution, that as soon as the River falls there be a general cleaning out of the colored population who have no honest means of support," and proposed their removal to Davis Bend—which was at that moment underwater—where they would be "provided with work."[84]

To men like Thomas, the women themselves were the dirt to be cleared out, and soldiers' wives were routinely characterized as vectors of immorality and disease. Colonel George Ziegler of the 52nd USCT strenuously protested the treatment of his men's wives and children. But the unit had already been moved for duty to another part of the Department of Mississippi and the Gulf. They were not mustered out until May 1866, and all that time the men were separated from their families. It was a "shame and a disgrace" to treat soldiers of the republic in such a fashion, Zeigler protested, demanding that the commissioner of freedmen see that "those women [were] attended to."[85]

Even as black soldiers made superhuman efforts to provide for their families while deployed, their wives were maligned and abused as indigents and vagrants; even as black soldiers' wives fought off sexual predation by white soldiers, they were denounced as prostitutes and their marriages as illegitimate. Women were liable to be labeled as prostitutes when they sought the support of a new partner in the absence of a husband who enlisted and disappeared. The formality of a marriage certificate did not dispel the kind of moral and sanitary threat they were thought to pose. Black soldiers demanded that the government live up to its promises to support their wives and children, and they threatened, and sometimes engaged in, mutiny when the government did not honor its promises and officers disrespected the sacredness of their family relations. "Mens wifes comes here [hundreds of miles] to see them and he will not alow them to come in to they lines," George Hanon informed General Lorenzo Thomas, speaking of his colonel. "Ever offiscer here that has a wife is got her in camps." "A collard man thnk jest as much of his wife as a white man dus of his." "We volentered and come in the servest to portec this government and also to be protected our selves . . . but col luster is treating us it don't seem . . . he thinks we are human."[86]

Government policy was based on an absurd expectation that black families—moments removed from slavery, separated by war, in the midst of war and military service, plagued by chronic disease and poverty—would instantly assume the form and conventions of the white, self-supporting middle-class family. A few, but only a few, in Union Army and policy circles voiced the absurdity of the idea. Black families are "totally unlike" white soldiers' families in their condition and configuration, one white officer protested to an assistant commissioner of the Freedmen's Bureau in 1865. If they were like "white Soldiers' families," he said sarcastically, then the bureau would have no reason to exist. Union officials and politicians feared the specter of dependency and social chaos more than they conceded any debt to the enslaved, so they yoked the terms of emancipation to marriage. At the same time, however, black soldiers' wives struggled everywhere to have the legitimacy of their marriages, so urgently recommended in policy, recognized and honored in reality. They struggled to secure rations, housing, and death benefits, and the massive set of pension applications housed in the National Archives robustly testifies to their tenacity, partial success, and individual and family lives during and after the war.[87]

However difficult it was for black women to insist on their identity as soldiers' wives, another group was cut off categorically and entirely from the government's promises, even on paper: the wives of black soldiers who belonged to loyal men. The Militia Act of 1862 purposely excluded these enslaved women, and the Emancipation Proclamation purposely excluded their owners.

In the winter of 1865, the second session of the 38th US Congress found itself back on the same unstable ground it had occupied in 1862. As it worked to pass the Thirteenth Amendment, it also debated the identity and claims of black soldiers' wives. That the congressmen ended up back here was in no small measure due to the actions of black soldiers' wives themselves, whose testimony to their brutal experiences and herculean difficulties piled up at military posts and, eventually, found its way into the congressional record. In particular, the experiences of black soldiers' wives at the hands of loyal masters commanded urgent attention in Congress and propelled the last major piece of military emancipation legislation: an Enlistment Act, passed on March 3, 1865, in which Congress was forced to go further and produce its own definition of slave marriage. President Lincoln signed the act into law the following day, along with the act that established the Freedmen's Bureau. Later that day he delivered his second inaugural address. As Lincoln prayed for the end of war and turned the nation's attention toward peace, the wives of Kentucky soldiers, and all other enslaved women in that state, waited still for a path out of bondage.[88]

The Militia Act and the Emancipation Proclamation exempted the four slave states in the Upper South (Maryland, Delaware, Missouri, and Kentucky) that had remained loyal to the Union in 1861. In those border states after 1863, as in Confederate areas exempted from the proclamation, military service remained the only available route to emancipation. For those unable to join the army, there was no legal route at all. The General Orders of October 1863 and 1864 that promoted recruitment had nothing to say about the status of wives, elderly parents, and children of border state recruits. That remained the case until individual states enacted emancipation statutes, as did Maryland and Missouri in January 1865. But in Kentucky, where loyal slaveholders regarded emancipation as a betrayal of their political trust, slaveholders fought that development to the bitter end. Recruitment of black soldiers did not begin until the spring of 1864. Slavery remained legal in Kentucky until the final adoption of the Thirteenth Amendment (without the state's assent) in December 1865. Unsurprisingly, with enlistment the only way to secure the title of free man, the state contributed more black soldiers proportionately than any other.[89] But Kentucky refused to act on the problem of their wives—women still held as slaves by loyal owners.

Slavery died hard everywhere in the United States. "I hear its expiring agonies & witness its contortions in death in every quarter of my District," Brigadier General Clinton Fisk wrote from Missouri. But nowhere harder than in Kentucky. In that state, enslaved women whose husbands had runaway to enlist were left to pay the price of their husbands' service. "R. L. more says he will kill every woman that he knows that has got a husband in the army," one enslaved woman reported of a local slaveholder. Union officers were fully aware of the problem. In Louisville, one reported that "colored men are willing to enlist" and go to the army but only if they were assured of protection for their families. "Attend to their wives and families and they would immediately rush to arms," he wrote. But the government did not deliver, and evidence of the shocking abuse of US soldiers' wives amassed. Eventually, it shamed even Congress. Black soldiers appealed for help, sometimes directly to the secretary of war, pleading for the army to intervene against vengeful masters; their officers did the same on the black soldiers' behalf, writing impassioned briefs on the conditions of the families of the men in their units and the powerlessness of men stationed far from home.[90] But women pressed their own case on the government too, emerging indisputably as actors in the political drama of emancipation to an extent unseen in 1862. Dragging their battered bodies into army posts, they presented themselves as evidence of their masters' violent retribution, then swore out official affidavits to document the consequences of the government's negligence toward the nation's soldiers.

By 1865, the figure of the black soldier's wife had assumed real, corporeal, collective form. "I am the wife of Nathan Johnson, a soldier in Company F. 116th U.S. Infantry," Frances Johnson testified. "I have three children and with them I belonged to Matthias Outon." The day after her husband enlisted, Mrs. Johnson testified, I "was brutally beaten by master." He had previously announced that "he and all the 'niggers' did might wrong in joining the army." Frances Johnson ran away to Camp Nelson, Kentucky, but she had to leave her children behind. "My children are still held," she made sure they knew. Patsey Leach, a soldier's widow, gave a similar affidavit, also at Camp Nelson, documenting the escalating abuse she suffered from her owner after her husband enlisted. "From that time he treated me more cruelly than ever whipping me frequently without any cause and insulting me on every occasion." After her husband died in the service, her owner beat her almost to death, declaring that he would "kill me by piecemeal." When he had finished whipping her, she testified, he said, "never mind God dam you when I am done with you tomorrow you never will live no more."[91]

The record of abuse was horrific and extensive. Frances Johnson, Patsey Leach, and many other women like them in Kentucky were living testimony to the consequences of congressional and presidential decisions taken in 1862 and 1863. "This is but one of dozens of similar applications of like character," an officer emphasized when reporting one such case. He begged to know what he could do for the women and children.[92] African American soldiers' wives clearly perceived some power in the Union Army. But the master's violent authority was local and immediate, the Union's often too far away. As late as March 1865, officers in Kentucky had no recourse against black soldiers' owners or legal means to free their wives.

Finally, belatedly, Congress acted. In December 1864, a bill came out of Henry Wilson's Senate Committee on Military Affairs. It began as a copy of the Militia Act of 1862, but by the time it was passed on March 3, 1865, it had acquired much more expansive form and language. As finally passed, the act declared "forever free" the wife and children of any person mustered into the Union Army or Navy, so long as "sufficient proof of marriage" existed. The law thus liberated the wives and children of black soldiers regardless of their owners' loyalty. At the very minimum, it confirms the concrete and long-lasting consequences of the first Militia Act, which, over Wilson's objections, had excluded the wives of black soldiers owned by loyal men. It also shows how black soldiers' wives had become a real political constituency. A selection of the women's testimony was read aloud on the floor of the Senate, breaking an impasse at a crucial moment in the debate over the bill.[93]

That debate was both nasty and protracted. It forced senators back into an argument about the existence and identity of the slave wife, but this time, it also forced them to *define* slave marriage so that the freedom claims of particular Kentucky women could be adjudicated. It is still easy to overlook or dismiss the matter of gender in history, so it is worth pausing to consider the scene in the Senate committee room. "Who is the wife of a slave?" John Sherman asked, returning to the issue that had dogged senators originally. "You must define who shall be considered the wife of a slave." "But which [wife] is to be the one?" Reverdy Johnson of Maryland responded, in predictable mocking mode. We can put in the proviso "that but one will be allowed," an abolitionist offered. The ridicule did not derail the bill but did refine it. In the end, the law stipulated that enslaved people who "lived together or associated or cohabited" until the day of the soldier's enlistment met the "evidence" of marriage. For the radical Charles Sumner, the emancipation of soldiers' wives was a simple matter: it was "inhuman" to do otherwise. But for his great adversary Garrett Davis, himself a Kentucky slaveholder, it was a matter of his constitutional rights, the takings clause in particular (which prevents the taking of private property for "public use" without compensation), and the old, still potent argument that there was no military rationale for the government confiscation of slave women. "Slave women and children were of no public use," Davis pointed out. He saw "no logic in [the] conclusion" that because a husband was liberated, Congress had the right to liberate his wife.[94] But by 1865, the logic was there.

In the end, Congress passed the act by a narrow margin, and President Lincoln signed it into law on March 4, 1865. The language of the act is so singular, to read it now is to recognize how the law marked racial difference, even as it extended equal recognition:

> It is hereby enacted that the wife and children . . . of any person mustered into the military or naval service of the U.S. shall, from and after the passage of this act, be forever free . . . ; and in determining who is or was the wife and who are the children of the enlisted person herein mentioned, evidence that he and the woman claimed to be his wife have cohabited together, or associated as husband and wife, and so continued to cohabit or associate at the time of the enlistment, or evidence that a form or ceremony of marriage, whether such a marriage was or was not authorized or recognized by law, has been entered into or celebrated by them, and that the parties thereto thereafter lived together or associated or cohabited as husband and wife, and so continued to live, cohabit, or associate at the time of the enlistment, shall be deemed sufficient proof of marriage for the purposes of this act.

The insecurity of ex-slaves' marriages and claims on their children persisted even in the act granting them freedom on the basis of the marriage bond.[95]

The Enlistment Act was not just a paper law. It tangibly and materially affected black women's lives—freeing at least fifty thousand women and children, mostly in Kentucky.[96] Garrett Davis fought it in state court and lost. The law was just one more piece of legislation in the long history of military emancipation in the Civil War. But coming after congressional passage of the Thirteenth Amendment, it is a powerful reminder of the enduring significance of marriage in shaping the terms of emancipation and citizenship in the United States. The black soldiers' quid pro quo gave his wife freedom, of a certain sort. As historian Amy Dru Stanley writes, "Her freedom represented something owed to him, a token of the exchange relation between the Union soldier and the national state."[97]

There was nothing new about this. Had not French republican commissioners said something similar in Saint-Domingue in 1793? Women enslaved in the United States did not win freedom as a human right or a natural right, nor did freedom endow them with the quality of self-possession. Instead, their husbands' rights to claim them prevailed over their masters' rights to the same. "Your wives shall have hereafter, a husband's protection and not a master's," the colonel of the 62nd US Colored Infantry declared to his men. With emancipation, black men secured the considerable rights of the husband as conferred in Anglo-American law. Rights for freedmen began with rights over their putative wives and children; the right to headship of a family fundamentally defined a "free" man. Freed into coverture, African American women were to be protected and governed under the laws of marriage, like all adult women. Emancipation was supposed to transform enslaved women into wives.[98]

In that sense, the final Enlistment Act, like all others that preceded it, speaks directly to the indispensability of marriage—and the patriarchal gender order—not simply as a tool of policymaking and politics but also of state-building and citizenship in the United States. The definition of marital and parental rights were foundational, not ancillary parts of the project of emancipation. At the very moment when slavery was permanently destroyed, and the US government moved to incorporate 4 million people of African descent into the nation, it took care to shore up and extend the institution of marriage. An act as radical as emancipation was unthinkable without that anchoring order, yoking men to the responsibilities of husbands, and subjecting women to the authority of particular men. It was virtually a condition of emancipation that slave husbands would assume the responsibility. Slavery had been built into the very foundation of the republic since its inception. In 1865, Republicans abandoned one kind of property in persons while clinging desperately to another. Freedom was unimaginable without marriage—a conclusion confirmed by the simultaneous debate over the Thirteenth Amendment.

Slavery and marriage were a twinned set of domestic relations with a long Anglo-American history. The law viewed slavery and marriage as symmetrical, both relations of domestic dependency. Not for nothing had proslavery ideologues in the United States relied on marriage to legitimate enslavement. But that equation or analogy could also be put to the reverse purpose: "If 'all men are born free,' how is that all women are born slaves," Mary Astell astutely asked in 1700. By 1865, there was an organized feminist movement pressing that very question about the slavery of sex. Slavery and marriage had been linked for so long as twin pillars of the social and political order that conservatives feared—and radicals hoped—that the dissolution of one would transform the other. And indeed, the two relations proved difficult to untangle. "Marriage is too much like slavery not to be involved in its fate," the proslavery sociologist George Fitzhugh had predicted in 1854.[99] If the language of the Thirteenth Amendment seems particularly cramped and ungenerous, this is in no small part owing to fears that, if not written carefully, the amendment might emancipate women as well as slaves. Charles Sumner's draft of the amendment wedged open that possibility. Versions of the amendment had been circulating since 1864; Francis Lieber, not surprisingly, had written one. The Senate Judiciary Committee had been working on a draft since the beginning of 1864 that copied the free-soil language of the Northwest Ordinance of 1787, language that survived in section 1 of the final text: "Neither slavery nor involuntary servitude, except as a punishment for crime whereof the party shall have been duly convicted, shall exist within the United States, or any place subject to their jurisdiction." But at a key moment in the debate, Charles Sumner, the Republican senator from Massachusetts, offered something far more ambitious than the negative injunction of the free-soil conceptualization. Borrowing instead from the French Declaration of the Rights of Man and the radical republican ideas of that document, he proposed this language for the Thirteenth Amendment: "All persons are equal before the law, so that no person can hold another as a slave; and the Congress shall have the power to make all laws necessary and proper to carry this declaration into effect everywhere in the U.S."[100]

The implications for women and marriage were not lost on anyone. Senators roused to the defense of their own most intimate prerogatives as men and husbands. Unlike prior congressional debates over emancipation, this time the opposition was not restricted to conservative slaveholders, southerners, Democrats, or border state men. Michigan senator Jacob Howard was a Radical Republican who had voted against the 1862 measure restricting emancipation to the wives of black soldiers owned by rebels, because it did not extend to all slaveholders. But he quickly pointed out the danger of Sumner's language: "I suppose before the law a woman would be equal to a man, a woman would be as free as a man. A wife would be equal to her husband as free as her husband before the law." That was precisely the problem. The amendment's advocates retreated amid such dangerous talk and scrambled back to safer free-soil ground, issuing reassurances that the legal abolition of a master's right of property in his slave would not diminish a man's property in the service of his wife. Similar arguments surfaced in the House debate as well. One minority Democrat, opposed to uncompensated emancipation, insisted that, when it came to property rights, the Constitution must defer to local laws. Their own prerogatives as men rested on the same ground as slaveholders, he pointedly reminded his non-slaveholding colleagues: "A husband has right of property in the service of his wife," and "all these rights rest upon the same basis as a man's right of property in the service of his slaves." He had a point. Property is what the government says it is, Henry Clay once said. Commitment to the bonds of marriage—and the subjection of women—had a broad political constituency in 1865. Not surprisingly, Sumner's "explicit language of equality under the law was rejected," historian Michael Vorenberg explains, "in part on gender grounds." The dangers of emancipation for marriage law and the rights of husbands were contained.[101]

In a period of Civil War–era constitutional revision in the United States so vigorous it can be called a second founding, when the idea of the nation and its citizens was fundamentally remade, marriage was carried over, carefully, into the new order. The explicitly hierarchical relationship of "man and wife"—and deliberately asymmetrical rights and obligations it modeled—were anything but obsolete in the re-United States of America. While the Thirteenth Amendment prohibiting slavery applied to men and women both, the Fourteenth Amendment defining the rights of free people and guaranteeing all citizens of the United States "the equal protection of the laws" would not be seen to have any application to women. The Fifteenth

Amendment right of citizens to vote did not apply to American women citizens of any race. It was not until 1971 that the Supreme Court for the first time interpreted the equal protection clause to invalidate a statute that discriminated on the basis of sex.[102] It took until 1920 and another amendment for US women to get the right to vote. By that point the process of black disfranchisement was so advanced that few African American women could exercise their right.[103]

The subjection of sex and men's rights of property in their wives were not threatened by emancipation. Instead, they were extended—to govern the relations of the millions of new American citizens whose freedom was confirmed by the Thirteenth Amendment. With emancipation, African American men came into the rights of free men and husbands. "What he has is his own. His wife is his," was how one white politician put it in debate over the civil rights bill. In ways that historians have not yet fully grasped, that principle would shape the raft of postwar legislation required to enforce the Thirteenth Amendment in the defeated Confederate states.[104] Marriage law would prove indispensable in the construction of a new postwar legal order in the South. In this the United States was no exception. Like lawmakers across the imperial world, they relied on marriage as the weight-bearing foundation of cultural and racial difference.[105]

African American women had fought for their peoples' freedom and their own and their families' survival in the American Civil War. They played a crucial part in the historical process of emancipation and Union victory. But their story never became part of the history of that war, except in so far as they were cast as wives and dependents. In the United States, following emancipation, marriage only gained salience as a tool of public policy and federal governance. So did the value of martial manhood. As newly freed African American men moved to claim the rights of citizens amid violent resistance by whites in the former slave states, they relied heavily on their record of service and sacrifice as soldiers in the nation's cause. "What higher order of citizen is there than the soldier?" one group of "colored citizens of Nashville" demanded to know.[106] Now they were self-possessing men with wives and children to protect and represent. And the history of the Civil War on which they relied was the soldiers' version—with the story of the soldiers' wives erased.

3

Reconstructing a Life amid the Ruins

The ends of wars, when they come, are always dangerous moments, ripe with possibilities of every sort. Peace must be made, armies dismantled, enemies held accountable, refugees returned, cities rebuilt, nations and individual lives reconstructed from the ruins. Everywhere after wars, women live those histories in ways particular to their sex.[1] In April 1865, the people of the Confederate States of America arrived at such a juncture. With war concluded but peace not yet made, the conquered and liberated alike awaited news of the victor's justice. The total military defeat of the Confederacy brought a decisive end to the national ambitions of the world's most powerful slaveholding class. It also threatened the very basis of their wealth and power. In the United States, slave emancipation was the war's legacy.

Emancipation in the United States reverberated globally, as evident in the sense of possibility for enslaved and bound workers on plantations and estates far beyond the American South, and in the failure of cotton brokers, from Liverpool to Bombay. At the very apex of world capital markets, partners in the London offices of Baring Brothers Bank scrambled to adjust, desperate for information on the condition of cotton plantations in the conquered South.[2]

Ella Gertrude Clanton Thomas, c. 1850s Courtesy of F. Michael Despeaux, Easley, South Carolina.

Far from the centers of global or national power, on a plantation six miles outside of Augusta, Georgia, one woman, Ella Gertrude Clanton Thomas, lived through it all: destruction, defeat, occupation, emancipation, political uncertainty, and, as would become clear, a long, grinding descent into poverty. Thomas kept a forty-one-year record of her life that captured the historical passage.[3] She knew she lived in radical times: "The fact is," she wrote shortly after surrender, "our

Negroes are to be made free and a change, a very [great] change will be affected in our mode of living."[4] Indeed.

In the American South in the spring of 1865, as so often happens in the aftermath of wars, the conquered and the liberated lived through the process of reconstruction in awful proximity. All wars involve an element of civil war, Tony Judt argues in his magisterial study *Postwar*, and "it is one of the traumatic features of civil war that even after the enemy is defeated he remains in place; and with him the memory of the conflict."[5] In the United States, where the enslaved were crucial allies of the Union victors, the postwar accommodation assumed an inescapably intimate form. Emancipation swept aside the Old South of masters and slaves. The 3.5 million people of African descent still enslaved to the Mrs. Thomases of the world emerged, liberated, from the ruins of the slaveholders' nation to face the staggering but promising task of building a free life and free homes. Their former owners emerged, conquered, to face the consequences of defeat: uncompensated emancipation or, as one put it simply, "the wreck of all."[6] In the postwar American South, reconstruction involved a revolution in every household and every family.

Writing that history now, and here, poses challenges that are both scholarly and political. One involves the problem of scale, specifically, the relationship between the global and the local. This history includes the consolidation of the new nation-state world system and the relentless movement of capital in a transnational cotton economy. But it also includes individual human beings within families and communities, in particular places such as Augusta, Georgia, who struggled to adapt to and redefine the new conditions of life—in work, family, property, racial laws, civil rights, and violence.[7] The global scope of Reconstruction is not entirely a new recognition, of course. More than eighty years ago, W. E. B. Du Bois wrote searingly of the "black reconstruction of democracy in America" as a test of labor and democracy itself worldwide. "Reconstruction," he observed, "was an economic revolution on a mighty scale and with world-wide reverberations."[8] In the new age of global history, however, when perspective is more likely established by capital or commodity flows than human labor, there is still something to be said for adopting the human-scale perspective—for reversing direction and seeing massive events from the perspective of a single place and life.[9] It is not only that the meta-history of "Reconstruction" has been brilliantly mapped over the past thirty years, and the complex structural developments in political economy clearly delineated.[10] It is also that such a perspective allows us to see how huge structural changes in land, labor, capital, and racial ideology were inextricably entangled with highly intimate matters of marriage and family, sexuality and love.

Without a doubt, we stand at a new juncture in the history of Reconstruction. Although it has not yet been laid out fully, it is increasingly clear that the frameworks that have structured debate in the field since the 1950s are collapsing under the weight of a new, early twenty-first-century accounting of racism and the legacy of slavery in contemporary life. Canonical formulations, such as the one offered by Eric Foner, which framed the entire tumultuous period of Reconstruction as an "unfinished Revolution," require a faith in the ongoing progress of black civil rights that is much harder to summon in 2018 than in 1988. Instead, scholars and writers from a variety of perspectives have challenged the idea of Reconstruction or emancipation as a definitive dividing line, or even an inflection, and have argued for profound and significant continuities across the eras of slavery and post-emancipation.

From one perspective, a recent wave of academic books on slavery in the antebellum United States has effectively eroded any basis on which to make claims about the distinctiveness of a southern system of social organization by assimilating slavery to other forms of capitalist organization. These works do not draw sharp distinctions between the exploitation of labor through market mechanisms and economic coercions (wage labor) and the *ownership* of persons (chattel slavery) as a permanent and hereditary condition for people of African descent in the United States. In these new accounts, slavery is wholly capitalist in nature, and capitalism, like slavery, is inherently, at its core, coercive. This body of literature, now collectively summed up as "slavery's capitalism," effectively dispenses with the historical divide of Civil War and emancipation, and reopens the matter of Reconstruction. If the South was fully capitalist before the war, then what did the defeat of the Confederate States of America and slave emancipation mean in US history? How significant a break was it historically, in terms of social organization, state power, race relations, and in the lives of the 4 million newly freed African Americans and their former owners, a now conquered and dispossessed master class? Never mind that the market in slaves was precisely the thing—the form of human capital—permanently destroyed by emancipation. Or that the cost to the South was staggering economically, plunging the region into a period of uncertainty so extreme that economic historians still identity it as the key feature of Reconstruction. Or, most importantly, that the transition to a new political economy and system of labor required a process so massive, disruptive, protracted, and contested that it defies any idea of capitalist "business as usual." Rejecting forty years of Marxist scholarship on the relationship between slavery and capitalism, this new scholarship unsettles the idea of Reconstruction as a fundamental divide or revolutionary juncture in American history.[11]

From a different scholarly perspective, the antiwar turn in interpretations of the war itself enforces increasing skepticism about the very concept of "Reconstruction" as a distinct period and process in American history and life. These scholars focus on the weakness of the federal government and the army of occupation, and on the pattern of unrelenting violence against African Americans, which suggest not a social and political revolution during Reconstruction but rather a continuous state of war.[12]

Perhaps the most compelling challenge to established views of Reconstruction and emancipation comes from the popular mobilization of the Black Lives Matter movement, and the searing analyses by African American writers that support it. This mobilization shows, too, that the historical question is not a narrow, pedantic matter but one that connects fundamentally to our lives and narratives today. Ta-Nehisi Coates's account of American history as the systematic plunder and pillage of black lives, bodies, and wealth—a view laid out in his memoir, *Between the World and Me*, and his celebrated essay in *The Atlantic* on the case for reparations—is, ultimately, a meditation on slavery and its half-life, if not its very persistence: "You cannot forget how much they took from us and how they transfigured our very bodies into sugar, tobacco, cotton, and gold." That "plunder of black life was drilled into this country in its infancy and reinforced across its history . . . a default setting," he says, "to which, likely to the end of our days, we must invariably return." The urgency of the historical question and legacy is equally apparent in Bryan Stevenson's work on the criminal justice system. And it is perhaps most directly articulated by the law professor Michelle Alexander, in her book *The New Jim Crow*, about the racialized systems of control in the United States that rendered Reconstruction transitory by definition: from her perspective, mass incarceration is the new Jim Crow, which was itself the new slavery.[13]

Taken together, this emphasis on the systemic nature of racial exploitation as a deep and persistent structure that provides the real through-line of US history is far more powerful than any previous argument for continuity in the long debate on the Civil War and Reconstruction. It represents a new cultural moment to be sure, and one that issues a profound challenge to historians who retain any conviction about emancipation as a meaningful break in historical time.

One white woman's life in the postwar maelstrom opens a small window on this vast landscape. Gertrude Thomas's is a planter-class perspective, and a woman's one at that, with all the limitations of vision that this implies. But precisely in its particularity, Thomas's personal, day-to-day account of reconstructing a life in the ruins of the Old South allows us to see the enormous disordering of public and private life, to see what persisted from the old regime, and to see what new possibilities emerged out this chaos. Among other things, it shows what freed people were up against as they tried to secure their freedom in the postwar South. People like Thomas did not simply accept the loss of their racial privilege or surrender their possessive claims on the people they had owned. As everything was wrenched away, her response mixed grief, loss, and rage in dangerous measure. Her personal history reveals a larger story.[14]

Thomas looked out on it all from a domestic—which is not to say private—space, and with a woman's perspective. She viewed the impact of social collapse and postwar reconstruction in personal as well as political realms.

In this respect her record defies the usual historiographical divisions between matters of political economy on the one hand, and women, gender, and the family on the other. The impossibility of separating political and domestic affairs had everything to do with the nature of what was destroyed in the revolution, that is, slavery and the world built on its foundation. To take the measure of Reconstruction, it helps to begin with a proper appreciation of what slavery was, as a social system, a system of labor and exploitation, and a foundation of subjectivity itself. "Will we ever settle quietly in our old peaceful domestic relations?" Thomas worried in November 1864, as the enemy bore down on her door. When Union soldiers arrived the convulsions started, and for her at least, for thirty years they did not stop. Slavery, like marriage, was a system of domestic relations, and when it was ripped up, virtually everything else was uprooted with it—not just the relationship between master and slave that constituted a massive proportion of the capital wealth of the South, governed the deployment of labor, gave value to agricultural land, grounded white supremacy and racial ideology, and shaped regional and national politics. In dismantling slavery, emancipation showed just what it had been—far more than a property regime or legal system—and how deep its roots had gone, penetrating and organizing every element of life and requiring their reconstruction as well.[15]

When "slavery became a thing of the past," Thomas explained in October 1865, she was "reduced from a state of affluence . . . to utter beggary." But if Thomas suffered from the financial loss, she suffered far more from the thought of what emancipation meant: that her eldest son and heir, deprived of education and put to the plow like any ex-slave, would now find as his equal or his better "his father's son by a woman a shade darker than *his* mother." For Thomas, emancipation was an excruciatingly intimate event, experienced as violation, provoking feelings of sexual humiliation, adultery, and its particular southern form, "miscegenation," which she understood as competition with mixed-race or "mulatto" women.[16] Slavery not only gave a terrible intimacy to war; it mingled property and love in ways that made its loss elemental. With defeat and the destruction of slavery, even the very notion of love and family had to be remade, and race (or white supremacy)—and all that it involved—reconstructed on new terms.

It is difficult to exaggerate how far Ella Gertrude Clanton Thomas fell. She was born in 1834, second daughter of Turner Clanton, one of the richest men in Georgia—cotton planter, businessman, owner of 12,000 acres and 400 slaves. At death his estate was valued at $2.2 million. When she married Jefferson Thomas in 1852, her father gave her twenty-three enslaved persons in her own name, and she got a further share of his estate as her own separate property when he died in 1864. But by 1888, she was fifty-four years old and, as she put it, "could not obtain credit for fifty dollars." Gertrude Thomas had been born into immense privilege and wealth but by this point, her second son, Jefferson Davis Thomas, was compelled to go to work as a clerk for a "Chinaman" in Augusta.[17] In many ways Gertrude Thomas's experience mirrored that of her class, albeit in exaggerated form.

The fall of the planter class is an epic story, one tied to the class's political fate within the re-United States.[18] Thomas's effort at reconstructing a living and a life was exquisitely syncopated with the chaotic process of experimentation in politics, labor, and familial forms that emancipation unleashed. For women, there was the added lack of control imposed by the dangers of the reproductive body, childbirth, and legal disabilities as wives. Gertrude Thomas's married life was punctuated by the additional perils of pregnancies, miscarriages, deaths of newborns and infants, and, in 1879, of her seven-year-old James Clanton. She gave birth to ten children, her last at age forty-one, six of whom survived to adulthood. It was an element of life largely out of her control.[19]

In the US South, as in so many other cases, war established the terms of the postwar world.[20] For Thomas the radical break arrived in late November 1864 with the army of General William Tecumseh Sherman. Flush from victory in the battle of Atlanta, Sherman's men fanned out in a swath of destruction that hit the Thomas plantations, first in Burke County and then in Richmond, both counties in the Georgia black belt. Thomas had lived in fear of this. Carrying Confederate bonds, silver spoons and forks, and her diaries, Thomas had moved into Augusta from her home plantation, Belmont, shortly before Sherman arrived. Like many other women in history, she met the crisis of war's end while pregnant. "Happening as it does in these troublous times I am sincerely sorry for it," she wrote. Finally, the moment of reckoning arrived, and within hours Sherman's men had accomplished "the destruction of our entire planting interest in Burke."[21]

With that began the slow disintegration of the master-slave relationship and the plantation household and family. Liberation and expropriation were one and the same, both structural and massively disorienting changes. At the Thomas plantations, the original loss was not an outside affair. It quickly emerged that Sherman's troops had been summoned by Henry, "one of our Negroes," as Mrs. Thomas described him, who had left the plantation the evening before, "joined the Yankees and the next morning conducted them to Cotton Town," one of the Thomases' two plantations in Burke County. Henry showed them where Uncle Sykes, "our Negro driver," had hidden the horses and mules. The repeated use of the possessive article gives some indication of the damage inflicted. In seizing the opportunity to turn their future onto a new path, Henry and other enslaved people took huge risks. Union columns did not provide certain protection, as recapture was common. And to the very last moment of the war, Confederate scouts prowled the countryside targeting and then murdering rebel slaves.[22] In South Carolina and Georgia there is hard evidence that Sherman's men destroyed the rice mills, big houses, and slave quarters at the specific request of local slaves, an orgy of burning designed to mark off the past as unrecoverable and shape the terms of reconstruction. Thomas recorded the details of those who were "burnt out" in her neighborhood around Augusta. At Cotton Town, Sherman's men burned the gin house and cotton screw, and destroyed all the corn and cotton. They left with Henry, dressed in a Union uniform and mounted on the Thomas's most valuable horse, to wreak the same damage on her brother-in-law's plantation.[23]

Such highly personal dramas of emancipation were enacted all over the Confederate South. Historian Eugene D. Genovese called them moments of truth.[24] Even before the war ended, these moments shattered "domestic relations" and aired truths violently suppressed under slavery. Thomas's losses were delivered at the hands of her slaves, prompting her to ask, "Who betrayed me?" Her particular accounting was not as obsessive as that of some others. But Thomas did go through the usual owner's inventory, trying to convince herself that "with the exception of Henry" and John Boss, "who drove us for five or six years after we were married," the others "proved most faithful."[25] For slaveholders all over the South, emancipation played out in the language of family loyalty and devotion. What slaves saw as victory and called liberation, owners experienced as personal betrayal.[26]

From that moment of emancipation forward, reconstruction would be a history of dispossession for slaveholders like Thomas, each loss freighted with meaning beyond the monetary or material. The material losses alone, however, were great. Thomas had long imagined an end to slave-owning and to her own liberation from its moral burdens, especially the way that unfettered access to slave women's bodies made planter men degenerate.[27] But hers was a fantasy future in which she gave up her slaves but retained their value; it was not so much emancipation as sale. The reality of defeat, of course, was otherwise. The total abolition of slavery was codified in the Thirteenth Amendment to the US Constitution and imposed on rebel states as a condition of readmission to the Union. It was "one of the largest liquidations of private property in world history," an estimated $4 billion, fully two-thirds of the capital wealth of southern states. In today's terms it would represent a loss of about $10 trillion in household assets. Georgia's losses alone from emancipation at the time amounted to $275 million.[28] Emancipation was the single biggest element of the staggering economic price the South paid for the war.[29] Gertrude Thomas lost almost everything: all of her original marital property, which she had taken in enslaved persons, "thirty thousand dollars ... invested in Negroes alone"; the increase of that human property over thirteen years (by 1865, she owned ninety slaves); and most of what was bequeathed in her father's will in 1864. "By surrender of the southern army," she said, "slavery became a thing of the past ... [and] we were reduced from a state of affluence to comparative poverty." She personally was reduced "to utter beggary." Thomas and her husband were also left holding $15,000 in repudiated Confederate bonds and a few thousand in worthless Confederate currency. By the beginning of May, nothing sold in the Augusta market except for silver or gold, gold had increased in value, and, as she noted starkly, "we have *not a dollar*."[30]

Slaveholders would nurture hopes of government compensation for slave property into the 1870s. Georgia legislators even advanced the argument that women, incapable of taking up arms in the rebellion, were innocents who should be fully compensated for the loss of their slaves. But there would be no compensation or reparations for Confederate slaveholders, male or female.[31] The losses were massive, they were permanent, and they were about a lot more than money.

In the postwar South, the antebellum form of the slaveholding family was dramatically broken. Between late November and the end of May 1865, Thomas witnessed the disintegration of her household at Belmont. On May 7, Yankee troops arrived in Augusta, and she watched through closed curtains as African Americans celebrated in the streets. The next day her husband gathered the "servants," informed them that "it was extremely probable that the Yankees would free them, that they would then be obliged to work," and that they might as well work for him. At this point most of the house servants were still there: America, who had just had a baby girl, and who had nursed Gertrude's son Jeff when he was born in 1861 and Gertrude had no milk; Tamah, the cook, whom Gertrude's eldest son called Mammy; Nancy, who had a daughter named Ella Gertrude and who had been wet nurse for Gertrude's daughter Cora Lou; Patsey; Milly, Cora Lou's nurse; a little girl, Betsey, whose mother Gertrude and her husband also owned; Daniel, their driver and butler; and Uncle Jim. By the end of the month none remained "out of all our old house servants," she noted, "except Patsey and a little boy Frank."[32]

As her household disintegrated, Thomas was thrust into unfamiliar negotiations with free servants. The morass of quotidian negotiations are the very picture of a revolution in process.[33] For months domestic servants preoccupied her—how to get them, what to pay them, and how to manage them. May began a period of uncertainty and adjustment to new household labor arrangements and relations. Thomas did not know what "a task" was in laundry, or how much to pay, and was so short of help she asked Uncle Jim, a farmhand from Burke, to wash clothes for her. "Good Lord, Missis," he said, "I never wash no close in my life." Throughout the month of May, she chronicled the departures of her former slaves and what these departures meant for her life. "The disordered state of things among the servants still continues," she noted. "I have done a great deal of housework today and startled Frank by saying I intended ironing." She made bread for the first time in her life. "My back ached when I was through," she declared; "it was about as hard work as I ever did." In late May after the exodus, she assisted Patsey in "wiping the breakfast dishes—a thing I never remember to have done more than once or twice in my life." After Tamah left she could not find a cook. She had to do without a baby nurse for her two-year-old daughter Cora Lou, who, as a result "fell down several times" and scarred her face. Clearly, Thomas was unaccustomed to the work of watching the child as well.[34]

Like many ex-masters who could not adjust to the new terms, she wanted to be done with black servants. She went to Dublin, the working-class, Irish section of town, looking for help, and even tried to get "a girl from the orphan's asylum" as a baby nurse, hoping for deliverance from negotiations with ex-slaves.[35] But none of that worked, and she was forced to learn to hire newly free African American women as domestic servants by the task and the day. On that score freedwomen prevailed. Housing was scarce, and some domestic workers continued to live in. But most insisted on living out, putting physical distance between themselves and their employers, and hard limits on the amount of work employers could demand. Living out was also a direct rejection of the domestic labor and spatial arrangements that had prevailed under slavery, which had allowed slaveholders to claim enslaved people as members of "the family." The new terms of domestic service in the postbellum South were a signal accomplishment in black southerners' struggle to give freedom substance.[36] Thomas would never quite get used to hired servants and their habit of making a priority of their own families' needs.[37] Nothing testified to defeat and emancipation quite as definitively as Gertrude Thomas in the kitchen.

As Thomas's household shrunk, her possessive claim to "her people" also died. With slavery, the form of the wealth had always been essential to its meaning; the same was true of its loss. Slaveholders had long cast their ownership of human beings in familial terms. It was a fundamental element of proslavery ideology throughout the antebellum period—historians call it "paternalism"—and though stripped of its material basis under slavery, planters continued to appeal to it when they became "masters without slaves."[38] A group of Savannah planters tried to strike the paternalist pose with General O. O. Howard, the head of the Freedmen's Bureau, in the summer of 1865, proposing involuntary contracts as best "for their State, and for that unfortunate race of people who have for generations composed a part of their families, and whose interest and happiness, have been so mutually dependent, and interwoven with each other."[39] Needless to say, this was not a view of family to which enslaved people or their descendants ever subscribed.

Like newly freed people all over the South, those enslaved at Belmont left to form their own free families out of the reach of their former owners. Every war creates waves of displaced people, and the Civil War was no exception. There were millions of refugees, many African American, in 1865. Some were refugees from war in the usual sense—people displaced by the movement of armies, occupation of territory, and general chaos. But in a deeper sense, African Americans were all refugees from slavery as well, and the forced separations of families in the African and interstate slave trades. Even before the war began, more than a million people had been forcibly moved from the eastern seaboard to the new cotton plantations of the deep South. Every single case involved the destruction of a family, the separation of mothers and fathers from their children, wives from their husbands, sisters from their brothers, grandmothers from their grandchildren.

Sometimes the only thing left was a memory. "I don't know who my grand folks were," the former slave Sallie Crane said, only that they "was all Virginia folks." Slavery left a trail of heartbreak and family members scattered everywhere from Accra to Maryland to Texas. This made lineage itself untraceable in a lot of cases. Historian and literary scholar Saidiya Hartman has written of the utter hopelessness of belonging once you had "lost your mother" in the slave trade. "I, too, live in the time of slavery," she writes, "by which I mean I am living in the future created by it." Slavery had wreaked havoc on people's lives, and most of the damage was irreversible.[40] By 1865, far too many family connections were irreparably broken.

In 1865, people moved first to search for and reunify their families. One Union official called it "the regathering." There was no central agency—no United Nations Relief and Rehabilitation Administration, as there was after World War II, no registry of displaced persons to check. What freed people had were their own memories, networks of people and churches, and the black press. Advertisements and notices—"Information Wanted" or "Lost Friends"—ran in black newspapers all over the United States, especially in the *Christian Recorder*, the publication of the African Methodist Episcopal church. Pastors read them from pulpits on Sunday mornings. People took to the roads, sometimes retracing slave traders' paths. By the summer of 1865, there was also the Freedmen's Bureau (formally called the Bureau of Refugees, Freedmen, and Abandoned Land), which had been created by Congress to oversee the transition of millions of former slaves to their new status as free people. It was charged with the return and care of refugees, black and white. Bureau offices received heartbreaking appeals for help from parents and children alike. The bureau tried to help the father in Arkansas who had not seen his children in seven years, forwarding his letter (it was addressed to the children) to the office in Augusta, Georgia, and then on to Florida, their last known whereabouts. The bureau was underfunded and understaffed, but it served as the official government network of communication and transportation for displaced people attempting to find surviving family members. It was a monumental undertaking. What was it to be free if you couldn't find your mother?[41]

In the spring of 1865, the roads around Augusta teemed with people, among them Gertrude Thomas's former slaves. Over the years, Gertrude and her husband had sold the people they owned far away from the Augusta area, without regard for family relations. Some of those people were never heard from again, including Isabella, separated from her children in 1857 when the Thomases sold her as punishment for theft. Other families had been separated locally, scattered to Clanton and Thomas holdings across three counties.[42] With emancipation, former slaves attempted to reverse the process and gather up their people, contributing one small stream to the larger migration.

Gertrude Thomas experienced it all as a personal loss and a repudiation of her possessive claim. Two days after Jefferson Thomas's begrudging announcement of freedom, Daniel, who had accompanied Gertrude's husband to war, took all of his clothes and left in the middle of the night "without saying anything to anyone." Nancy also left, taking her two children. Then "Betsey, a little servant," was sent to town to get the newspaper and never came back. At first Thomas thought the girl had been taken by her father. But then she discovered "it was a concerted plan between Sarah [her mother] and herself." Sarah, who had also been enslaved at Belmont, had been charged with stealing meat and sent down to the Cotton Town plantation in Burke County as punishment. "Mr. T. wouldn't sell her," Gertrude noted, implying that she would have done so. Separated from her daughter for more than a year, Sarah laid plans to reclaim Betsey and an infant child still on the Burke plantation. The overseer, Sykes, left Cotton Town, Thomas noted of this development, "seduced by the wiles of a Delilah"—Sarah—who "wishing someone to bring her baby to town persuaded him to run off with her." "He had left an ugly faithful black wife" to follow Sarah, "a good looking mulatto or brown complected woman." Gertrude thought that Susan, her mother's most trusted servant, was "influenced" to leave by her husband, but she recalled that her father had said that "in case of a revolt among the Negroes," which is clearly what this exodus felt like to her, "Susan would prove a ringleader." Her mother's cook and driver left too. The latter, Thomas added, is now "cutting a fine Beau Brummell figure as he gallants a coloured demoiselle or walks up the street with his cigar in his mouth."[43] This process of family reunification was essential, an existentially urgent need, to African American liberation in the postwar South, and Thomas recorded it—ridiculing every move of her family's former slaves as illegitimate and casting efforts at family reunification as defection, seduction, and insurrection

Clearly, it was not just capital or physical labor Gertrude Thomas lost, notwithstanding the "slavery's capitalism" scholarship that construes homogeneity and seamlessness between slavery and wage systems. All over the South, African American parents had to fight their old owners' claims of possession and go to court to reclaim their children.[44] Sarah was forced to steal her daughter back because, as Thomas saw it, Betsey belonged to Gertrude's family, not Sarah's. "I felt interested in Betsey," Thomas wrote the day her mother took her. "She was a bright quick child and raised in our family would have become a good servant. As it is she will be under her mother's influence and run wild in the street." Slaveholding, the owning of persons over lifetimes and generations, had real, subjective effect. "To an affectionate colored woman it must be a hard struggle between the love for her husband and the [white] children she has raised," Thomas observed once of a neighbor's servant named Caroline. Slaveholders such as Gertrude Thomas had a distorted view of love and family belonging. What she called love was the expropriated emotional and maternal labor of enslaved women in their daily work in the plantation household. It was a characterization those women decisively rejected, and which they expressed definitively in 1865 through actions such as the exodus from Gertrude Thomas's household.[45]

By the turn of the twentieth century, white southern women would be able to comfort themselves with the romantic myth of mammy, the black woman who loved the white family as much as or more than her own. It was one fictive element of the wholesale rewriting of the history of the slave South. But Gertrude Thomas's account of black women's devotion to her and her family was not the product of an early twentieth-century Lost Cause propaganda machine. Nor in 1865 was such a comforting fiction even possible, in the face of so much evidence to the contrary. Finally, freed people could openly claim their bodies and children as their own and put the needs of their own families first. Which is exactly what they did, quickly and at every opportunity, definitively and unequivocally repudiating ex-slaveholders' possessive claims. The shift of black women's maternal labor and attention to their own children was a crucial dimension, and symbol, of the transition from slavery to freedom, not lost on anyone at the time. Even as Gertrude Thomas claimed Betsey as her own, she was fully aware of all the black mothers around her fighting ferociously to reclaim, protect, support, and educate their children. Many former slave owners reacted to the frontal challenge, as Thomas did, with a bitter sense of betrayal and a tenacious, determined hold on privilege that could turn brutal.[46]

In the years right after the war, dispossessed slaveholders like Gertrude Thomas articulated beliefs about love and belonging embedded deep in the social relations and ideology of slave society. "I never liked extorted love or labour," Thomas would say a few years later, after all of her former slaves were gone.[47] But she did like extorted love. Slavery was hard to replace. To her, the people who left in 1865 were not just property or labor. They had nursed her as a child, driven her on her wedding day, attended her father on his death bed, delivered all of her babies, and taken her newborns to their breasts. Gertrude Thomas could not bear the claims of family made by servants upon "her negroes."[48] Slavery had set the terms of family life, love, and belonging in the plantation household. Now, all the terms had to be reset.

Against claims of love and possession by old owners, freedmen and -women had new and meaningful civil rights. They could make binding claims on each other as husband and wife, and, as parents, on their children. By early 1866, the Georgia legislature had devised a new post-emancipation legal order that recognized free families of "persons of color." By a series of laws written and passed in a session in March 1866, it invented that racial category—"free persons of color"—and defined it as all those "having one-eighth negro, or African blood, in their veins." It recognized freed people's marriages, which had been illegal under slavery; legitimized the children born of those relationships; and stipulated that the binding out of children required parental consent. Although coupled with punitive provisions, including against interracial marriage, this raft of laws gave African American parents new legal instruments.[49] And after the summer of 1865, they had an official federal agency, the Freedmen's Bureau, and an army of occupation to back up those rights with force.

But if the law made free families a possibility, it was not easy to extricate individuals from the plantation households in which they had been held. As early as June, Captain John Emory Bryant, an agent of the Freedman's Bureau in Augusta, issued a public warning about "complaints . . . that certain parties refuse to allow wives to leave their premises with their husbands, or parents to take charge of their children." Such people were put on notice that "freedmen in this regard have the same right that white citizens have," and any interference would be met with "severe punishment."[50] In the Augusta area, and especially in Burke County (where Jefferson Thomas had plantations), African American parents filed so many complaints against their former owners and the apprenticeship practices of the local courts that the assistant commissioner of the Freedmen's Bureau for Georgia, Colonel C. C. Sibley, ordered an investigation. The subsequent report identified the "growing evil in this county of the total disregard of its inhabitants to the laws established for indenturing children," including parental consent, and raised fears of a system that encouraged treatment "as severe as they received under the bondage of slavery." A local bureau agent, T. R. Littlefield of Burke County, had openly colluded with local planters to violate the law. In the aftermath of the report, Sibley ordered the cancellation of a whole slew of apprenticeships, including one "done without the mother's consent."[51] For generations, in many different moments of emancipation, parents, and especially mothers, had been the first line of defense in securing their children's fragile claims to freedom.[52] Things were no different in the United States in the summer of 1865. Notwithstanding the Thirteenth Amendment, freedom could not be taken as a right; it had to be seized and made real.

Many of the planters refusing to give up African American children to their parents simply wanted to control their labor. But some also made a case for continued possession based on belonging, as Gertrude Thomas had for Betsey.[53] Across the South ex-masters made claims of paternal care that had not lost all power. The children are "kindly treated and are doing well where they are," as one Freedmen's Bureau agent noted in answer to a mother's attempt to get her children back from a man, likely her former owner, who addressed her simply as "Mary."[54] Gertrude Thomas also claimed that Betsey would be better off with her. Generations of racist-paternalist thinking were not easily undone.

Perhaps the most disturbing element of freed people's struggle in the postwar South owed to the intimate character of the ties they had to sever to make their own free families. By the very nature of what slavery had been, a great many cases involved the disentangling of relationships like those Thomas described: people bearing the same last name, with years of belonging (quite literally for the enslaved) to the same "family," and familiarity with the intimate details of each other's lives, every case shot through with the power relations of masters and slaves, and generations of sexual violence. Servants now had their own names, Thomas noted in 1869, but before they had had only their master's. There were certainly freed people around Augusta— formerly owned by the Thomas and Clanton families—calling themselves Thomas in 1865 or Clanton or Walton, another surname from the extended Clanton family. There was nothing unusual about that. Troubling, even traumatic, complications leap off the page of postwar documents. In Augusta, Rachel Jones needed the intervention of the Freedmen's Bureau to get her children, George and Ella, back from Jenk Jones, her former owner. "Jones refuses to give them up," the bureau agent noted. One wonders why. The aunt and grandmother who brought a child into the bureau office bearing the marks of a whipping from the man to whom she had been apprenticed were, as he explained, "formerly his slaves." The adult women had left, but the ex-master held onto the child. The full nature of the "familial" ties were usually unclear to federal officials, men new to the area, but they surely explain why contests with ex-masters could be so violent.[55]

The making and unmaking of family was no small undertaking. In Augusta, as everywhere else, freed people were forced into direct and potentially deadly confrontations with their former owners. Planters were not accustomed to being challenged by their "servants." Thomas's brother, Buddy Clanton, pulled pistols on his former slaves when he found a group of them on the road heading off the plantation. He caused so much alarm that Gertrude's husband had to rush over to calm things down. It is no wonder that so many of Thomas's former slaves did not leave Belmont until mid-May 1865, when the US Army was encamped on the plantation and Augusta was garrisoned by black troops, or that so many left in the middle of the night and later returned to collect their possessions accompanied by Union soldiers, or that others, like Sarah, resorted to subterfuge to get their children back.[56] It took the full power of the new legal order to enforce freed people's parental rights against the possessive claims of old owners, some of whom were themselves fathers of the children in question. The explosiveness and violence of the postwar process was inseparable from the long prior history of rape, sexual violence, and coerced intimacy under slavery—and the presence of children born as a result. The Thomas family's "secret" history is a case in point.[57]

Gertrude Thomas was unmoored by emancipation. Her response tapped a deep well of anxiety about sex and slavery. That much was clear in an extraordinary letter she wrote to General Sherman's wife, Ellen Ewing Sherman, at precisely the moment his troops hit her plantations in Burke County. The letter, which she proposed to publish, exacted revenge for Sherman's destruction of her life by informing his wife of his alleged affair with a "Mulatto girl." "Enquire of Gen Sherman when next you see him who has been elevated to fill your place," Thomas taunted, referring to his "companion du voyage," the woman "spoken of by the Negroes . . . as 'Sherman's wife.'" Northern women would learn what emancipation meant, Thomas insisted, now that "*your* husbands are amongst a colored race whose reputation for morality has never been of the highest order." Southern women would be "avenged," and Ellen Sherman and white women at the North would drink from the same "bitter cup of humiliation" that had long been forced to the lips of cultivated southern women.[58] A primal manifestation of Thomas's anger over slavery, Yankee conquest, and male domination, the letter revealed that for her, emancipation (like slavery itself) was always about sex, adultery, and, inevitably, sex between white men and black women.[59]

Thomas's unbalanced screed to Sherman's wife was not the first time she had broached the delicate subject of sex and slavery. In ways unusual for women of her class, she had done so repeatedly since she was married, usually when confronted with evidence in the appearance of enslaved children on the plantation. Such had been the case with the enslaved woman Lurany's two daughters, Amanda and Lulah, who were, Thomas said, "as white as any white child." Lurany's case weighed on Thomas, as well it might. Lurany and her children were owned by Thomas's beloved father, Turner Clanton. Thomas pitied enslaved women like her ("more sinned against than sinning") and blamed them simultaneously. She held distinctly unflattering views of the vast majority of white men as predatory beings, with terrible power over enslaved women's bodies. She understood the southern white man's horror of marriage across the color line; what she could not understand was his "indifference to having the same [negro] blood flowing through the veins of a race of descendants held in perpetual slavery—perhaps by other men." For her, "the white children of slavery" were a living indictment of southern morality and a threat to the Christian family, including her own. There was "some great mystery about Lurany's case," Thomas acknowledged. Her children clearly had white fathers. But who? Gertrude Thomas spent much of her adulthood fending off the fear that her father and husband were not exempt from the general depravity of their sex. In 1859, confronted with Lurany and her children, Thomas had thought immediately of her father: "When I look upon so many young creatures growing up belonging to Pa's estate as well as others—I wonder upon whom shall the accountability of their future state depend."[60]

In 1864, shortly before her unhinged letter to Sherman's wife, Gertrude Thomas got the answer to that question. The knowledge nearly killed her. On Monday April 1, 1864, Gertrude's father died. (Woodrow Wilson's father was the minister attending at Clanton's deathbed.) Sometime between then and the following August, she was subjected to the reading of his will. After that there was no mystery about Lurany's case. The event precipitated a crisis of religious faith unlike any other in Gertrude Thomas's life. For almost four months she said nothing on the subject, then wrote one anguished entry about her father's will, the language tortured and opaque, the handwriting half-erased, barely legible.[61]

What had Gertrude Thomas learned? The acquisition of new wealth was contaminated by some knowledge of her father's life gained along with it. "As God is my witness," she wrote, "I would rather never of had that additional increase of property if . . . I would have been afraid [of] the knowledge which was communicated at the same time." She never said exactly what information—it is the "secret" that has fascinated many historians. But the knowledge was so damning, so unspeakable, that though she never fully revealed it, someone—perhaps she herself—subsequently attempted to erase the passage.[62]

Turner Clanton's will is on file in the courthouse in Richmond County, Georgia.[63] It leaves little mystery about the paternity of Lurany's children or the source of Gertrude Thomas's crisis.[64] There is only one way to read the will. Turner Clanton's will is dated March 16, 1861. There were short codicils added, the last one a week before his death. He left money and property to his wife and sons, and to his daughters, including Gertrude, in private trust. And then there was this, item 17, written in the original will of 1861 and never rescinded:

> To my friends Dr. Thomas B. Phinizy and Thomas J. Jennings, I give and bequeath the sum of three thousand dollars to be equally divided between them; together with the following negro slaves, to wit: Loraine, about thirty-eight years old, and her child, about three years old, together with any and all children she may have at my death; Amanda (wife of Stephen Walton) about twenty-five years old and all children she may have at my death; Laurence about twenty-three years old; Columbus about twenty-one; Geneva, about nineteen; Hampton about thirteen, Tallulah, about seven years old, and my faithful servant Cyrus about forty-eight years old; together with any and all children who may be born to said female slaves, at my death.

Turner Clanton did not will his own mixed-race children to his heirs as property. Instead, perhaps fearing incest—he had adult sons—Clanton deliberately moved his enslaved children and their mother (or mothers) out of the family, awarding ownership and custody to men presumably apprised of their parentage. It is entirely possible that Clanton gave those gentlemen additional instructions about his intentions for Lurany and her children either orally—they were his near neighbors—or in a separate document. There is no evidence that he emancipated them. Lurany died soon after. Amanda remained in the Augusta area with her husband, Steven Walton; they raised their children there, and Gertrude Thomas periodically saw them. Besides Cyrus (whose relationship to Clanton is unclear), Lurany and her children—Amanda, Laurence, Columbus, Geneva, Hampton, and

Tallulah—were the only enslaved persons mentioned by name in Clanton's will. He anticipated resistance: item 22 stipulated that any of his heirs who challenged the execution of the will would be disinherited. Clanton appointed his wife, sons, and sons-in-law as executors, but also Phinizy and Jennings. There was nothing abstract about Gertrude Thomas's crisis, the letter to Sherman's wife, or her lifelong association of slavery and sex, emancipation, and miscegenation. Her obsession with mulatto women came from a deep place. Amanda and Tallulah and the others were her half-sisters and -brothers, her father's children by another woman, a shade darker than her mother.[65]

The challenge presented by "white slave children" was hardly peculiar to Gertrude Thomas or the Thomas family. There were 588,000 "mixed blood" people in the United States in 1860, the historian W. E. B. Du Bois pointedly noted. In *Black Reconstruction in America*, he took dead aim at the southern planter class, puncturing every one of its claims to superiority in matters of culture and honor, Christianity and civilization. "Sexually they were lawless," he wrote, "flattering the virginity of a small class of women of their social clan" while "keeping at command millions of poor women," white and black. "Sexual chaos was always the possibility of slavery": "We southern ladies are complimented with the names of wives; but we are only mistresses of seraglios," he quoted one woman as saying. Turner Clanton's household fits the description. In 1860, the slave schedule of the census showed his home plantation (where Gertrude had grown up) to contain a disproportionate number of "mulattos," including women and girls who fit the profile of Lurany, Amanda, and Tallulah. Lurany and her daughters and their husbands and partners and children had to live with that knowledge. So did Clanton's wife and, by 1864, his daughter Gertrude, whose own household at Belmont had some of the same characteristics.[66]

Turner Clanton's will brought his enslaved children to public knowledge. In 1864, that personal event merged in Gertrude's life with a historical one: the devastation of defeat and slave emancipation. With the end of the war and emancipation, the secrets of slavery could no longer be kept and the accounting began. In 1864, *Harper's Weekly* published a series of photos of the "white slave children" of New Orleans. By that year, the technology of photography carried such knowledge far beyond individual plantation households and the realm of local gossip directly into national political culture. Men like Turner Clanton wreaked havoc on their families, creating such chaos in southern society that matters of lineage could never be sorted out or the fear of incest allayed. A series of paternity cases brought by African American women against their former owners in the years immediately after the Civil War provided further evidence, if any was needed, of the sexual lawlessness of southern masters.[67]

Emancipation was an excruciatingly intimate process for all parties. It involved the dismantling of family ties violently established over generations. For freed people, like Amanda Walton, Lurany's daughter, it meant the chance to establish free families, putting husbands, wives, and children under the same roof, establishing distance from those who had owned them, separated them, and violated them at will. For slaveholders like Gertrude Thomas, it meant betrayal, dispossession, and loss, but also sexual humiliation. For Thomas, persons owned body and soul had always mingled property and love in confusing measure. Emancipation played out in the same terms. Her property in slaves had come to her from her father, whose wealth had been increased, quite literally, by the birth of slave children. Her personal wealth, received as a token of his love, had always been burdened by the knowledge of its source and the terrible power it gave white men over slave women's bodies—women like Lurany. After 1864, Thomas had no place to hide from that knowledge. Her association of emancipation and illicit interracial sex came from a deep place. It was a hurt sustained at home. The damage from the sexual violence of slavery set a deep explosive charge beneath every negotiation over freedom in postwar American society.

The US South is hardly the only postwar society in which reconstruction centrally implicated the family. The challenge to gender order that came with war often provoked a backlash and the promotion and defense of the traditional family in the aftermath.[68] Elements of this postwar conservatism are evident in the postwar politics of the United States as well, particularly in the resistance to women's suffrage and, within the South, in the gender politics of the Lost Cause movement. Gertrude Thomas, an unrepentant rebel and founding member of the Ladies' Memorial Association of Augusta, did her bit in this regard.[69] But in the postwar South, emancipation put hard limits on the extent of family restoration. Gertrude Thomas's loss was her former slaves' gain. In fact, difficult as it was to accomplish, the formation of free black families was the most successful part of the entire reconstruction process. Those immediate postwar gains were never given back even after the brutal overthrow of Reconstruction. The antebellum forms of the slaveholding household were irrevocably destroyed, and the reconstruction of the family assumed fundamental dimensions, as it did for Thomas.[70]

Thomas never sent the letter to Sherman's wife. A year later, in one of her habitual re-readings of the diary, she stumbled back on the entry and was clearly shocked. "Reading that now I can see how my nervous system was completely unstrung."[71] And so it was. Thomas had lived through a revolution and reacted to it all in proportion to its devastating effects and meanings. It was a social revolution and an epistemological one. It played out not just in public but in the most intimate realms of family life. Thomas's diary offers a gendered history of defeat. She navigated the currents of change from her position as a slaveholder, a woman, and a wife. Gertrude Thomas does not tell us everything we would want to know by any means. But in its focus on women's relation to power, her account of reconstructing a life begins to show how deep the changes went.

Emancipation set but did not exhaust the penalties for treason. The terms of reconstruction under which the defeated South was to be governed was a highly volatile matter in 1865 and 1866, unknown and uncertain even to the power players in Washington. Like everyone else in the postwar South, Gertrude Thomas would have to "learn to live under the new order of things." But what order was that?[72] To the usual chaos of any immediate postwar moment in the United States was added the April assassination of the sitting president, Abraham Lincoln, a mere six days after General Robert E. Lee surrendered.

If ever there were hopes of a gentle peace, the assassination seemed to doom it. "The South must be literally swept with the sword," Francis Lieber raged. He saw no hope for self-reconstruction—any voluntary embrace of emancipation or self-directed political reform by the defeated Confederate states.[73] Andrew Johnson's ascendancy to the presidency roiled the fragile country, North, South, and West. But it had particularly potent meaning for former masters and mistresses in the occupied South. For if Johnson was known for anything, it was his hatred of the southern "aristocracy" and determination to punish traitors. On ascending to the presidency, Johnson refused to ratify the peace treaty signed by Generals William Sherman and Joseph E. Johnston in North Carolina, which offered generous terms to ex-

Confederates—terms, Gertrude Thomas insisted, that would alone have secured "a lasting and honourable peace."[74]

What followed war thus was not peace but military occupation. White southerners did not hold their fate in their own hands. "It is humiliating, very indeed, to be a conquered people," Thomas wrote in early May 1865. "Now that we have surrendered—are in a great degree powerless we can count with certainty upon nothing. Our negroes will be freed our lands confiscated and imagination cannot tell what is in store for us."[75] Land confiscation was the all-consuming fear of the immediate postwar period. Rumors abounded. "A failure to plant will cause the land to be confiscated," she noted in panic in early May. Thomas swore it was white southerners' duty to avoid politics and "provide sustenance for our familys," but the two—property and politics—were inextricably linked in the postwar world. Johnson's Reconstruction plan was revealed at the end of May 1865. It kept the southern ruling class firmly in his grip. His Proclamation of Amnesty and Pardon excluded former rebels who owned more than $20,000 of property, barring them from public life and leaving them subject to all the penalties for treason, including confiscation of property. To escape such debilities, each had to apply individually for a pardon. His name "stunk like carrion in the nostrils of the Southern people," Thomas said. Whether *anything* [would be] left us" to raise and educate our children was an open question.[76]

In 1865 and for a number of years thereafter, members of the old southern ruling class faced conditions of historical contingency extreme by most measures. Two years after the war, matters in the United States were still so unpredictable that the British foreign secretary, Lord Edward Henry Stanley, looked on in horrified fascination at "the singular scene which American politics present." "The American Revolution," he called it, "for the practical change in their government amounts to nothing less." "The world," he reported to the minister at Washington, "has nothing like it." What justice would require for former slaves and what disposition would be made of conquered Confederates and their property was an entirely open matter in those years, fought out at every level of the American political system. Indeed, the very question of what constituted property was itself a subject of political contestation. One valuable category of property—in persons—had already been nullified by law in the new Republican regime. Planters' right to what remained of their wealth, which consisted primarily of agricultural land, was also a subject of open political debate in a new world in which they did not hold sway.[77]

In the immediate postwar period, southern planters fought for their survival as individuals and as a class. Among other things, their struggle can be seen as one essential part of the larger historical process by which agrarian elites in western Europe and Asia struggled to hold on to national political power and keep rural labor in subjection during the transition to modernity.[78] In the United States, as elsewhere, the fight of landlords for power, on estates, in the region, and in the nation, was elemental and vicious. Gertrude and Jefferson Thomas played their part in that pitched battle. For the freed people who worked for them and other planters in the Augusta area, emancipation ushered in a long, brutal struggle to claim and enforce black southerners new status and full array of constitutional rights as citizens. Even with the federal government, US Army, and Freedmen's Bureau formally on their side, the former slaves were overmatched. The laws were never fully enforced, and freed people were subject to a campaign of racial violence that amounted to a counterrevolutionary force.[79]

The planter class faced radically new land and labor conditions in the immediate postwar years. Over the course of a bloody quarter century, southern planters managed to gouge back enough power to reassert dominance in local and regional politics. But they never regained their commanding position in national politics. In that sense, they were destroyed as a ruling class. Those individuals who managed to hold onto their land, control labor, and make cotton planting return a profit did so on new, more arduous terms. As a class, they were transformed in the process.[80] In the difficult postwar economic environment, many planters faced ruin. Lost capital, scarcity of currency and credit, failed crops, and new structures of entrepreneurship posed formidable challenges for everyone involved.[81] To survive economically required an ability to adjust and management skills that many simply did not possess.

Jefferson Thomas did not. To be sure, the Thomases' economic loss was far more drastic than most planter families. Their decline into poverty represents an extreme case of the general fall of the planter class. It is a potent reminder of the scope and latitude that historians must concede to individual variation and of the complicated intertwining of personal and political histories in this unstable postwar moment. Jefferson Thomas had never been successful in the plantation business, even in favorable antebellum circumstances when merchants, factors, and banks deferred to cotton planters and allowed them to carry enormous debts on the books for years. As would become painfully clear to Gertrude, her husband had been kept afloat by her father's generosity and constant borrowing from relatives. After the war, he proved incapable of the broad changes in personal economy, labor management, and business practices and acumen required to retain property and social position. His wife's account of planters' brutal struggle to defeat freed people's alternative visions of social organization and reassert dominance on the land and in political life leaves no doubt about how fundamental the challenge was.

Confiscation was a real possibility in the political life of the nation in 1865 and 1866. Freed people looked to the federal government to distribute confiscated land as a return on loyalty and military service, and as a firm material foundation for their freedom. In Georgia, where General Sherman had issued his famous Special Field Order No. 15, they had a particularly strong case. "Sherman's Reserve" was a thirty-mile-wide swath of land that ran south along the coast from Charleston to northern Florida. It had been seized from rebel owners by the US government and handed over to the control of the Freedmen's Bureau for the settlement of freed people. At the end of the war, the bureau controlled more than 800,000 acres of land, half of it in South Carolina and Georgia. Other land remained subject to seizure for taxes or abandonment. Land tenure was extremely insecure.[82] Unable to take the oath because of the terms of Johnson's amnesty, the Thomases, like the entire planter class, faced confiscation. Their situation was hardly the worst. Unlike fellow planters in more coastal parts of Georgia and South Carolina, they at least kept possession of their plantations. John Berkley Grimball and his wife, Meta Morris Grimball, were another couple who struggled to hold onto their property, much of it also inherited from her father. But their land fell within Sherman's Reserve. The Grimballs had fled Edisto Island just ahead of the Union Army in December 1864, abandoning their plantations to the enslaved people who lived on them. It took until January 1866 to get them back. It was on Edisto, where his Grove and Pinebury plantations were located, that freedmen fought hardest for title to the land they had occupied and cultivated during the war.[83]

The defeat of the freed people in Sherman's Reserve, by which the Grimballs regained possession of their plantations, came directly at the hands of Andrew Johnson. It was a dramatic turning point in Reconstruction. But the uncertainty surrounding land title dragged on into 1866, when Congress took up the debate.[84] Gertrude Thomas was well aware of the sentiment in northern public opinion that confiscation was necessary to break the power of the old slaveholding class. "I don't care to learn anything of that economy or Christianity either which will confiscate any more of my property," she fretted in October 1866. "Times are gloomy and threatening," and there could be no doubt about the "plans radicals propose."[85]

Andrew Johnson, in a significant turn, emerged as the unlikely savior of the southern planter class. "The rebels have again their heads up like kissing mares," Francis Lieber wrote with disgust. "Johnson has revived them." Johnson's liberal use of the pardon power was crucial, as was his directive to restore land to all pardoned owners. About fifteen thousand people applied for presidential pardons, most because of the value of their property, and about seven thousand were granted.[86] At some point in those volatile postwar years, Jefferson Thomas also received one. It is not clear whether Gertrude had to apply individually, as did other planter women possessed of property in their own name.[87] Meta Morris Grimball did because of all the inherited property was in her name. As Grimball's husband noted, the pardon prevented "the confiscation of her property" and left her "enough to support the family." The text of the pardon document she signed included a striking official recognition of women's political sovereignty and culpability: "Margaret Ann Grimball . . . by taking part in the late rebellion against the Government of the U.S. has made herself liable to heavy pains and penalties," it stated, and granted "a full pardon and amnesty for all offences by her committed," provided she took the oath of allegiance and never again claimed any "property in Slaves."[88] In this document, signed by a property-owning wife, one can discern a fissure in coverture and the emergence of new postwar domestic relations, not just between former masters and slaves but, potentially, between husbands and wives.

Johnson's policies reestablished planters as a landed class. But without slaves land had uncertain value. In passing measures for debt relief, the Georgia legislature referred to the destruction and liquidation of the state's wealth (in crops, stock, public debt, and capital in slave labor), and to "the prospect of successful agriculture, the basis of all value, now dependent on the voluntary labor of the freedmen," as "a question of doubt and experiment." And indeed, land values plummeted all over the former cotton states, an estimated 55 percent in Georgia by 1867. Land that previously sold for sixteen to twenty dollars an acre could command perhaps fifty cents an acre right after the war.[89] Georgia planters faced three consecutive seasons of drought with severe ramifications for cotton harvests, the region's only cash crop and source of currency and investment capital. For the Thomases, as for the rest of their class, the struggle to hold onto their land and make it yield a living was only beginning in 1865. In the grinding, decades-long, and ultimately failed process, Gertrude Thomas would lose a lot of property but also the shelter it provided elite women from involvement in plantation business.

Before the war, when she was newly married and all the couple owned was provided by her father, Gertrude Thomas idealized her dependence on her husband. He had, she said, "just such a master will as suits my woman's nature, for true to my sex, I delight *in looking up* and love to feel my woman's weakness protected by man's superior strength." As slavery crumbled, so did that proslavery vision of marriage and wifely love. For the entire extent of their marriage, most of what the Thomases owned was legally hers—her slaves, her land, her town lots, her houses, her bonds, her property, but, as she thought of it, "Mr Thomas's affairs."[90] However slowly, reluctantly, imperfectly, and begrudgingly, Gertrude Thomas expanded her knowledge of plantation business and her husband's indebtedness. Her diary of this process provides an index of sorts to the fundamental reconstruction of public and private life in these years.

The plantation business changed dramatically in the immediate postwar years. Planters, including Jefferson Thomas, were forced into a radical experiment in how to grow cotton with laborers who were no longer enslaved and whose right to make free contracts the federal government was, for the first time, pledged to protect. Freed people had their own deeply alternative visions of a future, individual and collective, that would preclude the need to sell their labor to their old masters. "I think they have an idea of possession," Mary Jones of Liberty County said of her former slaves' claim on their home plantation. Even where they lost possessory titles, freed people resisted planters' efforts to reassert ownership and control. J. R. Cheves reported to General Davis Tillson, the assistant commissioner of the Freedmen's Bureau in Georgia, that he faced a virtual "Landsturm" when he tried to return to his plantation in the Ogeechee District. People allegedly under contract to him surrounded his house, drowning out his attempts to speak and declaring "that there was no master on the plantation. . . . These freedmen, in actual possession, declared they 'would work for no man.' They would have the land & nothing but the land would satisfy them." On Edisto, where freed people had been sold out by the government, they refused to go back to work for John Berkley Grimball. Grimball kept title to his plantation, the Grove, but lost it when he could not make payments on the mortgage.[91] As Freedmen's Bureau personnel opened their office in Augusta in the summer of 1865, they found themselves in the middle of an existential struggle between planters and freed people over the terms of labor, production, and civil rights in the post-emancipation South.

The Thomas family plantations were a case in point. From the moment of emancipation, when Jefferson Thomas urged his former slaves to remain and work for him, he tried to find and keep field laborers at Belmont (the home place), and in Burke and Columbia Counties. He was unaccustomed to government oversight or to negotiating for what he formerly commanded. But like all area planters, he was required to sign contracts with his workers (including his former slaves) and to submit them to Captain John Emory Bryant in Augusta. Facing widespread destitution of black and white southerners, bureau agents, including Bryant, urged freed people to return to work for their old owners and to sign contracts for the balance of the year. Indeed, Bryant, who was known by planters as a radical, had written an important memo on the terms of such contracts that circulated widely in the region in 1865.[92]

The terms Bryant laid out were by no means lenient for workers. His prototype contract lectured freed people on the "burdens and duties" of freedom and specified their obligation to support themselves and "their wives and children," and to contribute to the support of the "non-workers." Field hands were to work six days a week, domestic servants six and a half; they were warned of the penalties for nonfulfillment of contractual obligations. Dreams of land distribution were quashed. The only way to own land, they were told bluntly, was to save money and buy it. "Idleness and vagrancy will not be tolerated" (state laws already criminalized those non-wage options), and "the government will support none, able and yet unwilling to work." According to Bryant and the bureau, waged agricultural labor was the freed peoples' assigned future. Mere months after the end of slavery—a two-hundred-year system that expropriated all the fruits of their labor—the government lectured freed people on the virtues of industry, sharply curtailed welfare, and insisted on immediate self-reliance. Model contracts such as Bryant's deployed a punitive liberal conception of free waged labor and contract freedom.[93]

But Bryant's contract also set terms for employers, a fundamental innovation in southern society. Contracts were to be strictly voluntary and money wages to be paid on an established schedule: $7 per month for male hands, $3.50 for male half hands, $6 for female hands, and $3 for half hands. The retention of slave-era labor terms did not obscure the radicalism of this concept. The "colored laborers," the circular stipulated, "are free in all parts of the State of Georgia and South Carolina, and their rights as freedmen will be protected by the whole military force of the U.S. government, if necessary." Every act of injustice was to be investigated and wrong-doers punished. Bryant issued warnings against planters who were violating freed people's new civil rights by refusing to "allow wives to leave [plantations] . . . with their husbands, or parents to take charge of their children." "Freedmen in this regard, have the same right that white citizens have," he specified. The inadequacy of enforcement does nothing to change the fact that the very idea of contracts between former masters and former slaves, of black workers as freely contracting individuals, involved a recognition of freed people's humanity and rights that had the potential to set history on a new course. However limited, labor contracts were a radical departure from the past.[94]

To planters like Gertrude and Jefferson Thomas, the very idea of an "equitable contract"—or any to which their former slaves were a party—was a radical affront. Planters signed them—they had to—but with little intention of abiding by their terms.[95] Just a few months into the experiment in free labor, Jefferson Thomas was hauled in front of the Freedmen's Court of Claims by his employees, charged with violating the terms of their contract on one of the Burke County plantations. The court had been established by Captain Bryant, and judgment in the case of "Willis Thomas Col'd vs J. Jefferson Thomas" was recorded on his docket on July 31, 1865. Bureau records confirm that Bryant ruled in favor of the plaintiffs and ordered Jefferson Thomas to pay Willis Thomas $46.50 in back wages plus court costs. Jefferson's labor practices were typically criminal, the characteristic behavior of men unaccustomed to answering to laborers or the law. According to Bryant, Jefferson had driven Willis and the other workers off the plantation in July, then claimed they had violated the terms of their contract. It was "a swindle" widely perpetrated in Burke and surrounding counties in that first postwar summer. Indeed, this case was one of two hundred heard by Bryant in July alone, most for the same cause. "It was at a time when the crop had been 'lain by,'" Bryant reported to his superiors in August, and despite the fact that they had signed annual contracts, planters were turning away their hands without pay in hundreds of cases. In every case heard, Bryant explained, "the freedman who brought the suit was entitled to recover pay for work."[96]

The summer of 1865 proved a brutal learning curve for Gertrude and Jefferson Thomas and everyone else involved in the experiment in free labor in Augusta, Georgia. Bryant and his superior, General Davis Tillson, had begun the summer optimistic about the prospects of their work, concerned mostly about their ability to discipline freedmen to wage labor on cotton plantations. As late as October, Tillson had seen the planters as his allies, even authorizing the hiring of local white men as civilian agents of the Freedmen's Bureau. Tillson was by no means the most radical of bureau commissioners, but even his policies directly challenged planters' assumptions about the control of labor. In fact, both the degree and kind of resistance by planters

J. Jefferson Thomas   Courtesy of F. Michael Despeaux, Easley, South Carolina.

to the most basic of civil rights for African American laborers blind-sided bureau officials. Like Bryant, they came to see the freedmen as "just complainants" against a pattern of planter fraud and violence that threatened the very future of free labor and postwar peace. Willis Thomas and the Burke workers had a lot of company. "Four fifths of those who labored under that [annual contract] system the past year have been swindled out of their years labor," one agent reported to the bureau in Augusta. Bureau files bulge with the evidence. Milly Hopkins and other former slaves on her place were turned off without pay by their employer, Cornelia Hopkins. Similarly, Reef Velard had a contract with Dr. William Velard for half the crop but was turned off "with nothing in the world." Every freed person on the plantation witnessed his complaint. Planters had so discredited and violated the system that at the beginning of the new year, they could not find laborers willing to sign annual contracts. "Of 3,000 hands in Burke County," one planter complained to General Tillson, "there are not 50 who will even talk of making arrangements for the next year."[97]

It took tremendous courage for freed people such as Willis Thomas to press charges against their old owners and insist on the recognition of their new rights by employers. But they did. In the face of brutal violence, they exercised their rights to personal mobility, to marry and claim their children, to choose their employers, to enforce wage clauses in contracts, to hold public meetings, and even to bear arms. The planters' violent response acutely demonstrates the challenge that even contract freedom posed, even as scholars of slavery's capitalism envision a continuum or continuity between slavery and wage labor. When one worker protested his employer Edward Beniet's fraud (he had paid only half of the corn contracted as wages), declaring to his face that "it was not justice," Beniet drew a pistol and told him "he would blow his brains out." Israel Kelly filed an affidavit swearing that his employer, John Kelly, had hit him with the butt of a gun and threatened to blow his brains out. Mary Ann Walker likewise swore that Calvin Ward, her employer, hit her twice with an axe and set his dogs on her because she "refused to allow him . . . to have elicit intercourse with her." Green Jones testified that Dr. Benjamin Friar of Burke County violently assaulted Jeannus Friar, chasing her with dogs, tying and gagging her when caught, and then whipping her cruelly with switches while another white man stood on her face. Men "so disguised that the deponent could not recognize them" searched one man's house for arms, and when they could not find any, dragged him and his son into the woods, stripped them naked, and beat them with a saddle stirrup strap. In that first summer, John Emory Bryant received numerous death threats; one of his assistants was murdered.[98] To men accustomed to complete control over the labor of slaves, to strict deference, to unbridled access to African American women's bodies, and to a monopoly on violence, even something as simple as a request to pay wages due could provoke a lethal response.

As battered freedmen made their way from plantations in outlying Burke and other counties into the Augusta office, and agents such as Bryant and his assistants sat at their desks taking affidavits, issuing summonses, and hearing cases, the evidence piled up. The pattern of planter fraud and violence was so widespread and stunning that even General Tillson, the original defender of planter self-reconstruction, reversed his position. By December 1865, he proposed a plan for the military reconstruction of Georgia determined "to teach whites 'some regard for the law.'" He also took to spelling out freed people's right to defend themselves. "All men, without distinction of color, have the right to keep arms to defend their homes, families or themselves," he declared in a public pronouncement. The following March, Tillson reported the dire state of affairs in Georgia to the head of the Freedmen's Bureau, General O. O. Howard. Specifically citing wage fraud and the onslaught of assaults and murders, he requested immediate military assistance. It was a blunt assessment of conditions: The freed people can only "be enabled to realize and enjoy their freedom by the presence, at least temporarily, of a sufficient force to compel their employers to give them a reasonable compensation or allow them to go where it can be obtained."[99]

Even as Tillson began to take the measure of Augusta planters, his talk of freed people and employers shows that he had little sense of the entangled histories that made labor conflicts so explosive in the postwar South. One of the most striking things about the labor complaints bureau agents heard is just how many of the workers carried their employer's—and former owner's—family name. It says little about emotional attachment or belonging, but it does speak to power. Like Willis Thomas, a lot of freed people were working for the same man on the same place as before, while attempting to shape new lives on new terms, to make a new history nonetheless. Twice Willis Thomas had to personally deliver a summons to Jefferson Thomas, his former master.[100] Gertrude was on hand on both occasions. Amid her own preoccupation with domestic servants in the summer of 1865, she took note of the extraordinary historical moment when the field hands from Burke arrived at Belmont and handed Jefferson Thomas "a letter . . . from Captain Bryant summoning [him] to answer to the demand of these Negroes for wages." Thomas sent them off dismissively, they "hollor[ing]" as they left the yard. "This too *we* had to endure," she added. Not familiar with "the Burke negroes," she failed to recognize Willis Thomas. But more than a year later, when Willis returned, this time alone, with another summons on her husband for the same back wages, still unpaid, she asked a servant Patsey his name. Told it was Willis, she said, "not a family Negro or I would have remembered him but a man Pa bought and gave to us when we were married." But Jefferson Thomas knew him. Willis Thomas had been enslaved to Gertrude and Jefferson Thomas for thirteen years and their employee for only two months when he brought the first summons. That face-to-face confrontation took guts. On one occasion when Jefferson had encountered Willis on the road, Gertrude reported, her husband had tried to convince Willis that "it was a foolish thing trying to sue him last year," that he still "took more interest in him than anyone else." But Willis Thomas exposed that threadbare paternalism as a planter fraud, risking retribution and going to law and outside parties to construe his old master as a mere employer, bound to pay him for his labor. The destruction of the slave plantation system and the reconstruction of labor on new terms was inescapably fraught—and intimate. The blacks see Bryant "as a Savior," Gertrude Thomas acknowledged, but she blamed him "for sowing broadcast the seeds of dissention between the former master and slave and caus[ing] what might have continued to be a kind interest to become in many cases a bitter enmity."[101]

The full extent of Gertrude's husband's troubles emerged only slowly, but already by the end of 1865 there were signs enough to intrude on her ignorance of what she still called "his" affairs. She knew he struggled: to get labor, to pay it, and to manage it. Jefferson Thomas had gone down to Burke "to have a settlement with the Negroes," she mentioned at the end of December. "They have made nothing and he has little inducement to plant." "Indeed he does not know what to do," and seems like other southerners, "waiting for something to turn up."[102] In many respects, Thomas's difficulties did illustrate generally the "condition of the southern people," as his wife suggested: bad cotton crops in 1865, 1866, and 1867; cratering land values; impossibly tight money supply; and new rules for credit that exposed land to seizure for debt.[103]

But, as she increasingly realized, there was something else going on. Jefferson Thomas reached for some of the same solutions as his peers to the new power of black labor. He formed a company to promote labor immigration and served as its president; he formed an agricultural society for Richmond County; he tried to rent out their land at Belmont and elsewhere to bypass the labor issue and make it yield an income; and he went into business in town, investing in a china and glassware company—Mosher, Thomas & Straub—a move his wife clearly approved of. But with land as their most plentiful asset, there was no real alternative to cotton planting and so, over the course of three years, he and most other cotton planters tried to adjust by moving to a system of farming on shares, which divided up the land to be worked by separate families, who paid with part of the crop.[104]

As the country prepared for the presidential election of 1868, the first ever in which male freedmen could vote, the South was a powder keg. White men in Augusta were armed to the teeth, Jefferson Thomas prominent among them. African American men in the former Confederate states had been enfranchised by congressional passage of the Military Reconstruction Acts. In the spring of 1867 and under military supervision, Freedmen's Bureau officers were ordered to register them to vote. In Richmond County, which included Augusta, where Jefferson Thomas voted, freedmen outnumbered registered white voters by 3,276 to 2,271, and in neighboring Burke and Richmond Counties by even higher proportions.[105] Augusta whites now faced a black majority electorate.

Soon, freed people showed their strength, including at Belmont. In Augusta, the African American community was well organized and proactive, with a leadership intent on exercising every right, including the right to bear arms. Among that leadership group was Sam Drayton, a black preacher whom Gertrude had known and admired for years.[106] By 1866, they had already formed a network of Republican political clubs and militias, the latter an indication of the unavoidably paramilitary nature of southern politics. For more than a year before the presidential elections tensions had been building. In March 1867, immediately following passage of the Military Reconstruction Act, a group of "black citizens" attempted to register to vote in the upcoming election for mayor and city council. When denied, they took their case to the Freedmen's Bureau. That election was subsequently cancelled, under orders of General Ulysses S. Grant, and a new mayor and board of alderman appointed by General John Pope.[107]

Freed people were eager to exercise their right to bear arms. In August 1866, a group had demanded the right to parade to a barbecue organized in military companies, a move clearly designed to show their political presence and military strength, and to impress their new identity and rights on the community. Although General Tillson had already made a public statement about freed people's second amendment rights, the white mayor denied permission on the grounds that "any military display on the part of the colored people" was an impolitic and inflammatory provocation. Indeed, in Camilla, Georgia, a town in the southwestern part of the state, freed people who held such a parade in the run-up to the November election were massacred by local whites. As was the case all over the South in 1867 and 1868, Augusta area freed people who attempted to arm themselves and defend their right to bear arms faced a phalanx of opposition from whites, fully aware that their political survival depended on it.[108]

By the time of the presidential elections in 1868, freed people had already won significant victories in two elections that made Republicans' political strength in Georgia demonstrably clear. The party had racked up big majorities in both cases, defeating white Democrats decisively and then using their power in the state convention to write and ratify a radical constitution and install a Republican governor and legislature that included the state's first elected black representatives.[109] Black male voters had demonstrated their power decisively. As a majority within the state and voting solidly Republican, they would not easily be dislodged by electoral means. After the April 1868 elections, the new (white) Republican mayor of Augusta, Foster Blodgett, tried to contain a white backlash that seamlessly intimidated blacks as both laborers and voters. "Many colored people in this and adjoining counties have been discharged by their employers for voting the Republican ticket at the last election," he wrote, "and in some instances, women have been discharged because of their husbands vote." Appealing to the military, he begged to know what could be done "for their protection."[110]

White Democrats responded to radical Reconstruction with a campaign of violence so extensive that its leading historian, Allen W. Trelease, bluntly refers to it as "terrorism." Violence against African Americans, including by white men who disguised their identities, had started in 1865, as bureau records confirm. But the pattern of violence escalated steeply with the onset of black electoral politics and radical Republican rule. By 1867, it constituted a highly organized campaign of arson, torture, mutilation, sexual violence, and murder. Indeed, the Ku Klux Klan, as the movement became known, was so organized and lethal that it still constitutes *the* primary example of domestic terrorism in the history of the United States. Trelease offers the informed judgment that the Klan's role in the overthrow of Republican control was greater and more decisive in Georgia than in any other part of the South. Within the state, the campaign of terror against Republicans, and especially black Republicans, reached its vicious "apotheosis" precisely where Gertrude and Jefferson Thomas lived—in the black-majority districts in the eastern part of the state, including Richmond and Columbia Counties.[111]

That campaign of political violence not only reached, but also radiated out from, Gertrude and Jefferson Thomas's home plantation. As election day approached and white Democrats prepared themselves for a pitched battle, "radicals" at Belmont, led by two men, Isaiah and Mac, were organizing on the plantation in preparation for voting the Republican ticket. They had plans to "meet at the creek tomorrow night," Gertrude was informed, "to march to town the next day with uncle Isaiah as captain." "Things are rapidly approaching a crisis," she noted two days before the election. "It is reported that all of the houses in the neighborhood are to be burnt up." Her informant among the Belmont freed people, a teenager named Ned, told her that "uncle Mac said if he had a son who was willing to be a Democrat he would cut his throat."[112]

Arrayed against each other, and amid rumors of violence and arson, white and black at Belmont prepared for the coming fight. The night before the election, Jefferson Thomas went out to patrol with the local militia company "of which he is captain," his wife noted proudly. Before he kissed her goodbye, he asked to have his guns brought up. There they sat, stacked in the corner of the kitchen. When her husband left, Gertrude expressed her hope that that there would be "no necessity for force. . . . Only absolute necessity [would cause] southern men to resort to force," she noted that night. It was a claim refuted by a long history.[113]

On election day, everyone girded for violence. "No wonder the great heart of the South throbs at the thought of how much will depend upon the vote of today," Gertrude noted nervously that morning. "Mr. Thomas went to Pine Hill to vote," she added. "Mr T." would have a leading role to play as she knew: he was "captain of the [militia] company in Augusta," and in this neighborhood "president of the Democratic club."[114] It was a damning admission, as Virginia Burr, the editor of Thomas's diary, was quite aware. Burr omitted that entry entirely from the published diary, as she did earlier references to Jefferson Thomas's role as captain of the militia during the violent campaign of voter suppression and a later one to Gertrude's brother Buddy, known by local black Republicans as "one of the Ku Klux." The published diary has been scrubbed clean. Those critical entries lie buried among more than two thousand manuscript pages in the Rubenstein Library at Duke University.[115]

But it is impossible to inoculate Gertrude Thomas from her family history. And it is impossible to inoculate family history from political history: the existential political battle of Reconstruction unfolded not just in public places and institutions but within the households and homes of southern planters and laborers. The Klan was effectively "a terrorist arm of the Democratic party," and it had been built up and organized around a network of "Democratic clubs" and rifle clubs such as the one Jefferson Thomas led. They had been formed after Republican victories in the April 1868 elections and were extremely active around Augusta, targeting black voters before the November elections. "Virtually every night prior to the election the Klan rode out in parts of Richmond, Warren, Columbia, Lincoln and Greene Counties," Trelease explains, "searching for guns among the freedmen, whipping and threatening death to any who voted Republican."[116]

Klan members wanted a violent overthrow of the state government and an abrogation of electoral democracy in the presidential contest.

Jefferson Thomas played a leading part in his precinct as captain of the militia company and president of the Democratic club. In 1868, white militias, Democratic clubs, and the Klan were instrumental in Republican electoral defeat in Georgia. In Columbia County, the Republican candidate for governor, Rufus Bullock, garnered 1,222 votes in the April elections; in November, Republican presidential candidate General Ulysses S. Grant got exactly 1. On election day companies of armed whites, with Jefferson Thomas commanding at Pine Hill, assembled around the polls, confiscating Republican ballots and intimidating voters. Black voters had to run the gauntlet just to get to the poll. "In Columbia county," Trelease confirms, "they even intimidated the soldiers who had been sent there" as poll watchers. Notwithstanding the efforts of sharecroppers such as Isaiah and Mac, who marched to the polls en masse and armed, Republicans around Augusta could not match the firepower of men such as Jefferson Thomas. In Augusta, there was violence on election day, a riot with "the white men" (as Gertrude put it) lined up on one side facing down the black men who were attempting to come to town to vote. "Yankee" soldiers, fittingly, were in the middle. The deputy sheriff was shot. Mac, the sharecropper at Belmont, came back and proudly reported that he had voted the Republican ticket. When he was asked to name the candidate he had voted for, Gertrude claimed he turned to her son Turner and asked whom he had voted for. Hearing the answer, Mac said, "Then I voted for the other side."[117]

By that point any fiction of mutual interest was gone. We trusted ourselves to "the coloured people" earlier "during the war," Gertrude Thomas wondered. "Why not now?" But the answer was clear: because black laborers were now free to express their views of the relationship, opinions that had been violently silenced under slavery. Freed people were no longer required to maintain the pose of devoted family servants. They had staked out their own position in the conflict between capital and labor. And they had given political force to their interests as newly freed African Americans and enfranchised male citizens through the Republican Party.[118]

Relationships Gertrude Thomas had always regarded as internal to the household, as personal bonds of attachment—hierarchical but mutual—were nakedly exposed as public economic relations—antagonistic and defined by power. These relations were now compensated with a wage and regulated by the market. Emancipation made visible the violence that had always characterized the relationship of master and slave, turning social and political life into an armed struggle. As Thomas's perspective on the election of 1868 confirms, political violence was as much a household as a public affair. Thomas would continue to denounce federal interference in southerners' "domestic affairs," but really, there was nothing domestic about them anymore.

Gertrude Thomas's sense of personal loss as she fiercely clung to white power and privilege cannot be disentangled from her husband's violent contribution to the so-called redemption of the state from "black" Republican rule. They were all manifestations of the desperation to forge a new kind of white supremacy equal to the new terms of social and political life. Gertrude Thomas shared—though not entirely—her husband's racist perspective on the political revolution of Reconstruction. The one difference was that she understood why "the Negroes vote the radical ticket" because, disfranchised herself as they were formerly, she knew the value of the vote:

Think of it, the right to vote, that right which they have seen their old masters exercise with so much pride and their young masters look forward to with so much pleasure is within their *very grasp*—they secure a right for themselves, which it is true they may not understand, but they have children whom they expect to educate. Shall they secure this right for them or sell their right away? . . . Who can guarantee that right will ever have it extended to them again.

From her perspective as a woman denied political rights, Gertrude Thomas could see the issue from the other side. "If the women of the North once secured to me the right to vote whilst it might be 'an honor thrust upon me,' I should think twice before I voted to have it taken from me," she declared.[119] And by this point Gertrude Thomas had good reason to think about the value of self-representation.

For Gertrude Thomas reconstruction proved much harder to survive than war. For her, reconstruction was more like deconstruction—a relentless process of loss, subtraction, and diminution in wealth and class distinction. The year 1868 was the turning point, the moment when she was first "brought to bankruptcy" and began to grasp the extent of her husband's financial troubles. The following year, the Thomases went under the sheriff's hammer for the first time—and the dunning did not stop until they had lost everything. Their personal history paralleled that of the region and reveals its new political powerlessness within the national and global financial order.[120] Gertrude knew times were hard for all cotton planters, but she also knew that many managed better than her husband. Jefferson Thomas was pursuing the usual course of action for the planter class, but there was something different about their condition. "In my own conscience,

I think a great deal of what we call bad luck is bad management," she noted bluntly. In the midst of their financial crisis, she observed that "this is infinitely worse than Sherman." Then "it was so general a loss that we could sympathize with each other but this trial I am undergoing now is lonely."[121]

For women such as Gertrude Thomas, their dependence on men immeasurably deepened the uncertainty of the postwar years. Indeed, white women's financial dependence on their husbands was much greater than black women's, a point Thomas observed and resented. Jefferson Thomas was not a winner in the postwar scramble; he was not among the men able to remake themselves and their class to meet the new day. Gertrude knew as much but was tied to him nonetheless. Amid the tectonic shifts of the postwar world, her fate was still fixed as much by marriage as any other institution. In that sense, her perspective underscores once again the stubborn continuity of marriage in an era of radical change, and the importance of gender and its meanings in the making of the postwar domestic political order.

Gertrude Thomas had to bury many hopes in her newly straitened circumstances, including, as she lamented, "my woman's ambition in the success of my husband."[122] The wholesale damage that indebtedness wreaked on her marriage and family relations is a commonplace but little noticed part of the story of the fall of the planter class. By the very nature of their property and wealth, the Thomases were in debt not just to strangers that Gertrude vaguely identified as "the man from New York," or corporations such as the Bank of Augusta, but to beloved members of both families, including Gertrude's brother Buddy, who had signed a loan for Jefferson with his own plantation as collateral. The Thomases were in debt for loans incurred before the war, the china business in Augusta, and eventually for supplies and advances to run the various plantations, pay back taxes, and cover workers' unpaid wages. Over the course of an awful thirty years, they were sued by a New York supplier of fine china; various national and local banks; Jefferson's Savannah factor, a Mr. Stark; a score of Augusta grocers and furnishing merchants; the estate of Turner Clanton; and every one of their relatives. "Sued by my mother, my sisters and brothers, Mr. Thomas' sister and brothers," Gertrude wrote in 1871, "with Stark's lien for which I am responsible added to it, I rebel and turning to my children for comfort, I think they too may sue me some day." In 1897, they did.[123] The postwar trial of debt changed her view of her husband and her marriage, devastated her relations with her family, and exerted excruciating pressure on her role and identity as a mother.[124]

By the end of 1868, Gertrude Thomas still did not fully grasp the reality of their financial situation, and she still maintained a tenuous and selective relationship to information. "I have heard so much of homestead bills, bankruptcy, state courts and so on I understand nothing of it," she wrote in November of that year. But she knew enough to panic. "Mr. Thomas' affairs are so complicated and he is so depressed, 'run to death' as he expresses it." "For a long time," she admitted, "I have known of his pecuniary embarrassments." That year her husband's china business failed, and he was forced into bankruptcy by Dun and Bradstreet, the credit rating agency. The sheriff's sale was advertised in the newspaper. Their home, Belmont, was also at risk.[125] That humiliating development coincided fatefully with the final settlement of Gertrude's father's estate, the event that brought everything to a head. Gertrude's recognition of how heavily her husband had borrowed against their share dramatically shifted her fortunes and her view of her husband.

By 1868, married women's legal status had changed significantly. In 1866, as part of a raft of legislation, Georgia passed "An Act to

Protect the Rights of Married Women," which guaranteed that property brought into a marriage remained "the separate property of the wife" and was not "liable for the payment of any debt . . . of the husband." In 1868, that law was bundled with a homestead exemption and made part of the state constitution.[126] As Thomas would later joke, the bill "securing a married woman's property had been passed now that most of the women in Georgia had nothing to lose—like locking the stable door after the Horse has been stolen."[127] The laws were hardly irrelevant, but as the context confirms, they were passed as a response to "the critically widespread indebtedness of the postwar years." The laws were not designed to emancipate women. Their goals were strictly protective, to shore up a new racial order by protecting white men's property from sale for debt repayment. In Georgia, the laws themselves did not suggest that women could do anything with their property other than possess it. In this sense, they were no different from separate estates or trusts, one of which Gertrude Thomas already possessed. Long deployed by wealthy fathers to protect daughters' inheritances from incompetent husbands, they invested power in trustees who could do a lot or a little, depending on how the trusts were written. Jefferson Thomas was one of Gertrude's trustees.[128] Thus, by 1868, when her father's estate was settled, Gertrude did not lack legal rights. But neither old-fashioned trusts nor the new married women's property acts could protect her from the catastrophic consequences of her husband's management of her property.

In 1868, Gertrude Thomas still owned a good deal of property in her own name, most of it land and town lots inherited from her father. She relied on Jefferson, however, for the security of her property. This was both clear and deeply problematic. "He may do as he pleases and will of course," she declared after one disagreement, "but I have an individuality of my own." Thomas's new assertiveness put her marriage under tremendous strain. She tried to check herself. No living being ever heard her utter a word of censure against Mr. Thomas for "the manner in which our affairs are involved," she vowed one day, even as she reproved him privately for involving her brother. He told her "not to interfere," she confessed at one low point, "and I try to obey him & be indifferent." But she could no longer obey, and she had lost the luxury of indifference. Her husband "complain[ed]" that her "manner" was "too decided." "You are so emphatic," he charged, "it spoils everything."[129]

For the rest of her life, Thomas, a devout Methodist, struggled to maintain the proper posture of a wife. As she went through the trial of reconstructing her life, she ended up with a very different view of marital unity. She abandoned talk of masters' will and womanly subjection, but even so, there were real limits to her ability to control events. The 1860s statutes did not destroy coverture so much as modernize it. The law and social relations were still inseparable.[130] Gertrude Thomas's fate was entwined with her husband's, but they were not equals. She lost confidence in his judgment. She came to see him as a bad manager.[131] But it did not matter. She could watch, but never avert, the collapse.

Thomas periodically deluded herself that the worst was over, but for thirty relentless years, there was no relief. First, Jefferson Thomas lost the china business and both of the Burke plantations, which were sold to settle the claims of her sister-in-law Julia Scales and the Bank of Augusta. Gertrude pasted the notices of the sales into the cover of her diary, to better absorb the shocking reality. Then they lost the town home in Augusta, the plantation in Columbia County, four town lots, and eventually Gertrude's lifetime interest in her father's estate.[132] In 1870, Belmont, her home place, was to be sold at a sheriff's sale to settle her debt to her siblings on her father's estate. She copied that one in too—but the sale was averted. They lost the house in a fire in the 1870s. When her son Julian was born in 1868, she barely had money to buy a layette. In 1869, her eldest, Turner, who was sixteen years old, was taken from school and put to work on the farm. The 1870s were so devastating that, although she kept a diary, someone destroyed the two volumes. The 1878 diary resumes with the poignant question, "How shall we live?"[133] By that point she was living in an unplastered wooden house called "The Farm," inherited from her father. She had built a room on the side and was working for a living teaching school. She had one servant. Gertrude earned thirty dollars a month, more when she had boarders. Her wages went to support and clothe the children but also to pay taxes, interest on notes at the bank, even supplies for "the Negroes in Columbia."[134] Her husband's credit was so destroyed he could not get an annual advance on the crop from local merchants. Her second son, Jefferson Davis, was "clerking for a Chinaman by the name of Loo Chong." "It was," she noted sadly, "the only situation he could obtain."[135] At some point the sheriff started to serve the papers on her personally. The first time it was a terrible shock, and the man was embarrassed. Thomas taught school for five years and lived paycheck to paycheck. "I am always glad when Friday afternoon comes for I think I am that much nearer gaining the month's salary," she noted in 1880. She watched every penny, counted every gallon of kerosene, every peach that came off the tree. But even that standard of living was insupportable, and by 1893, after a long struggle, she and Jefferson gave up the fight and went to live with their son Julian in Atlanta.[136]

Jefferson Thomas had tried and failed to adjust to New South ways. Behind his own troubles lay a profound disruption of the credit and factorage system that had underwritten the South's prewar cotton economy. Unlike the antebellum period, when capital in slaves provided sufficient security for loans, after the war there was only land and the crops growing in the fields. New York and London bankers turned off the spigot of investment money that had poured into the cotton South. Factors and increasing numbers of interior "furnishing" merchants who advanced money and supplies began to require mortgages or liens on the crop to secure an advance. After three terrible crop years and the collapse of land values, merchants expected liens "even from gentlemen." As planters failed and newspapers filled with foreclosure notices, those merchants accumulated a great deal of cotton land in their hands. Jefferson Thomas was hardly the only southern cotton planter who failed to rebuild his fortunes after the war. "Not all planters were successful in their efforts to rent out parcels of land and to open a store," the historian Harold Woodman confirms. Indeed, as historians have made clear, the planters who survived in the postwar South often did so by becoming something else—merchants, mostly, some of whom, over time, became a new landlord class. They made profits not so much off of the land but by furnishing supplies to their tenants at the region's high interest rates.[137]

But Jefferson Thomas could not manage it. For too long he had financed his—and his wife's—lifestyle on a mountain of debt. His debts to the estate of Turner Clanton extended back before the war. He borrowed from everyone until eventually no one, not even his mother-in-law, would lend him money. "She did not wish to run any risk," a mortified Gertrude noted. In 1878, Gertrude was still trying to repay money he had borrowed from a seamstress before the war. He had multiple mortgages on every piece of land they owned and had been forced to give liens to furnishing merchants on the crops and mules. In the new, unforgiving landscape of the Reconstruction South—when cotton wasn't king—merchants called the shots, and interest rates routinely reached 20 percent. Debts were called in, and Jefferson Thomas lost everything. "With the Civil War," W. E. B. Du Bois famously observed, "the planters died as a class." Jefferson Thomas's personal financial failure both speaks to that history and illuminates its very personal contingencies and permutations.[138]

Jefferson Thomas took Gertrude and the children down with him. The legal protections her father arranged amounted to nothing. In 1897, the Richmond County Court heard the case of *Turner C. Thomas v. Gertrude Thomas.* Turner was Gertrude's eldest son. The son sued the mother, charging the wasting of their inheritance. When the case was settled, court officers valued the estate at $22,000. It sold for $4,900. After all the creditors were paid, Turner Thomas and his siblings received $70.62.[139]

Gertrude Thomas certainly played her part in the downfall. For a long time, she was willfully ignorant about the extent of their indebtedness and painfully slow to adjust to straitened circumstances. For at least three years after the end of the war she lived in denial, renting a big house in Augusta for $1,200 in gold per year, retaining a good deal of household help, and keeping up appearances. "I am only afraid he is more liberal than he can afford to be," she said of her husband with a tinge of pride. She routinely ridiculed black women's extravagant investment in dressing themselves well—"the servants are such improvident creatures," she observed—but it was a bit rich coming from a woman whose diary teemed with references to brocade and gloves, hats and trim. Even as the contents of her husband's store were at public sale, she went to town and bought herself a "'love of a bonnet' . . . and a dove coloured barege," a bolt of expensive cloth to make a dress. She continued to go to the theater and opera, even in 1870 when the Burke and Belmont plantations were advertised for sale. That drew a stinging criticism from her mother. "Money is too scarce," she told her daughter, "and you ought not to go Gertrude." "Ma says I am singularly short sighted in money matters," she acknowledged. But her sense of entitlement died hard.[140] A great deal rested on it for her and the children: on the education, clothing, carriages, magazines, and summer travel to the North. The gentility of it all anchored her social identity and sense of distinction. She suffered terribly from the loss of things. "It is infinitely more easy to be amiable when one is rich," she observed tartly one day in 1880, while attempting to bear the disorder of a poor household: peeling plaster, bad furniture, and bare floors in winter. She renamed her place "Dixie Farm," but with cotton growing up to the front door it was a far cry from Belmont.[141]

Among the many things destroyed in Gertrude Thomas's fall were her relations with her family. She never could forgive her husband for involving her brother in his debts, and it was a source of constant tension between the couple. Buddy had co-signed a note for Jefferson without requiring any collateral and stood to lose his own plantation when the note was called in. "Poor dear Buddy," Gertrude wrote, "his generous act of endorsing for Mr Thomas will involve him in trouble. Ma blames him that he did not require security . . . but I blame Mr Thomas more." In late 1870, when Buddy lost his share of his father's estate in settlement of Jefferson's debts, Gertrude staggered under the burden of guilt—like Jesus, she said, under "the cross." And in April 1871, when her husband told her that her brother would lose his plantation, Gertrude was inconsolable. But if she blamed her husband, neither could she forgive her siblings for suing her. In 1870, at the same time that the Burke plantations were sold to settle debts to her sister-in-law, Julia Scales, the Thomas's home at Belmont was also levied upon by her siblings and mother to recoup Jefferson's debts to her father's estate. "Did *you* know of this execution," she demanded of her mother when she saw the sale advertised in the papers. There were eight legatees, she noted, and each would get very little, but she would be evicted from her home. Gertrude could not understand how they could do this to her and was certain "that I would have spared one of my own sisters' husband this humiliation, for that sister's sake." "I know it is legal," she admitted, "I do not forget that. But this is against all nature. I get bewildered." Gertrude's mother gently rebuked her. You do your siblings "an injustice," she wrote.[142]

The complications and entanglements of Jefferson Thomas's debts left his wife torn between her obligations to her husband and children on the one hand, and her brothers, sisters, and mother on the other. She could not see her way through. She grew increasingly isolated from the people who had always supported her, ashamed at how her children had become "the poor relations of the family," and afraid to ask for sympathy that she would not get. For thirty years this was her life. She would not wish on her worst enemy "any greater trial than to be encumbered with debt," she declared at the beginning of it all. Will "I ever breathe the air of a freedman," she wondered, then crossed out the "d."[143]

Gertrude Thomas was an astute observer of the relations of power that shaped her world. After the war, her read on men's patriarchal prerogatives sharpened to a point. She insisted on representing the wife's perspective on the trial of debt in the context of women's dependence. It was, among other things, a bid for the legitimacy of women's perspective in history. "I wonder if it ever occurred to anyone to realise or imagine how a proud woman feels under such circumstances?" she wrote. "A woman who is identified so completely with the interest of her husband that his success or failure is hers." Her view of marital unity and hierarchy changed dramatically. She raged about Jefferson's progressive wasting of her inheritance. "Most men dislike to admit that their wifes own anything," she fumed at one point. "It is all the masculine 'my' and 'my own' which they use and in polite circles it would be considered bad taste for a woman to say 'my plantations' 'my horse' 'my cows' altho they really are as much her own as the dress she wears." Freedwomen, she said, had the better approach, insisting on keeping their accounts separate from their husbands. "What's mine is mine" and "wha's tother folks is tother folks," a farmhand named Mollie had told Gertrude when demanding a separate account from her husband. But African American women had a different family history behind them and had never had the luxury of dependence.[144]

Gertrude became less passive, more knowledgeable about legal details and procedures, and more openly critical of her husband's judgment. She fought him about signing the Burke properties over to her to avoid a settlement for debt. After questioning him closely on the details of a lien Stark held against their crops on two properties, she said, "I was and am not satisfied." Her husband said she lacked "confidence in his judgment," which by then she did. But even as she rebuked herself, her resentment and anger at her lack of control came through. She tried not to say anything publicly—"all my life I have tried to . . . hide from outside persons . . . anything which do[es] not reflect credit upon my family." But in private she expressed condemnation and shame—at her husband's irreligiosity, his profanity, and what was almost certainly his alcoholism. The latter condition she never named. As with her father and his mixed-race children, she spoke even to her journal only of secrets and skeletons in the family closet. "Every house" has "some subject which by mutual consent it is best to avoid," she declared. She saw "the mask off," she said of her husband at one point. She came to see him as a vain and undisciplined man. Once referring to two mares he had bought amid their financial troubles, she said his love of horses was as great as his love for "whom, shall I say—for—himself?" Jefferson Thomas's masterly will, and his wife's reliance on it, died with slavery and slaveholders' prerogatives.[145]

The whole experience turned Gertrude Thomas into an advocate of women's right to vote.[146] But in many ways, it made no difference. The demands of marital unity were unyielding. She knew that virtually everything her husband had came from "the property Pa gave into his charge for me and the children." She believed his "first debt" was to her and the children.[147] It was her property. She had legal title to it and knew her rights. She did not approve of her husband's decisions, but she was his wife, and when he asked her to sign them away, she could not refuse.

Gertrude Thomas first signed away her property rights in December 1868. "Mr Thomas said 'Gertrude here is a paper which I wish you to sign'" to allow a mortgage on one of the town lots. She knew it was a mistake, but he said "if this was not done the store would be . . . brought to bankruptcy. I signed it but did not read it." As the years went on and he kept putting the papers in front of her, she would argue, she *would* read them, but ultimately she would sign. Sometimes she took the papers to town to have her signature witnessed. Georgia did not require a privy exam, designed to ensure that women's consent had been freely given. Thomas was not physically coerced, but the power relations of marriage defy simple concepts of free will. Her mother warned her "to be careful how I signed papers in Mr T's embarrassed situation or I would lose the little sum I had settled upon me"—evidence of an obviously ongoing women's conversation about property rights. But he continued to ask, and she continued to sign until there was nothing left. By 1879, when her "lifetime interest" in her father's estate was sold to settle "a debt due by us," Gertrude, ever scrupulous, acknowledged the legitimacy of the claim. "As to whether I ought to have signed them," she said of the papers, "that is not the question involved."[148]

The real question is why Jefferson Thomas insisted. Among the most damaging of Jefferson Thomas's failures of judgment was his mishandling of his wife's property, a complicated legal terrain that other planters navigated more successfully. This error stands out even within a crowded field of poor judgment. John Berkley Grimball, in contrast, pursued a different path from similarly challenging circumstances. Grimball was in dire straits himself in the immediate postwar years. He was living in a boardinghouse in Charleston and sleeping on bare floors as he fought for the return of his plantations, which had been designated as abandoned lands. One of his daughters was teaching school, one son was trying (and failing) at the furnishing business, another was trying the auction business, and another (who had served in the Confederate Navy) was in exile in Mexico awaiting a pardon. His wife, Meta Morris Grimball, was living in Spartanburg in the South Carolina upcountry, where the cost of living was lower. Meta's relatives held a bond on John's plantation, the Grove, to secure the $38,000 he had borrowed from them. But even when he faced foreclosure and his creditors—that is, his wife's relatives—demanded that his wife "become surety for the debt" on the Grove, Grimball would not let her risk it. Instead, the couple worked together to construct an airtight trust that protected her wealth from his creditors. According to the trust deed, the property Meta inherited from her father, Lewis Morris, "no part of which has come into the possession of her husband," was secured to her sons with the consent of her husband and could not "be subject to his debts liabilities or engagements." The trust deed allowed Meta and her husband to draw income and profits from the property and to make gifts to their children from it. The decision was not comfortable for John—the whole family knew that he lived on his wife's family's wealth. One son, Berkley, who served as a trustee on the estate, referred to his father's plantation as "a burden on Mas property" and hoped that his father would find a way to become "self-supporting." The arrangement protected Meta's property and exposed John's. He tried and failed to "find a capitalist" to help him pay for labor to work the Grove. But after many unsuccessful efforts to find a solution, in 1870 he surrendered title in settlement of his debt. The personal cost to him was high, but the arrangement allowed the family to stabilize their losses and generate an income stream. In 1897, the Grimball sons were still drawing income from the trust and its diversified portfolio of investments, which included New York State bonds, and canal, waterworks, and railroad bonds.[149]

The contrast with Jefferson Thomas was a telling one. His insistence that Gertrude sign away her property rights sacrificed the family's inherited wealth and the only potential source of future income. It meant that Gertrude was perpetually torn between the "effort not to reduce my children to beggary . . . and my wish to oblige Mr. Thomas."[150]

The struggle to rebuild a life from the ruins of the old slaveholder's world involved even the realm of motherhood. Gertrude Thomas was thirty-one years old and pregnant when the war ended. She lost the baby, Charley, the day after he was born—to her relief. "Little darling," she wrote, "if I could have you back again I would not." The burden of debt corroded the natural forces of life as Gertrude saw things. She had three more children after the war, including one, Julian, in 1868 at the height of their financial troubles. Her husband did not want the baby; since "our change of fortune . . . Mr Thomas has thought we had children enough." He could not share her joy in Julian or the subsequent two, because, as she described it, "he has so morbid a dread of our having more mouths to feed, and little feet to cover that he chills my womanly heart and makes me untrue to my better nature."[151]

Aversion to childbearing was not an unusual reaction to the turmoil, uncertainty, and poverty of postwar life, especially for the defeated. In Germany in 1945, the German birthrate dropped precipitously, in distinct contrast to the baby boom among Jewish displaced persons who had survived the carnage of the Holocaust. Reproduction and maternity are essential elements of postwar histories. They both reveal and constitute changes in the domestic social and political order.[152]

Childbearing had never been easy for Gertrude Thomas. She had repeated miscarriages (which she called "abortions") before her first child was born, and more after. She gave birth to ten children, and only six survived to adulthood. But in the postwar period, pregnancy, childbirth, and motherhood were just as entangled with debt and financial loss as they had been with wealth and slaveholding in the prewar period. When her beloved seven-year-old Clanton died in 1879, Gertrude was at work. "Oh my God that is so hard," she wrote in her diary. "I was teaching other people's children when I ought to have been with my own child." She would periodically dream that she held him. Gertrude Thomas would fight for her children and their place in the postwar world. "Oh my God how a mother loves her child," she wrote in 1882, "and how I love Julian." As Julian hoed six rows of cotton to earn a little spending money, Turner worked the river swamp place with his own hands, and Jeff waited on people in Loo Chong's store, Gertrude took the measure of how far they had fallen.[153] Of all the things she lost in the new regime, she mourned none more than her ability to protect her children and their place in the postwar world—and the wealth that would have enabled her to do it, as her father and mother had done for her and her siblings before the war.

In the end, Gertrude and Jefferson Thomas and their children lost almost everything. She remained devoted to her children, and she remained with her husband, wedded as firmly in poverty as they had been in wealth. "What, I, the child of wealth and pride ... [to] suffer such degradation," she wrote of her postwar life path, a turning of "Fortune's Wheel" ever downward. She had been forced to drink from another "bitter cup," of poverty and debt, destined "to drink, and drink again until the dregs are consumed."[154]

Gertrude Thomas was an astute observer of the new postwar southern world. Her efforts at reconstructing a life from the ruins illuminates the revolution in process, especially, finally, between white and black southerners. Thomas was painfully aware that defeat and emancipation required the reconstruction of white supremacy itself, on new terms. Caste, she said in 1869, must be now "a real, substantial fact" of "social and mental superiority" and not a mere "imaginary idea."[155] But how was that to be produced? Among all the trials to which Thomas was subjected, none mattered more than her children's declining place in the world. By her own reckoning, white racial superiority now required real and cultural capital that she no longer possessed.

In 1935, W. E. B. Du Bois insisted that, ultimately, the challenge of Reconstruction was for white Americans to recognize that black people "were altogether human." Over the course of the twentieth century, the very best historians have identified this moment of Reconstruction as a pivotal one in the history of race or "racecraft," as Karen and Barbara Fields more accurately name the process: the production of claims about racial difference (read, inferiority) designed to legitimize practices of domination. African American freedom in the context of a *formal democracy* directly challenged white southerners' social and political power. It tested the idea of government by the people, a test met by white southerners with raw violence and a search for new ways to legitimate exclusion on the basis of racial inferiority. The destruction of slavery destroyed the old certainties of white supremacy; it took fifty years of experimentation to build a new system as serviceable as the old. In Reconstruction, "race" was resignified.[156]

Most of the historical literature on this process, and patterns of racial violence in riots such as New Orleans, Memphis, and Camilla, Georgia, and in the terror campaigns of the Ku Klux Klan, focuses on white men and the threat to white men's *political* power. Even work that tackles the sexual violence at the heart of Reconstruction typically insists that it was politically motivated. But Gertrude Thomas's scramble to find secure footing on the new ground shows the limits of that view. "Racist concepts do considerable work in political and economic life," Karen and Barbara Fields acknowledge, "but, if they were . . . without intimate roots in other phases of life, their persuasiveness would accordingly diminish."[157] Thomas's path to a new kind of racism was driven by concerns that were nothing if not intimate.

Thomas's panic about race and caste peaked later than the terrible first three postbellum years, in 1869 and 1870. These years were still the eye of the radical Reconstruction storm to be sure, but also, revealingly, coincided with Jefferson Thomas's first forced bankruptcy, when the couple's humiliation first came into public view. It was at this moment, in agonized diary entries, that Gertrude grappled with the vulnerabilities of the new social order, the rise of African American individuals and communities, and the real possibility of white social degradation.

Thomas fought hard for her children's future. Eventually she would go to work to support them. But over the course of her forty-plus years of postwar life, she had to face the fact that she and Jefferson had squandered their children's inheritance. She was not without material resources, especially at the beginning, but increasingly the children's advantages were provided by her mother: dancing lessons, new clothes, and trips North.[158] Gertrude could fasten a diamond pin to her eldest son Turner's lapel as he dressed for a party in 1869, but by that point she could not afford to keep him in school. As Turner was forced into fieldwork alongside "the negroes," his mother anxiously collected signs of his superiority, including a habit of reading on the job. Although his father complained, it was better, she insisted, that he "converse with an intelligent author to the illiterate negro who was driving" the cart. She was sustained for months when he won a jousting tournament in Augusta, riding as Henry of Navarre. She demanded that the "servants" address her son with respect—she expected them to answer "yes sir" when he called them—but they resisted these rituals of subordination and deference associated with slavery. With such everyday practices abandoned, and Turner laboring in the fields, there was nothing to organize relations of inferiority and superiority. She lectured workers about "the distinction to be made between Turner and ... the servants," but as long as her eldest son was "engaged in work which any Negro could have done as well," there was no meaningful distinction to be made. "Among all my troubles," she wrote in 1870, "none worried me more than" this.[159]

Gertrude's worries for her children's future converged explosively with the question of what racial order would emerge with black emancipation. To Thomas it was a frighteningly open and unsettled question. "We have the superiority of race by nature and education," she stated in 1869, but without the latter, she was not sure of what the former consisted. She saw a race of people, African Americans, on the rise, threatening to compete successfully in all arenas; the racial degradation she was witnessing involved southern white people. "What was it but blood and education which gave so much power to Aaron Alpeoria Bradley," the newly elected black congressman from Georgia, she asked pointedly at that sensitive juncture. At the same moment, white planter boys, presumably like hers, "descend . . . suddenly to the rank of the day laborer."[160]

Yet to Thomas, the most immediate, visceral threat of black equality came in the form of "mulatto" women, more than equipped to compete as wives and mothers with women like her. For Thomas, of course, that preoccupation was not new. But emancipation changed the calculations, as sexual relationships previously hidden, disowned, and illicit threatened to become public and legitimate.

Gertrude Thomas's thinking about race was grounded in the new realities of labor, law, and sexuality in the postwar order. This was vividly clear in May 1869, shortly after Turner had been taken out of school by his father and put to farm work, and at the very moment the local papers advertised the sheriff's sale of the contents of her husband's store. Thomas had an encounter with a light-skinned African American woman and her equally "bright" child that shook her to the core. It was the woman's obvious intelligence and gentility that triggered a stream of anxious reflection on the future. "I have never met with an educated coloured woman before this one," Thomas observed of the woman, formerly enslaved, who lived in the neighborhood with a white man, a Mr. Towns. Thomas did not believe Towns to be the father of the little girl because she bore "too strong resemblance to someone else," naming the woman's former owner. She worried that such open interracial relationships as the woman currently had with Towns were sure to become more common. The laws of the state currently "permit Negroes to vote and hold offices but forbid their marriage with white persons," but she was convinced that would change. It was only a matter of time until women with the best white blood in their veins, free of the stigma of slavery and raised with the "equalizing influence of education," were "received socially into some familys." As she noted bluntly, there had always been "a strong affinity for the two races" or there would not be so many mixed-race children among the black population. Now with freedom, she feared, those children would be the beneficiaries of an education her own sons did not have, and the girls would prove attractive to white men in marriage. If "we" do not maintain our superiority in "nature and education," she stewed, then all the laws against marriage would be useless: "As it is the law is almost an insult to Southern woman." Thomas saw herself in direct competition with mulatto women for white men as marriage partners, and she was not confident about the odds. She railed against the blindness of her own people: men who think only of how much they need their sons' labor in the fields. Her own husband could not have been far from mind: "To obtain a hand the boy's head suffers and he grows up an ignoramus while negro women toil and strive, labour and endure in order that their children 'may have a schooling.'"[161] There was a lot of respect for black women in that sentence.

Thomas broadly and fearfully perceived competition between mulatto and white women, and now that slavery was destroyed, saw it as an open fight for social distinction between their children. In May and June 1869 and for the entire year following, she displayed an obsessive interest in black women's bodies and sexuality (and absolutely none in black men's). She commented repeatedly on the complexities of freedwomen's sexual and marital histories, collecting examples of sexual relationships—marriages in all but name—between mulatto women and white men. The example of the "coloured" woman living with a Mr. Morris on her brother's land, who had been purchased by him ten years earlier, brought her to the point. "I expect she came between his wife and himself," she noted. "White women and mulattoes prove rivals, unconscious though the former may be."[162]

Gertrude Thomas's belief that she was living through the creation of a new racial order that would extend to interracial marriage was not entirely unfounded. Laws on interracial marriage *were* unsettled, particularly in the intense period when Republicans controlled southern state legislatures and wrote new constitutions. Georgia had put a ban on interracial marriage in the constitution of 1865 and then passed laws prohibiting such marriages in 1866. Such racist laws against "miscegenation," and the related claim that marriages across the color line were "unnatural," as historian Peggy Pascoe argues, were the very "foundation of ... white supremacy" for the long century that stretched from the end of the Civil War to the middle of the twentieth century. Thomas never used that toxic term "miscegenation," nor the antebellum antecedent "amalgamation." Instead, she talked concretely of marriages and relationships, those living as man and wife, and of affinity. She was not at all sure that interracial marriage was unnatural; quite the opposite, actually. She believed public opinion was moving more toward acceptance than proscription. And in fact, after the adoption of the Fourteenth Amendment in 1868 and guarantees of equal protection under the law, courts began to strike down those laws and legislatures moved to repeal them. The new 1868 Georgia state constitution written by a Republican majority (which now included black representatives) did not contain the previous ban. By the 1880s, after a decade of legal contestation and the so-called redemption of southern state houses by white supremacist Democrats, this period of progressive opening had closed and virtually every intimate relationship between people of a different race, including ones that involved white men, was again illegal and illicit. But the totality of Reconstruction cases refute the usual portrait of universal southern opposition to interracial marriage in the post–Civil War period and "reveal a moment when it might have been possible to remove racial dividing lines from American marriage law." It is worth noting that all of the liberalizing legal activity focused on precisely the coupling Gertrude Thomas found most threatening: black women and white men.[163]

In a volatile social and political order, and as her own family's fortunes plummeted, Thomas tried to make sense of the new reality. She found little comfort in new racializing myths, including the doctrine that blacks were a lower form of human life advanced in a popular book. On many occasions, typically prompted by the appearance of mixed-race children, she reflected on the relationship between color and intelligence. At times, she lazily associated blackness with baseness and assumed a hierarchy of civilization. But when, in the summer of 1870, she directly considered whether, as people say, "all the intellect [mulattos] possessed" could be attributed "to the white blood in their veins," she dismissed the idea as patently false. "One of the brightest intellects I have ever seen among the coloured people was Sam Drayton who used to preach down at this same church, and he was a black man." That day Gertrude, Jefferson, and their children had been special guests at a picnic at the "coloured" Baptist church attended by many of her former slaves. She had watched the children perform their exercises, comparing the black and "bright mulatto" ones, which led her to the observation about Drayton, a man she had long admired. The "negroes as a class have made little progress" in education she observed that day, adding that it was because there are not too many good teachers out in the country. Gertrude copied the invitation Jefferson Thomas had received from the black school superintendent into her diary, to "give you an idea of their capability." She commented on the difficulty the man had spelling the word "superintendent," but noted that he tried it a second time and got it right. Thomas's othering gaze—the us and them—clearly marked the racial divide, but her assessment in turn narrowed it. She was impressed by the man's efforts. She thought it "wonderful when the circumstances are considered under which this man received his education. There are numbers of wealthy white men who can do no better."[164] Gertrude Thomas was acutely sensitive on the subject of education, embracing a "Lamarckian" belief that environment mattered, and "that education and refinement are inheritable," as the historian Nell Irvin Painter explained.[165] Whites had lost their monopoly on education, and African Americans' evident capacity to embrace its opportunities profoundly distressed this white mother.

In the end, the weight of the past ineluctably shaped Gertrude Thomas's ability to face the future. The sexual terror of slavery, in particular, had lodged itself deeply and permanently in southern families. Given her family history, it is hardly surprising that for her, financial and sexual humiliation merged confusingly. Nor that her thinking about race and sexuality led her toward a new paternalist version of white supremacy. Gertrude was always quick to find evidence to confirm her low regard for black women's sexual morality. "The moral character of our negro race is so low," she expostulated one day. In this case, Thomas claimed that Diania, a woman working for her, had an estranged husband, a lover, a child with the lover, and a new man she planned to marry without the expense of a divorce. But Thomas knew too much about slavery and white men's sexual violence to entirely believe even her own line of reasoning. As always, her mind moved immediately to the culpability of white men: "If virtue be the test to distinguish a man from a beast," she wrote while on the apparent subject of black women's sexuality, "the claim of many Southern white men might be questionable to the claim of 'Man made in the image of his maker.'"[166]

Gertrude Thomas had little faith in white men, including her own husband. In the work of reconstructing whites' racial superiority, men—fathers—could not be trusted. In the summer of 1869, as the family's failures became public and as Jefferson took Turner out of school to work as a field hand, her focus on mulatto women and their white or mixed race children veered very close to home. Just how close is a matter of judgment. In a long, overheated, and wide-ranging entry about caste and what could secure white supremacy in the postwar world, Gertrude moved, seemingly involuntarily, from a general discussion of white fathers and their illegitimate mulatto children to a suspiciously specific observation. Venting about white fathers' abandonment of their sons' futures, she condemned a world in which white boys—like her sons—"born heirs to thousands plough daily side by side with the Negro who perhaps works for his victuals and clothes." What could this lead to but "degradation," she raged. She directed her rage dangerously at black women, but also at white men and, most assuredly, her own husband. If this continued, she pronounced darkly, "while he follows the plough, his education totally neglected," he would be surpassed by the "mulatto boy, perhaps his father's son by a woman a shade darker than *his* mother, let him receive an education . . . and where will caste be then in the respective influence those two men will exert, each voting each holding office?"[167]

The sense of betrayal was palpable. Thomas did not name Turner or his father, but the example did not seem hypothetical. It is difficult to know how literally to read it. Jefferson Thomas may well have had another child with a black woman. The evidence is far from conclusive. What is conclusive is Gertrude Thomas's knowledge of *her father's* adultery, his longstanding relationship with his slave Lurany, and their almost white children—knowledge enough to crater any earlier confidence that her father and husband were exceptions to the "general depravity" of men. Carolyn Curry, Thomas's biographer, insists that in terms of "miscegenation" within her own family, Gertrude Thomas "lived in denial like other women of the antebellum South." But this is palpably not true. Confirmed knowledge of her father's other family and children, and suspicions about her husband, were the bedrock reality of all of her thinking about race in the postwar southern world. White racial superiority had to be reproduced or her sons would sink and other, mulatto women's children would rise. White men could not be trusted. "Educate our boys," she concluded, "and all will be right."[168] But she could not. As she saw it, only wealth and education could make caste now. And in that race, Gertrude Thomas was afraid her children would lose.

Thomas's diary evinces none of the romanticizing of an Old South past common among postwar women's writings and Lost Cause propaganda. Her confrontation with her family history seems to have precluded that most common kind of postwar racism. But Thomas was a white supremacist nonetheless, and her relentless focus on black women's bodies and sexuality, on their alleged seduction of white men, was a dangerous element of a new racial ideology that would come to define Jim Crow modernity.[169]

We know a good deal more about southern women's role in the white supremacist movements of the late nineteenth and twentieth centuries than we do about the formative period of Reconstruction.[170] Gertrude Thomas's personal history, and that of her husband and family, begin to show the elements of that story: how, in a period of incredible uncertainty, in the first moment of open confrontation with the sexual legacy of slavery, white women's volatile mix of grief and rage at lost privilege was part and parcel of the violent process by which white southerners moved to reassert dominance and beat back African Americans' success at defining a new social order.

By the 1890s, when Gertrude Thomas was in her late fifties, the turbulent personal and public years of Reconstruction were far behind her. She emerged on the verge of the new century as a suffragist, a southern liberal, and a diehard Confederate. Her politics and thinking about race were shaped, as always, by intimate matters. Slavery and its sexual violence left a lasting legacy in American life, one felt by every southerner, white and black. Thomas's own particular, paternalist version of white supremacy was defined, not surprisingly, by a series of moral crusades: against male drunkenness, for the public education of black as well as white southerners, for white women's right to vote.[171] Combined with an unstinting commitment to the Lost Cause, these crusades remind us of how pieces of the past were carried forward to shape a new century.

There is only so far one life can take us toward a new history of Reconstruction, even one so richly recounted as Gertrude Thomas's. Old certainties about the revolutionary nature of these years have been undermined by a resurgent recognition of how deep the challenges of racism went—and go—in American life. But in a moment when we are inclined to think that emancipation did not represent a significant break in history, Gertrude Thomas's life and writings provide an intimate accounting of the ways in which it did. They leave little doubt about how utterly revolutionary it was to her life and identity to lose "possession" of her slaves. Given what slavery was, its undoing had to, and did, reach far beyond public and political arenas, into the most personal realms of life, touching on matters of love and belonging, marriage and motherhood, and subjectivity itself.[172]

As in other postwar societies, old elites did not easily surrender the levers of power. Reconstructions are always and ever partial in that respect. Southern whites such as Thomas were a conquered and expropriated people, fighting for their old racial supremacy in a new order. Eventually they achieved it, although it took a different form than slavery. In the American South those old elites clearly saw their former slaves as enemy collaborators, and the full wrath of defeated Confederates fell on them. It was a brutal struggle, and one that, like other postwar stories, does not lend itself to triumphalist narratives.[173]

But neither is it a story of continuity or predictability. In its outlines and especially its intimate details, Gertrude Thomas's ground level, unfolding, and emotional account is a valuable reminder of the volatility and uncertainty of the postwar southern and American world, and of the fundamental (even elemental) nature of the reordering underway.

Epilogue

Women are not just witnesses to war. Across human history, women have left no doubt about their political commitments, willingness to fight for them, and pay the price. They have also left plenty of evidence of how they suffered in wars, as countless people have, less interested in a cause than in survival. In all of this they have acted as individuals and members of communities, fully immersed in the currents of history, transformed by the conditions of military conflict, and acting in ways that shaped and changed the terms of war and peace. As Svetlana Alexievich says, they have been "actors and makers" in those histories.[1] Much of their part remains to be written.

The three Civil War stories told in this book contribute one small part to that far larger history of women and war. They leave no doubt about women's stakes in the national conflict. They amply demonstrate the ways in which women of many different kinds moved, out of choice or necessity, to shape their own destinies and their peoples' histories in the maelstrom of war. They also demonstrate the decisive impact of women's actions on all the major dynamics, processes, and outcomes of the war. Taken together, the stories provide a clear picture of the varied roles women played in the military conflict, most shockingly as enemy women in the war of resistance, but also as enslaved refugees who challenged the government's plans to exclude, control, and contain them in the emancipation process, and as defeated Confederates determined to shape the terms of the peace. There is no Civil War history without women in it.

Little about this should surprise us. But yet it does, in no small measure because most of that history was conveniently forgotten as soon as the war ended. Forgetting, or silencing, is always a part of how spoken and written histories are produced, but the process operates along particular lines of power. Mary Beard's recent blistering manifesto about the silencing of women's public voice and speech reveals a pattern of disempowerment, of attitudes, assumptions, and prejudices that are hardwired into our culture and millennia of our history. That pattern of gender and power accords enormous public authority to men (and none to women), dictating not just who speaks in public but who makes history and who writes it. Heroic national narratives, like that of the American Civil War, necessarily involve selective celebration along patriarchal lines. In those histories, stories of women's war have no place. As Ranajit Guha observed about nationalist histories of peasant insurgencies in India, they fail to honor women's role in the movement because to do so "messes up the plot." Tales of women's suffering and sacrifice can generally fit the plot line, but outside of those, the process of erasure and trivialization begins.[2]

This is not simply a matter of historians and the writing of history. The erasure goes much deeper than that. Indeed, the pattern of denying or suppressing knowledge of women's participation in military conflicts forms a striking and persistent pattern across a range of postwar societies in the nineteenth and twentieth centuries. The way women act during war, the capacities for violence and independent thought and action they show, even if just in surviving, force deeply uncomfortable recognitions on everyone involved. As in the American Civil War, such actions profoundly disrupt men's assumptions about women's innocence *and* about their normative identity as wives willingly subject to the authority of their husbands. Those principles are hard to live without; when war is over they have to be restored.

The writing out of women from histories of war reflects a deep investment in the gender order itself and a desire to limit the destructiveness of war. Even at the turn of the twenty-first century, with old certainties about gender identities and relations crumbling all around us, and in the face of an avalanche of evidence of women's participation in military conflicts, including directly as combatants, international organizations like the United Nations remain deeply invested in the idea that women are innocent victims entitled to special protections in war. They recognize women's agency not in waging war but only in making peace. The faith that women are outside war remains an indispensable one at odds with history.

We see how the process of erasure worked after the Civil War in the accounts of Francis Lieber. He was a central figure in Reconstruction policy in the years right after the war, called back to work for the government gathering evidence for Jefferson Davis's treason trial.[3] Lieber retained his broad sense of authority over Republican politics and policy. In the climate of fear that gripped the country after Lincoln's assassination, he worked ceaselessly to protect the achievements of our "heroic period," as he called the war, and to put the newly unified nation on a firm footing. Lieber had always attached a great deal of significance to marriage and the family as the indispensable basis of the state. He had said as much in 1838, and he felt no different in 1867. "Man and woman are made to complete one another," he wrote then, "to become 'one flesh and bone,' to establish the family, whence the state arises not only in primeval times, but every day anew."[4] It is hardly surprising that in a moment of national crisis, he stressed the necessity of returning American women to their "natural" sphere of the family and the home—and expelling them from the public sphere of politics and war.

The threat to the gender order had not ended with the war. Postwar deliberations involved their own dangers. For Lieber women's agitation for the right to vote during a period of profound constitutional revision was one manifest threat that had to be contained. In 1867, as New York prepared to hold a constitutional convention amid a national debate on "universal suffrage," Elizabeth Cady Stanton made a forceful push for women's right to vote in New York as an essential element of "reconstruction." In a speech delivered in person in the state assembly chamber, Stanton made her case that white men could not be trusted to legislate for women and "negroes" held under their "ban of inferiority." Equal rights was equal rights, she insisted, and "Reconstruction must begin at home." In demanding the right of self-representation for women as well as African American men, Stanton moved to collect on the debt the nation owed loyal women for their patriotic toil and sacrifice in the Union cause. Like everyone else in the suffrage debate that consumed the nation that year, Stanton linked war and politics, service, sacrifice, and political rights. Why, she asked pointedly, should immigrant men of every class and sort possess the right to vote "while the loyal mothers of a million soldiers whose bones lay bleaching on every Southern plain" did not? Women had earned the vote by the blood of their sons.[5]

But this was hardly Lieber's idea of what Reconstruction required. To him, the very idea of suffrage was an assault on women's nature. When Andrew Dickson White, the dean of the Columbia Law School, warned Lieber that Democrats were going to push through a proposal for women's rights (as a means of bringing their party back to power), Lieber waded into the fight. In speeches and articles first delivered by invitation at the Union League Club in New York, he defended the natural order of things, claiming the right to speak for women. Stanton had linked politics and war. For Lieber, too, those were inextricable domains exclusively under the control of men. "As long as politics is so vehement and involves wars and armies," and woman's delicacy is valued, he insisted, she ought to be represented in her husband. If woman entered the arena of politics, she would lose her "legitimate influence in the proper sphere." Indeed, such a thing would "unwoman her," as it had so many French women before, from the "fish women in the revolution to a Pompadour." Reaching for that already predictable trope of political immorality, of women out of place, he asked, "Who wishes this of his own mother, his wife, his sister, or his daughter." "How would we like a woman president?"[6] Lieber's woman was always singular, the bourgeois wife and mother, like his own spouse. In war, she was the one left on the homefront, guarding the values that would be needed with the return to peace.

In this account of women's nature and sphere, the recent history of the war presented an awkward set of facts. As Lieber knew better than most, in times of war women stepped onto the wall and looked the enemy in the face. He had lived through the Napoleonic Wars at the beginning of the century, and he knew about women's military resistance to the French in Spain and Prussia. He admitted that in Prussia he had fought "by the side of a woman sergeant, so brave that she received successively several orders of distinction." He kept a list in his files of "Great Women," beside his examples of "women the weaker sex." That file included a clipping on "the girl who fought for Hungary" in the celebrated but suppressed revolution of 1848. And, of course, in the middle of the American Civil War, he had been forced to write a code of laws that acknowledged enemy women as a military threat and held them accountable for treason. Lieber acknowledged very little of that recent history and actively disavowed what he knew of the Civil War. That there were "exceptional" cases in history he was willing to admit, as indeed he had done in 1838. But even as the number of exceptions piled up, he insisted that was not the way women's influence was practiced in history, including in the last war. "We all recollect what the mothers and sisters and daughters have heroically done in our last struggle for our Country," he wrote, "and no nobler type of humanity can be imagined than a patriotic mother or wife who with hot tears of affection in the last embrace, still says: Go or who goes to the hospital and gives herself up to the work of comforting and assuaging and healing while her husband or her father may be fighting either near or far away."[7] With all the inconvenient women written off as exceptions, and women's role in the Civil War culled down to a single theme of womanly sacrifice and service to men, Lieber had an usable history for the postwar order. Despite all he knew, he stuck willfully to the script that women had played no part in the war except as patriotic mothers, wives, sisters, and daughters. Lieber's postwar investment in restoring the gender order involved a great deal of forgetting and a version of women's war that bore little resemblance to the messy, urgent original.

Lieber's view of women's nature and right to vote did not go unchallenged. One female interlocutor ridiculed the "illogic" of his argument in the pages of *The Nation*. She insisted that women had as much interest as men in just war and righteous peace, and deserved the vote to register their views. But even her feisty response conformed to the narrow account of women's Civil War that had already taken hold by 1867. In making her case for women's right to vote, she offered the "sacrifices" and service women had made to the national cause "in the working rooms and on the executive committees of the Sanitary Commission . . . and in the care of the wounded in hospitals and on the field."[8] That was the approved script. Even radical women's rights advocates like Elizabeth Cady Stanton and *The Nation* author did not venture too far out of bounds. There were hard limits to what women's rights advocates could say about women's war. By 1867, the process of forgetting, erasure, and trivialization was already well advanced.

Lieber's version of women's war was deeply tied to his investment in restoring the gender order at home. But it also reflected his desire to shore up a view of marriage and the family that undergirded the international order and anchored efforts to limit the destructiveness of war. It was part of woman's nature, as he defined it, to "want and naturally seek a protector." The definition of women as "women-in-need-of-protection" has had a long life in international law. It was a principle already embedded in Lieber's code, particularly in article 37, which prohibits rape. It provided the baseline meaning when "civilians" were first extended definite provisions for protection in the Fourth Geneva Convention in 1949 for which Lieber's code was the "avowed model." In the Protocols Additional to that convention passed in 1977, when the concept of the "civilian" was first formally defined— "Civilians are what combatants, members of armed forces, are not"— the obvious problem of the distinction was yet again anchored in the assumed innocence of women and children. In need of a visually observable means of making the distinction, the protocol included the rule that there must be "a heavy presumption that women and children are protected civilians."[9]

But perhaps the most striking recent evidence of the durability of the idea that women are outside war comes from United Nations Security Council Resolution 1325, adopted in 2000 in the aftermath of the wars in Bosnia and Rwanda. Titled a "Resolution on Women,

Peace and Security," Resolution 1325 calls on all parties to a conflict "to take special measures to protect women and girls from gender-based violence, particularly rape and other forms of sexual abuse." It also "affirms the important role of women in the prevention and resolution of conflicts, peace negotiations, peace-building, humanitarian response and post-conflict reconstruction," and stresses the importance of "their equal participation . . . in all efforts for the maintenance and promotion of peace and security." In a preamble and eighteen separate recommendations, there is only one mention of "female . . . ex-combatants." Seventeen of the eighteen specific recommendations speak of special protections to be accorded women and girls as civilians and in their role as peace-makers. Resolution 1325 talks consistently of the impact of armed conflict *on* women and girls but never of women and girls *in* armed conflict. The Gender, Policy and Strategy division of the US Institute of Peace, which aims to implement this resolution in US policies, cites its fight against the persistent invisibility of women in stories of war, but most of its work focuses on the "work of ending or preventing wars," which is "weakened when women are excluded."[10]

Feminist activists and scholars have mostly embraced Resolution 1325, seeing in it a vital tool by which to protect women in military conflicts and empower them in the negotiation of peace and security measures when they end. They view the resolution as "a radical step forward in the language of the Security Council," and critical to "the empowerment of women and sustainable peace," which they believe to be connected. But the resolution leaves the question of women as combatants and the complicated and diverse experiences of women unacknowledged. Feminist peace and security scholars recognize its limits, particularly expressing discomfort, as one put it, with the way 1325 conceptualizes gender and gender security as "women-in-need-of-protection" and with the assumption that women are "natural peace-makers by virtue of their femininity." The problems of the resolution are acknowledged and real, but it is not easy to counter the effect it has of relegating women to the status of civilians, or as one theorist described it, "those who suffer distress and weakness, despite the evidence to the contrary."[11]

It is astonishing to realize how much of the history of women and war has to be overlooked to make this claim work. As the peoples' wars of the early nineteenth century gave way first to modern industrial war in the American Civil War, and then to the logic and technologies of total war in the twentieth century, the distinction between civilian and combatant dissolved entirely, including the assumptions of women's innocence on which it had always depended.

By the end of World War II, when the full horrors of that conflict were known, even the presumption that women were civilians had been utterly obliterated. Somewhere between 800,000 and 1 million women fought in the Soviet Army and many more in partisan forces. They were tank drivers, infantrymen, machine gunners, snipers, military pilots, scouts, cryptographers, radio operators, airplane mechanics, field nurses, surgeons, doctors, laundresses and cooks, militia fighters, partisans, liaisons to partisan forces, munitions workers, and engineers. Vasily Grossman's account of Stalingrad and Svetlana Alexievich's oral histories of Soviet women testify to the many womanly faces of war. Those women came home and never spoke of their experiences. Until Alexievich solicited their testimonies in the late 1970s and 1980s, they had never told their war stories to anyone. In Greece, Italy, France, Britain, Germany, and the United States as well, women served in huge numbers in regular armed forces or in reserve and support capacities. They played a prominent part in the resistance to Nazi occupation across the sweep of that empire. Nor was their role any less prominent in the wave of anticolonial wars that swept across large swaths of the world after 1945. In Algeria, as in Northern Ireland and many other places, women were active participants in resistance movements and wars of national liberation. None of this has changed in the present moment.[12]

Women, like all humans, suffered in all of these wars, as they do in Syria today. They lost husbands and sons in combat and watched their children die of starvation and disease. They were the particular target of campaigns of sexual violence, including rape, as they were in Francisco Franco's Spain, in the Soviet invasion of Germany, and in Bosnia and Rwanda.[13] They suffered through bombings and invasions, and were forced to flee their homes and live precariously as refugees. Many of them surely wanted peace even if it came with defeat, although Gertrude Thomas could not be counted among that number.

But even in the American Civil War, in the middle of the nineteenth century, when the nature of modern war manifested itself, women's experiences of war encompassed far more than the role of victim. To survive the conflict required more of them than that. Wars sweep everyone into their maelstrom, and force everyone—male and female alike—to fight. In the American Civil War, as we have seen, women fought for a variety of causes, and in the process they helped to define the very nature and meaning of the conflict. They fought for the Confederacy, for the Union, for liberation from slavery; they fought to protect themselves and their children and sometimes their husbands; they fought to keep body and soul together and survive, somehow, until the war was over; and when, finally it was, they fought to stem its losses or reap its gains, for themselves and their children. If we think of the history of war as the history of human beings in war, then we will need the version with the women still in it.

Notes

Acknowledgments

Index

Notes

Prologue

1. Svetlana Alexievich, *The Unwomanly Face of War: An Oral History of Women in World War II*, trans. Richard Pevear and Larissa Volokhonsky (New York: Random House, 2017), p. xvi. Alexievich says "about a million women fought in the Soviet army" (xii).

2. Francis Lieber to Senator John C. Calhoun, n.d., in *The Life and Letters of Francis Lieber*, ed. Thomas Sergeant Perry (Boston: James R. Osgood, 1882), p. 230; Francis Lieber, *Manual of Political Ethics, Designed Chiefly for the Use of Colleges and Students at Law*, vol. I, ed. Theodore D. Woolsey (1838; reprint, Philadelphia: J. B. Lippincott, 1911), pp. 138–139.

1. Enemy Women and the Laws of War

Quoted in Michael Fellman, *Inside War: The Guerilla Conflict in Missouri during the American Civil War* (New York: Oxford University Press, 1989), p. 203.

1. Francis Lieber, General Orders No. 100, "Instructions for the Government of Armies of the United States, in the Field," War Department, Adjutant General's Office, Washington, D.C., Apr. 24, 1863, in US War Department, *The War of the Rebellion: A Compilation of the Official Records of the Union and Confederate Armies* (Washington, D.C.: Government Printing Office, 1880–1901) (hereafter *O.R.*), ser. 3, vol. 3, pp. 148–164, http://ehistory.osu.edu/books/official-records/124

/0148; Geoffrey Best, *Humanity in Warfare* (New York: Columbia University Press, 1980), p. 171. See also Frank Freidel, *Francis Lieber: Nineteenth Century Liberal* (1947; reprint, Gloucester, Mass.: P. Smith, 1968), pp. 387–417.

2. On Lieber's code in the history of the laws of war, see Best, *Humanity in Warfare*, pp. 206–211; Helen M. Kinsella, *The Image before the Weapon: A Critical History of the Distinction between Combatant and Civilian* (Ithaca, N.Y.: Cornell University Press, 2011); and John Fabian Witt, *Lincoln's Code: The Laws of War in American History* (New York: Free Press, 2012). The Germans called it *Volkskrieg*, war of peoples. On the Napoleonic Wars as inaugurating the age of "total war," see David Bell, *The First Total War: Napoleon's Europe and the Birth of Warfare as We Know It* (Boston: Houghton Mifflin, 2007). On debate about the American Civil War, see Mark Grimsley, *The Hard Hand of War: Union Military Policy toward Southern Civilians, 1861–1865* (New York: Cambridge University Press, 1995), and Mark E. Neely, Jr., *The Civil War and the Limits of Destruction* (Cambridge, Mass.: Harvard University Press, 2007).

3. Best, *Humanity in Warfare*, p. 265; Kinsella, *Image before the Weapon*, pp. 2, 3.

4. Witt, *Lincoln's Code*, p. 233. Witt deals with the distinction but not its embedded assumptions about gender.

5. Ibid., pp. 4, 241, and throughout.

6. Best, *Humanity in Warfare*, p. 180. For discussions about the necessity for the code, which cite a wide range of issues, see Lieber to General Henry Halleck, Feb. 7, Nov. 13, Dec. 31, 1862, box 27; Halleck to Lieber, Nov. 15, 1862, box 9, Francis Lieber Papers, 1815–1888, Huntington Library, San Marino, Calif. (hereafter FLP, HL). Lieber had already prepared two memoranda at the request of the War Department on guerilla warfare and on the use of free blacks and fugitive slaves in the Union Army. See Lieber to Halleck, n.d. (in response to Halleck to Lieber, Aug. 6, 1862), in *O.R.*, ser. 3, vol. 2, pp. 301–309, http://ehistory.osu.edu/books/official-records/123/0301; and "A Memoir to Mr. Secretary Stanton," enclosed in Lieber to Halleck, Aug. 10, 1862, box 27, FLP, HL. John Witt acknowledges that "the warrant for violence was daunting," but the implications for the distinction is not his concern. See Witt, *Lincoln's Code*, pp. 234, 241.

7. Kinsella, *Image before the Weapon*, pp. 84, 88–89. The point at which it gave way, she argues, was where discourses of civilization trumped those of gender, as

in the indiscriminate massacre of Cheyenne and Arapaho women and children by the Union Army at Sand Creek, Colorado, in November 1864. See pp. 82–104.

8. Francisco de Vitoria, "On the Law of War," in *Political Writings,* ed. Anthony Pagden and Jeremy Lawrance (Cambridge: Cambridge University Press, 1991), pp. 293–327, esp. Question 3, pp. 314–317; Hugo Grotius, *De jure belli ac pacis libri tres (The Laws of War and Peace),* trans. Francis W. Kelsey (Oxford: Clarendon Press, 1925), vol. 2, bk. 3, chap. 11, pp. 733–735, 733 (quotation); Emer de Vattel, *The Law of Nations; or, Principles of the Law of Nature, Applied to the Conduct and Affairs of Nations and Sovereigns, with Three Early Essays on the Origin of Nature and Natural Law and on Luxury* (London: G. C. and J. Robinson, 1797), bk. 3, chap. 8, secs. 145, 147, 72 (quotation). Vattel writes of "women, children, feeble old men, and sick persons" that "we have no right to . . . use any violence against them," a principle he says of all "civilized" nations. Lieber, General Orders No. 100, art. 19 and especially art. 37.

9. The term "gender and innocence" comes from Kinsella, *Image before the Weapon,* p. 54. Best, *Humanity in Warfare,* p. 55.

10. Kinsella, *Image before the Weapon,* pp. 3, 83; on self-evidence, p. 22; Christine de Pizan, *The Book of Deeds of Arms and of Chivalry,* cited in Kinsella, *Image before the Weapon,* p. 47; Grotius, *De jure belli ac pacis libri tres,* vol. 2, bk. 3, chap. 11, pp. 734–735.

11. Linda Kerber, *No Constitutional Right to Be Ladies: Women and the Obligations of Citizenship* (New York: Hill and Wang, 1998); Kerber, "The Paradox of Women's Citizenship in the Early Republic: The Case of Martin vs. Massachusetts, 1805," in *Toward an Intellectual History of Women* (Chapel Hill: University of North Carolina Press, 1997), pp. 261–302; Kerber, "A Constitutional Right to Be Treated Like American Ladies: Women and the Obligations of Citizenship," in *U.S. History as Women's History,* ed. Linda Kerber, Alice Kessler-Harris, and Kathryn Kish Sklar (Chapel Hill: University of North Carolina Press, 1995), pp. 17–35. On the normative status of adult women as wives—even those who were unmarried (widows, for example)—see Ariela R. Dubler, "In the Shadow of Marriage: Single Women and the Legal Construction of the Family and the State," *Yale Law Journal* 112, no. 7 (May 2003): 1641–1715. On the contradiction of the citizen-wife, see Stephanie McCurry, "Review Essay," *Signs: Journal of Women in Culture and Society* 30, no. 2 (Winter 2005): 1659–1670.

12. Hendrik Hartog, *Man and Wife in America: A History* (Cambridge, Mass.: Harvard University Press, 2000), p. 263.

13. A point developed powerfully by Nancy Cott, *Public Vows: A History of Marriage and the Nation* (Cambridge, Mass.: Harvard University Press, 2000), p. 7 and throughout, and by Sarah Barringer Gordon, *The Mormon Question: Polygamy and Constitutional Conflict in Nineteenth Century America* (Chapel Hill: University of North Carolina Press, 2002), p. 4 and throughout. See also Dubler, "In the Shadow of Marriage." Lawmakers, she says, look "to marriage as a public policy tool capable of privatizing women's economic dependency" (1654).

14. Hartog, *Man and Wife*, p. 100.

15. Linda K. Kerber has revisited the Martin case repeatedly since she first treated it in *Women of the Republic: Intellect and ideology in Revolutionary America* (Chapel Hill: University of North Carolina Press, 1980), pp. 133–136. The fullest account is in *No Constitutional Right to Be Ladies,* chap. 1, but she offers a sharp account in "The Paradox of Women's Citizenship." For the Sullivan quote, see "Paradox," p. 292; for Sedgwick, see pp. 294, 301, 289. According to Kerber, "The story of Martin vs. Massachusetts suggests that the early national period was Thermidorean" ("Paradox," p. 301). *Shanks v. Dupont* in 1830 rendered a different decision but was quickly reversed. See Kerber, "Paradox," pp. 298–301.

16. John Adams to James Sullivan, May 26, 1786, in *The Feminist Papers: From Adams to de Beauvoir,* ed. Alice S. Rossi (Boston: Northeastern University Press, 1988), pp. 13–14.

17. Lieber to Senator John C. Calhoun, n.d., in *The Life and Letters of Francis Lieber,* ed. Thomas Sergeant Perry (Boston: James R. Osgood, 1882), p. 230; Francis Lieber, *Manual of Political Ethics, Designed Chiefly for the Use of Colleges and Students at Law,* vol. 1, ed. Theodore D. Woolsey (1838; reprint, Philadelphia: J. B. Lippincott, 1911), pp. 138–139, 140; Lieber, *Manual of Political Ethics, Designed Chiefly for the Use of Colleges and Students at Law,* vol. 2 (1838; reprint, Boston: C. C. Little and J. Brown, 1911), pp. 253, 269–270, 254, 259–260. See also clippings and notes in folder "Women's Suffrage," FLP, HL. For references to Mary Wollstonecraft (named in the text) and Angelina Grimké (unnamed), see Lieber, *Manual of Political Ethics,* 2:267. The reference is clearly to Angelina Emily Grimké, *Letters to Catherine E. Beecher, in Reply to An Essay on Slavery and Abolitionism* (Boston: I. Knapp, 1838), letter 12. Francis Lieber, "Reflections on the Changes Which May Seem Necessary in the Present Constitution of the State of

New York, Elicited and Published by the New York Union League Club, May 1867,"
in *The Miscellaneous Writings of Francis Lieber*, vol. 2, *Contributions to Political Science, Including Lectures on the Constitution of the United States and Other Papers*, ed. Daniel Coit Gilman (Philadelphia: J. B. Lippincott, 1881), pp. 181–219. On "the family as the social institution prior to all states," see Lieber, "Reflections on the Changes," p. 208.

18. Reva B. Siegel, "She the People: The Nineteenth Amendment, Sex Equality, Federalism and the Family," *Harvard Law Review* 115, no. 4 (February 2002): 982; Siegel, "The Modernization of Marital Status Law: Adjudicating Wives' Rights to Earnings, 1860–1930," *Georgetown Law Journal* 82, no. 7 (Sept. 1994): 2127–2130 and throughout. See also Hartog, *Man and Wife*, and Dubler, "In the Shadow of Marriage," p. 1654. On changes in the law, see Kristin A. Collins, "'Petitions without Number': Widows' Petitions and the Early Nineteenth Century Origins of Public Marriage-Based Entitlement," *Law and History Review* 31, no. 1 (February 2013): 1–60. On divorce, see Norma Basch, *Framing American Divorce: From the Revolutionary Generation to the Victorians* (Berkeley: University of California Press, 1999). On married women's property rights, see Suzanne Lebsock, "Radical Reconstruction and the Property Rights of Southern Women," *Journal of Southern History* 43, no. 2 (May 1977): 195–216, and Carole Shammas, "Re-Assessing the Married Women's Property Acts," *Journal of Women's History* 6, no. 1 (Spring 1994): 9–30. The literature on the women's rights movement is substantial but for one excellent account, see Christine Stansell, *The Feminist Promise: 1792 to the Present* (New York: Modern Library, 2010), chap. 4.

19. Fellman, *Inside War*, p. 203.

20. An issue developed in Stephanie McCurry, *Confederate Reckoning: Power and Politics in the Civil War South* (Cambridge, Mass.: Harvard University Press, 2010).

21. Vattel, *Law of Nations*, bk. 3, chap. 8, sec. 145; Grotius, *De jure belli ac pacis libri tres*, vol. 2, bk. 3, chap. 6, p. 646; chap. 9, pp. 734, 735; H. W. Halleck, *International Law; or, Rules Regulating the Intercourse of States in Peace and* War (San Francisco: H. H. Bancroft, 1861), p. 428; Lieber, General Orders No. 100, arts. 37, 102. Women are innocents to be spared in war, Grotius wrote, "unless they have been guilty of an extremely serious offence" or "take the place of men" (735).

22. For the term "violent secessionism," see G. Mott Williams, "Letters of General Thomas Williams, 1862," *American Historical Review* 14 (Jan. 1909): 320. On women's reputations, see also Stephen V. Ash, *When the Yankees Came: Conflict*

and Chaos in the Occupied South, 1861–1865 (Chapel Hill: University of North Carolina Press, 1995), pp. 42–43; Charles Royster, *The Destructive War: William Tecumseh Sherman, Stonewall Jackson, and the Americans* (New York: Vintage Books, 1993), pp. 86–87; Drew Gilpin Faust, *Mothers of Invention: Women of the Slaveholding South in the American Civil War* (Chapel Hill: University of North Carolina Press, 1996); and Women's Loyal National League, *Proceedings of the Meeting of the Loyal Women of the Republic, Held in New York, May 14, 1863* (New York: Phair, 1863). For a fuller treatment of the issue of women spies and the protection accorded Confederate women, see McCurry, *Confederate Reckoning*, chap. 3.

23. Sheila R. Phipps, *Genteel Rebel: The Life of Mary Greenhow Lee* (Baton Rouge: Louisiana State University Press, 2004); Cornelia Peake McDonald, *A Woman's Civil War: A Diary, with Reminiscences of the War, from March 1862*, ed. Minrose C. Gwin (Madison: University of Wisconsin Press, 1992). Lee was sister-in-law to the Confederate spy Rose O'Neal Greenhow, who was arrested in the summer of 1861. Greenhow was on the Confederate payroll. See McCurry, *Confederate Reckoning*, p. 103, and E. P. Alexander to Jefferson Davis, Sept. 11, 1861, in *The Papers of Jefferson Davis*, vol. 7, *1861*, ed. Lynda L. Crist and Mary S. Dix (Baton Rouge: Louisiana State University Press, 1992), p. 356.

24. Quoted in Royster, *Destructive War*, pp. 86–87.

25. Ari Kelman, *A Misplaced Massacre: Struggling over the Memory of Sand Creek* (Cambridge, Mass.: Harvard University Press, 2013). My comments on African American refugees draw on the forthcoming book by Thavolia Glymph, "Women at War: Race, Gender, and Power in the War over Slavery" (unpublished manuscript in possession of the author). I take up the issue more directly in chapter 2.

26. General Orders No. 46, By Command of Major-General Halleck, Department of the Missouri, St. Louis, Feb. 22, 1862, in *O.R.*, ser. 1, vol. 8, pp. 563–564, http://ehistory.osu.edu/books/official-records/008/0563.

27. Halleck, *International Law*, pp. 427–428, 375–379, 270–288, 73–74. On Halleck, see John F. Marszalek, *Commander of All Lincoln's Armies: A Life of General Henry W. Halleck* (Cambridge, Mass.: Harvard University Press, 2004), p. 98 and throughout.

28. Halleck, *International Law*, pp. 383, 73; emphasis added.

29. *Los Desastres de la Guerra*, collection of originals held at the Calcografía Nacional of the Real Academia de Bellas Artes de San Fernando, Madrid. For the publication history, see Ronald Fraser, *Napoleon's Cursed War: Popular Resistance in*

the Spanish Peninsular War, 1808–1814 (New York: Verso, 2008). On the Mexican War, see Peter Guardino, *The Dead March: A History of the Mexican-American War* (Cambridge, Mass.: Harvard University Press, 2017).

30. General Orders No. 28, Department of the Gulf, New Orleans, May 15, 1862, in *O.R.*, ser. I, vol. 15, p. 426, http://ehistory.osu.edu/books/official -records/021/0426; Benjamin F. Butler, *Butler's Book: Autobiography and Personal Reminiscences of Major-General Benj. F. Butler* (Boston: A. M. Thayer, 1892), p. 418. On the military threat, see Butler to J. G. Carney, July 2, 1862, in Benjamin F. Butler, *Letters of Butler* (Norwood, Mass.: Plimpton Press, 1917), 2:35–36, and Williams, "Letters of General Thomas Williams," pp. 320–332. General William Sherman had the same view of elite women from his time in St. Louis. See Michael Fellman, *Citizen Sherman: A Life of William Tecumseh Sherman* (New York: Random House, 1995).

31. Phipps, *Genteel Rebel*, p. 159 and throughout; Michael G. Mahon, ed., *Winchester Divided: The Civil War Diaries of Julia Chase and Laura Lee* (Mechanicsburg, Penn.: Stackpole Books, 2002).

32. Davis to Lee, July 31, 1862, in *The Papers of Jefferson Davis*, vol. 8, *1862*, ed. Lynda L. Crist, Mary S. Dix, and Kenneth H. Williams (Baton Rouge: Louisiana State University Press, 1995), p. 310.

33. General Orders No. 41, Department of the Gulf, New Orleans, Jun. 10, 1862, in *O.R.*, ser. I, vol. 15, pp. 483–484, http://ehistory.osu.edu/books/official -records/021/0483; Major General Benjamin F. Butler to Secretary of War Edwin M. Stanton, June 17, 1862, in *O.R.*, ser. 3, vol. 2, p. 159, http://ehistory .osu.edu/books/official-records/123/0159. For the numbers in New Orleans, see James Parton, *General Butler in New Orleans* (New York: Mason Brothers, 1864), p. 121. On Winchester, see McDonald, *Woman's Civil War*, p. 126, and Phipps, *Genteel Rebel*, p. 177. For the text of the oath, see General Orders No. 30, Department of the Missouri, St. Louis, Apr. 22, 1863, in *O.R.*, ser. I, vol. 22, pt. 2, p. 243, http://ehistory.osu.edu/books/official-records/033/0243.

34. Ash, *When the Yankees Came*, p. 60.

35. Linda Kerber notes that oaths of allegiance were not imposed on women during the Revolutionary War: "Although framed in terms of all residents, oaths seem almost always to have been selectively imposed on men." See Kerber, "Paradox of Women's Citizenship," p. 274.

36. William Blair, *With Malice toward Some: Treason and Loyalty in the Civil War Era* (Chapel Hill: University of North Carolina Press, 2014), p. 144; Best, *Humanity in Warfare*, p. 114.

37. See, for example, Report of Major Emory S. Foster, June 17, 1862, in *O.R.*, ser. I, vol. 13, pp. 124–125, http://ehistory.osu.edu/books/official-records/019 /0124. For a comprehensive treatment of guerilla warfare in the Civil War, see Daniel E. Sutherland, *A Savage Conflict: The Decisive Role of Guerrillas in the American Civil War* (Chapel Hill: University of North Carolina Press, 2009). Michael Fellman's study of guerilla warfare in Missouri is still valuable, not least for its attention to gender matters. See Fellman, *Inside War.*

38. Constitution of the United States, art. III, sec. 3; Blair, *With Malice toward Some*, pp. 16, 52, 56, and throughout. In General Orders No. 1, issued January 1, 1862, Halleck authorized the use of military commissions to try "military offenses" of a treasonable character; he did not yet talk of "military treason." *O.R.*, ser. I, vol. 8, p. 477. Blair makes the important point that popular understandings of treason far exceeded constitutional limits and definitions, and that attempts to punish it were pursued by all three branches of government, state governments, local authorities, and the US Army. On treason, see also James Willard Hurst, *The Law of Treason in the United States: Collected Essays* (Westport, Conn.: Greenwood, 1971); Witt, *Lincoln's Code*, chapters 9–10; and Mark E. Neely, Jr., *The Fate of Liberty: Abraham Lincoln and Civil Liberties* (Chapel Hill: University of North Carolina Press, 2011).

39. Lieber to Halleck, July 23, 1862, box 27; Halleck to Lieber, Aug. 6, 1862, box 9, FLP, HL; Lieber to Halleck, Aug. 6, 1862, in *O.R.*, ser. 3, vol. 2, p. 301, http://ehistory.osu.edu/books/official-records/123/0301. See also Lieber to Halleck, Jan. 30, Feb. 19, 1862, box 27, FLP, HL. Blair notes that it was in Missouri that military commanders learned the lesson about "the problems of combatting treason through courts." Blair, *With Malice toward Some*, p. 55. On the confusion, see Witt, *Lincoln's Code*, p. 270.

40. On Halleck's experience in Missouri, see Marszalek, *Commander of All Lincoln's Armies*, pp. 110–111; Sutherland, *A Savage Conflict*, pp. 58–65; and Fellman, *Inside War*, p. 88, chap. 3.

41. "Guerilla Parties Considered with Reference to the Laws and Usages of War," in Lieber to Halleck, n.d. (in response to Halleck to Lieber, Aug. 6, 1862), in *O.R.*, ser. 3, vol. 2, pp. 308–309, http://ehistory.osu.edu/books/official-records/123/0304.

42. Ibid., pp. 304, 305; emphasis added.

43. Lieber to Halleck, n.d. (in response to Halleck to Lieber, Aug. 6, 1862), in *O.R.*, ser. 3, vol. 2, p. 309, http://ehistory.osu.edu/books/official-records/123/0309.

44. Halleck to Major General William S. Rosecrans, Mar. 5, 1863, in *O.R.*, ser. 1, vol. 23, pt. 2, pp. 107–109, http://ehistory.osu.edu/books/official-records/035/0107; Lieber to Halleck, Mar. 17, 1863, box 27, FLP, HL.

45. Halleck quoted in Marszalek, *Commander of All Lincoln's Armies*, p. 168; Halleck to Major General Horatio G. Wright, Nov. 18, 1862, in *O.R.*, ser. 1, vol. 20, pt. 2, pp. 67–68, http://ehistory.osu.edu/books/official-records/030/0067; Wright to Brigadier General Julius White, Feb. 14, 1863, in *O.R.*, ser. 1, vol. 23, pt. 2, pp. 69–70, http://ehistory.osu.edu/books/official-records/035/0069; and Governor James F. Robinson to Wright, Mar. 1, 1863, in *O.R.*, ser. 1, vol. 23, pt. 2, pp. 96–97, http://ehistory.osu.edu/books/official-records/035/0096. On the effect of the Emancipation Proclamation in Kentucky, see Aaron Astor, *Rebels on the Border: The Civil War, Emancipation, and the Reconstruction of Kentucky and Missouri* (Baton Rouge: Louisiana State University Press, 2012).

46. Reynolds to Rosecrans, Feb. 10, 1863, in *O.R.*, ser. 1, vol. 23, pt. 2, pp. 54–57, http://ehistory.osu.edu/books/official-records/035/0054.

47. Major General George H. Thomas to Rosecrans, Feb. 11, 1863; Rosecrans to War Department, Feb. 18, 1863, both in *O.R.*, ser. 1, vol. 23, pt. 2, pp. 54–57, http://ehistory.osu.edu/books/official-records/035/0054. Lieber started drafting General Orders No. 100 in late December 1862. See below.

48. Lieutenant Colonel and Provost Marshal General F. A. Dick to Colonel William Hoffman, Mar. 5, 1863, in *O.R.*, ser. 2, vol. 5, pp. 319–321, http://ehistory.osu.edu/books/official-records/118/0319. For the broader context, see Kristen L. Streater, "'They Have Five Ladies at Alton': The Politics of Imprisoning Confederate Women during the Civil War" (unpublished paper in possession of the author); Kristen L. Streater, "'She-Rebels' on the Supply Line: Gender Conventions in Civil War Kentucky," in *Occupied Women: Gender, Military*

Occupation, and the American Civil War, ed. LeeAnn Whites and Alecia P. Long (Baton Rouge: Louisiana State University Press, 2009), pp. 88–102; and Thomas P. Lowry, *Confederate Heroines: 120 Southern Women Convicted by Union Military Justice* (Baton Rouge: Louisiana State University Press, 2006). The latter is useful but interpretively unreliable. On St. Louis, see also Louis S. Gerteis, *Civil War St. Louis* (Lawrence: University Press of Kansas, 2001).

49. Lowry, *Confederate Heroines,* pp. 104, 150; Streater, "'They Have Five Ladies,'" p. 26.

50. On the use of female detectives, see, for example, Colonel A. C. Harding and Colonel S. D. Bruce to Rosecrans, Feb. 5, 1863; Chief of Police Sam Truesdail to Rosecrans, Feb. 13, 1863, in *O.R.* ser. I, vol. 23, pt. 2, pp. 46, 64, http://ehistory.osu.edu/books/official-records/035/0046, http://ehistory.osu.edu/books/official-records/035/0064; and Lowry, *Confederate Heroines,* pp. 98–101 (Anna Johnson), 147–150 (Jane Ferguson). On networks in refugee camps, see Fellman, *Inside* War, pp. 71–72. For the spy claiming Confederate rank, see Lowry, *Confederate Heroines,* pp. 99–100. For evidence of women spies on Confederate government payrolls, see E. P. Alexander to Jefferson Davis, Sept. 11, 1861, in Crist and Dix, *Papers of Jefferson Davis,* 7:356, and McCurry, *Confederate Reckoning,* p. 105.

51. For an excellent account of women's centrality to guerilla war and a discussion of Ewing's order, see LeeAnn Whites, "Forty Shirts and a Wagonload of Wheat: Women, the Domestic Supply Line, and the Civil War on the Western Border," *Journal of the Civil War Era* I, no. 1 (March 2011): 56–78. Whites emphasizes women's role in the supply line; see p. 63. According to Thomas Lowry's Index Project, nineteen women were subject to military commission trials for harboring guerillas and deserters. Others were tried for encouraging desertion. For a description of the Index Project and the military commission and court martial records, see Thomas P. Lowry, "Research Note: New Access to a Civil War Resource," *Civil War History* 49, no. 1 (2003): 52–63. For Halleck's explanation of the use of "military tribunals" and procedures for military commission trials, see Halleck to Rosecrans, Mar. 20, 1863, in *O.R.,* ser. 3, vol. 3, pt. 1, pp. 77–78, http://ehistory.osu.edu/books/official-records/124/0077.

52. On Smith and Callahan's band, see Streater, "'They Have Five Ladies,'" pp. 29, 27–28. On Beattie, see Rosecrans to Abraham Lincoln, Nov. 11, 1864, in

O.R., ser. 2, vol. 7, pp. 1118–1119, http://ehistory.osu.edu/books/official-records /120/1118; and Lowry, *Confederate Heroines*, pp. 8–11. On the ambush, see Fellman, *Inside War*, p. 201. The examples of women guerillas are constant but scattered throughout the literature. For another example, of Nancy Hart, a known "rebel leader" in West Virginia, see Sutherland, *A Savage Conflict*, p. 31. For a fictional account, see Paulette Jiles, *Enemy Women: A Novel* (New York: William Morrow, 2002).

53. Here I differ from Kinsella. For her view on race, civilization, and the distinction in the American Civil War, see Kinsella, *Image before the Weapon*, pp. 82–103.

54. The phrase "hard war" is Sherman's. See Sherman to Halleck, Dec. 24, 1864, in O.R., ser. 1, vol. 44, p. 799, http://ehistory.osu.edu/books/official -records/092/0799.

55. The total number of military commission trials are provided in Lowry, "Research Note," pp. 52–63. The number tried specifically for violations of the law of war are derived from summaries of case files from the Index Project. See Lowry, "Research Note," pp. 58–59. For Halleck's justification of "military tribunals" by the common usages of the laws of war and explanation of proce- dures for military commissions tribunals, see Halleck to Rosecrans, Mar. 20, 1863, in O.R., ser. 3, vol. 3, pp. 77–78, http://ehistory.osu.edu/books/official -records/124/0077. Lieber explains the difference between military commission trials and courts martial in article 13 of General Orders No. 100.

56. For the numbers in St. Louis, see Thomas F. Curran, "'Making War on Women' and Women Making War: Confederate Women Imprisoned in St. Louis during the Civil War," *The Confluence: A Publication of Lindenwood University Press* 2 (Spring–Summer 2011): 4–15. On the provost marshal system, its many levels, and disorganized nature, see Blair, *With Malice toward Some*, chap. 4.

57. Women's cases represented 3.6 percent of the military commission trials conducted by the Union Army during the war. Numbers calculated based on totals included in Lowry, "Research Note," pp. 54, 58.

58. John Keegan, *A History of Warfare* (New York: Knopf, 1993), p. 76.

59. Quoted in Streater, "'They Have Five Ladies,'" p. 32; Dick to Colonel William Hoffman, Mar. 5, 1863, in O.R., ser. 2, vol. 5, pp. 319–321, http:// ehistory.osu.edu/books/official-records/118/0319; Kinsella, *Image before the Weapon*,

pp. 79–80. According to Thomas Lowry, several death sentences were handed down but there is no evidence that any besides Mary Surratt were executed. See Lowry, *Confederate Heroines*. On Surratt, see Witt, *Lincoln's Code*, pp. 289–294. Men find little honor in waging war against women, Kinsella says. See Kinsella, *Image before the Weapon*, pp. 79–80. Grotius made the same point. On the reaction of German soldiers to engagement with Soviet women in combat roles, see Isabel V. Hull, *Absolute Destruction: Military Culture and the Practices of War in Imperial Germany* (Ithaca, N.Y.: Cornell University Press, 2005).

60. See Major T. Hendrickson to Hoffman (with enclosures), May 15, 1863, in *O.R.*, ser. 2, vol. 5, pp. 619–624, http://ehistory.osu.edu/books /official-records/118/0619; Colonel J. Hildebrand to Hoffman, Feb. 16, 1863, in *O.R.*, ser. 2, vol. 5, pp. 277–278, http://ehistory.osu.edu/books /official-records/118/0277; Hendrickson to Hoffman, in *O.R.*, ser. 2, vol. 6, pp. 149–150 (with indorsements), http://ehistory.osu.edu/books/official -records/119/0149. I was alerted to the case by Streater, "'They Have Five Ladies.'" The same observation could be made about the secondary literature on the Civil War.

61. John Fitch, *Annals of the Army of the Cumberland* (Philadelphia: J. B. Lippincott, 1863), pp. 501–507.

62. Indorsement of Captain and Provost Marshal General William M. Wiles (included in military correspondence on Judd case), Jan. 13, 1863, in *O.R.*, ser. 2, vol. 5, p. 621, http://ehistory.osu.edu/books/official-records/118/0621; Hildebrand to Hoffman, Feb. 16, 1863, in *O.R.*, ser. 2, vol. 5, pp. 277–278, http://ehistory.osu.edu/books/official-records/118/0277; Rosecrans quoted in Streater, "'They Have Five Ladies,'" p. 35. Judd was rearrested and confined to a female military prison in Louisville. For the full story, see Streater, "'They Have Five Ladies.'"

63. Provost Judge John Fitch to Wiles, Jan. 13, 1863, in *O.R.*, ser. 2, vol. 5, pp. 620–621, http://ehistory.osu.edu/books/official-records/118/0620; Fitch, *Annals of the Army of the Cumberland*, p. 502.

64. Fitch, *Annals of the Army of the Cumberland*, pp. 501–507.

65. William M. Wiles, Jan. 13, 1863, indorsement on Fitch to Wiles, Jan. 13, 1863, in *O.R.*, ser. 2, vol. 5, p. 621, http://ehistory.osu.edu/books/official-records /118/0621; Hildebrand to Hoffman, Feb. 16, 1863, in *O.R.*, ser. 2, vol. 5,

pp. 277–278, http://ehistory.osu.edu/books/official-records/118/0277. For Clara Judd's statement (dated May 11, 1863), see *O.R.*, ser. 2, vol. 5, pp. 621–624, http://ehistory.osu.edu/books/official-records/118/0621. For the debate about her release, see Hendrickson to Hoffman, May 15, 1863 (with enclosures from "And. Wall" to Hendrickson, May 12, 1863), in *O.R.*, ser. 2, vol. 5, pp. 619–620, http://ehistory.osu.edu/books/official-records/118/0619; and Hendrickson to Hoffman (with indorsements), Jul. 25, 1863, in *O.R.*, ser. 2, vol. 6, pp. 149–150, http://ehistory.osu.edu/books/official-records/119/0149.

66. Halleck to Rosecrans, Mar. 5, 1863, in *O.R.*, ser. 1, vol. 23, pt. 2, pp. 107–109, http://ehistory.osu.edu/books/official-records/035/0107. The term "military traitor" does not appear in the *O.R.* before this date and again later only in reference to Halleck's instructions of March 5, 1863. "War rebel" had been used by Lieber in the guerilla memorandum. See Lieber to Halleck, n.d. (in response to Halleck to Lieber, Aug. 6, 1862), in *O.R.*, ser. 3, vol. 2, pp. 301–309, http://ehistory.osu.edu/books/official-records/123/0301. Halleck's letter was reprinted in the *New York Times* on March 15, 1863. See "The Conduct of the War; Letter from Gen. Halleck to Gen. Rosecrans on the Treatment of Disloyal Persons within Our Lines," *New York Times*, Mar. 15, 1863, http://www.nytimes.com/1863/03/16/news/conduct-war-letter-gen-halleck-gen-rosecrans-treatment-disloyal-persons-within.html.

67. See Kinsella, *Image before the Weapon*, pp. 88–89, chap. 4.

68. After Halleck's first use on March 5, 1863, the term "military treason" appeared a few times before its adoption in Lieber's code. See Halleck to Major General E. V. Sumner, Mar. 17, 1863, in *O.R.*, ser. 1, vol. 22, pt. 2, pp. 158–159, http://ehistory.osu.edu/books/official-records/033/0158, and General Orders No. 30, Department of the Missouri, St. Louis, Apr. 22, 1863, in *O.R.*, ser. 1, vol. 22, pt. 2, pp. 237–244, http://ehistory.osu.edu/books/official-records/033/0237. On March 31, Halleck wrote Major General Ulysses S. Grant expressing his view that "the character of the war has very much changed within the last year. There is now no hope of reconciliation. . . . We must conquer the rebels or be conquered by them." He had used almost identical words in a letter to Lieber. He now advocated the turn to hard war, by which he meant a policy of slave emancipation and bringing war to disloyal civilians. See Halleck to Grant, Mar. 31, 1863, box 9, FLP, HL.

69. Special Orders No. 399, War Department, Adjutant General's Office, Washington, D.C., in *O.R.*, ser. 3, vol. 2, p. 951, http://ehistory.osu.edu/books /official-records/123/0951. He had previously been informed by telegraph from Halleck. See Lieber to Halleck, Dec. 7, 1862, box 27, FLP, HL.

70. Lieber, General Orders No. 100, arts. 15, 29; Witt, *Lincoln's Code*, p. 234. The text of article 37 reads, "The United States acknowledge and protect, in hostile countries occupied by them, religion and morality; strictly private property; the persons of the inhabitants, especially those of women: and the sacredness of domestic relations. Offenses to the contrary shall be rigorously punished."

71. Lieber quoted in Witt, *Lincoln's Code*, p. 170; Lieber to Halleck, Oct. 3, 1863, June 13, 1864, box 28, FLP, HL; Hartigan, ed., *Lieber's Code and the Law of War*, p. 77. Lieber expressed the distinction between *volkskrieg* (war of peoples) and war of cabinets. David Bell describes "cabinet wars" as set-piece battles between standing professional armies. See Bell, *The First Total War.*

72. Best, *Humanity in Warfare*, p. 200; Witt, *Lincoln's Code*, p. 233; Kinsella, *Image before the Weapon*, pp. 88–89.

73. Lieber to Halleck, Nov. 13, 1862, box 27; Halleck to Lieber, Nov. 15, 1862, box 9, FLP, HL. Trials by military commissions had been authorized since the beginning of the war, most surprisingly in the case of the Dakota War of 1862. Such trials became more common after the adoption of General Orders No. 100. On the case of the Dakota trials, see Maeve Herbert, "Explaining the Sioux Military Commission of 1862," *Columbia Human Rights Law Review* 40 (2009): 743–798, and Carol Chomsky, "The United States–Dakota War Trials: A Study in Military Injustice," *Stanford Law Review* 43, no. 1 (1990): 13–98.

74. Lieber to Halleck, Feb. 20, June 21, 1863, box 27; Lieber to Halleck, Oct. 3, 1863, box 28, FLP, HL.

75. Lieber to Halleck, Nov. 25, 1862, box 27, FLP, HL; Lieber to Judge Amos M. Thayer, Feb. 3, 1864, in Perry, ed., *Life and Letters of Francis Lieber*, pp. 339–341, 341 (quotation). To Lieber the American Civil War was a war of national unification like that of Italy or, later, Germany; he talked of "the national side" and the "southern side" in the Civil War. Lieber to Senator Charles Sumner, June 16, 1864; Lieber to Dr. S. Tyler, Jan. 14, 1867, in Perry, ed., *Life and Letters of Lieber*, pp. 348, 367. Lieber's views of national sovereignty and state unity

were of transnational interest. See his communications with Johann Kaspar Blunctshli and Édouard Laboulaye in FLP, HL, and Stephen W. Sawyer and William J. Novack, "Emancipation and the Creation of Modern Liberal States in America and France," *Journal of the Civil War Era* 3, no. 4 (2013): 466–500.

76. Lieber insisted that slavery had legal standing only as a municipal institution, that the institution had no standing in international law. Lieber, General Orders No. 100, art. 42. On that see also the recent argument of James Oakes, *The Scorpion's Sting: Antislavery and the Coming of the Civil* War (New York: Norton, 2014), pp. 158–599.

77. Lieber to Halleck, Feb. 20, 1863, box 27, FLP, HL.

78. LI 182B (photostat of Halleck copy), FLP, HL; emphasis added. Draft article 19 states, "The United States acknowledge and protect, in hostile countries occupied by them, religion and morality; unmixed private property . . . the persons of the inhabitants, especially those of women; and the sacredness of domestic relations." The edited draft was sent around March 13, 1863. See Halleck to Lieber, Mar. 13, 1863, box 9, FLP, HL, and Witt, *Lincoln's Code*, p. 231. Halleck's invitation to Lieber is described in Witt, *Lincoln's Code*, p. 229. Witt uses the expression "age of democratic nations and mass armies."

79. Lieber to Halleck, Mar. 4, 17, 23, 1863, box 27; Halleck to Lieber, Apr. 8, 1863, box 9, FLP, HL. The long version referenced here is LI 182A, FLP, HL.

80. Lieber, General Orders No. 100, arts. 90, 91, 92, 102, 155, 156, 157.

81. It seems too obvious a point to require documentation but on the Peninsular War, where women's role became part of national mythology, see Fraser, *Napoleon's Cursed War.* On the Italian wars of unification, see the example of the "Garibaldiennes" (noted but treated as an absurdity) in Best, *Humanity in Warfa*re, pp. 197–198. On the Spanish Civil War, see Paul Preston, *The Spanish Holocaust: Inquisition and Extermination in Twentieth-Century Spain* (London: Harper Press, 2012), and Preston, *The Spanish Civil War: Reaction, Revolution, and Revenge* (New York: Norton, 2007). On Algeria, where women's roles were prominently featured in Gillo Pontecorvo's famous 1966 film *The Battle of Algiers*, see Alistair Horne, *A Savage War of Peace: Algeria, 1954–1962* (New York: Viking Press, 1977). It would require a collective effort to assemble the master list.

82. For the quote and an excellent statement of the state of the field from a historical perspective, see Elizabeth D. Heineman, ed., *Sexual Violence in Conflict*

Zones: From the Ancient World to the Era of Human Rights (Philadelphia: University of Pennsylvania Press, 2013), p. 18. For a more contemporary perspective emphasizing the need to get beyond simplistic dualities (men as perpetrators and women as victims), including in scholarship and development policies, see Caroline O. N. Moser and Fiona C. Clark, *Victims, Perpetrators, or Actors: Gender, Armed Conflict and Political Violence* (Chicago: University of Chicago Press, 2001), and Kathleen Kuehnast, Chantal de Jonge Oudraat, and Helga Hernes, eds., *Women and War: Power and Protection in the 21st Century* (Washington, D.C.: United States Institute of Peace Press, 2011), pp. 1–18. For one fascinating early grappling with the issue, see the focus on women terrorists in Julia Kristeva, "Women's Time," trans. Alice Jardine and Harry Blake, *Signs: Journal of Women in Culture and Society* 7, no. 1 (1981): 13–35, esp. 28. I address the subject more fully in the epilogue.

83. Kinsella, *Image before the Weapon*, p. 136. On the Algerian War as prototype of wars of decolonization, see Horne, *A Savage War of Peace*.

84. On the Philippines, see Witt, *Lincoln's Code*, pp. 353–365, and Paul Kramer, *The Blood of Government: Race, Empire, the United States, and the Philippines* (Chapel Hill: University of North Carolina Press, 2006). Kramer seems unaware of the earlier history of guerilla war that shaped the powers accorded the US Army in wars of occupation by General Orders No. 100.

85. Frank Freidel, Lieber's biographer, says that the Bluntschli 1866 treatise was "little more than a translation." See Freidel, *Francis Lieber*, pp. 340, 402–403. On the "Hague track" and the overlooked nineteenth-century German and Russian lineage of the law of war and international humanitarian law, see Peter Holquist, "'Crimes against Humanity': Genealogy of a Concept (1815–1945)," presentation at the Russian, East European and Eurasian Center (REEEC), University of Illinois, Champaign, Feb. 5, 2015. Lieber's correspondence with Bluntschli, Édouard Laboulaye (who translated the code into French), and the Belgian scholar and jurist Gustave Rolin-Jaequemyns is in his papers at the Huntington Library. In April 1872, Lieber was officially consulted by the International Committee of Geneva. See Perry, ed., *Life and Letters of Lieber*, 422. Lieber died in 1873 just before the first Brussels meeting, but nonetheless Martti Koskenniemi counts him as one of founders of the field of international law. See Koskenniemi *The Gentle Civilizer of Nations: The Rise and Fall of International Law, 1870–1960* (New York: Cambridge University Press, 2002), p. 92.

86. Quoted in Sawyer and Novack, "Emancipation and the Creation of Modern Liberal States in America and France," p. 492; Laboulaye to Lieber, July 31, 1863, box 16, FLP, HL. Laboulaye wrote articles on the Civil War for the French press, including one on the election of 1864 emphasizing its significance not just to the United States but to France and Europe. He continued to follow Lieber's work on Reconstruction and on black suffrage as meaningful for French efforts in democracy and self-government. Laboulaye to Lieber, Oct. 4, 1864, Sept. 28, 1865, box 16, FLP, HL.

87. John Witt says the American code "had made the laws of war safe for the powerful states of late nineteenth century Europe, just as it had for the Indian wars in the American west." But that argument follows far more directly from section X of the code than the emancipation articles on which his thesis turns. Witt, *Lincoln's Code*, pp. 345–346.

88. James A. Seddon to Colonel Robert Ould, Jun. 24, 1863, in *O.R.*, ser. 2, vol. 6, pp. 41–47, http://ehistory.osu.edu/books/official records/119/0041.

89. Seddon to Colonel Robert Ould, June 24, 1863, in *O.R.*, ser. 2, vol. 6, pp. 41–47, 42, 43, 46 (quotations), http://ehistory.osu.edu/books/official-records/119/0041; Jefferson Davis, Annual Message to Congress, Dec. 7, 1863, in *The Papers of Jefferson Davis*, vol. 10, *1863–August 1864*, ed. Lynda L. Crist, Kenneth H. Williams, and Peggy L. Dillard (Baton Rouge: Louisiana State University Press, 1999), pp. 103–104; Witt, *Lincoln's Code*, pp. 249, 250–284. My analysis of the Confederate response offered here differs in emphasis from that of John Witt, who argues that "the parts of the code that most provoked Confederate authorities" ("the most prominent of the matters treated in Order No. 100," to quote Seddon) were those that took up the slavery question. See Witt, *Lincoln's Code*, pp. 245–246.

90. On the torture of Confederate women, see McCurry, *Confederate Reckoning*, pp. 85–132; Phillip Shaw Paludan, *Victims: A True Story of the Civil War* (Knoxville: University of Tennessee Press, 1981); and Victoria E. Bynum, *Unruly Women: The Politics of Social and Sexual Control in the Old South* (Chapel Hill: University of North Carolina Press, 1992). Lieber was shocked much later to uncover evidence in Confederate archives of violence of Confederate troops toward women in North Carolina. Lieber to Halleck, Mar. 20, 1866, FLP, HL.

91. William T. Sherman to Halleck, Dec. 24, 1864, in *O.R.*, ser. I, vol. 44, p. 799, http://ehistory.osu.edu/books/offical-records/092/0799; William T. Sherman to John Sherman, Sept. 22, 1862, in *The Sherman Letters: Correspondence between General Sherman and Senator Sherman from 1837 to 1891*, ed., Rachel Thorndike (New York: C. Scribner's Sons, 1894), p. 162; William T. Sherman to Assistant Adjutant General Roswell M. Sawyer, Jan. 31, 1864, in *Sherman's Civil War: Selected Correspondence of William T. Sherman, 1860–1865*, ed. Brooks D. Simpson and Jean V. Berlin (Chapel Hill: University of North Carolina Press, 1999), pp. 598–602, 599, 602 (quotations).

92. Lieber to Halleck, Feb. 11, 1865, box 28, FLP, HL.

93. Halleck to Sherman, Sept. 28, 1864, in *O.R.*, ser. I, vol. 39, pt. 2, p. 503, http://ehistory.osu.edu/books/official-records/078/0503. Sherman's orders in Savannah also insisted explicitly on loyalty as a condition of protection. See Field Orders No. 143, Division of the Mississippi, Savannah, Dec. 26, 1864, in *O.R.*, ser. I, vol. 44, pp. 812–813, http://ehistory.osu.edu/books /official-records/092/0812. Far from seeking to constrain Sherman, Halleck egged him on: "Should you capture Charleston, I hope that by some accident the place may be destroyed, and if a little salt should be sown upon its side it may prevent the growth of future crops of nullification and secession." See Halleck to Sherman, Dec. 18, 1864, in *O.R.*, ser. I, vol. 44, p. 741, http://ehistory.osu.edu /books/official-records/092/0741. On Sherman's march as the embodiment of the new law of war, see also Witt, *Lincoln's Code*, chap. 9.

94. Sherman to Halleck, Sept. 4, 1864, in Simpson and Berlin, eds., *Sherman's Civil War*, p. 697.

95. Mayor James M. Calhoun, E. E. Rawson, and S. C. Wells to Sherman, Sept. 11, 1864, in *O.R.*, ser. I, vol. 39, pt. 2, pp. 417–418, http://ehistory.osu .edu/books/official-records/078/0417; Hood to Sherman (enclosure), Sept. 9, 1864, in *O.R.*, ser. I, vol. 39, pt. 2, p. 415, http://ehistory.osu.edu/books /official-records/078/0415. The mayor pled the case of poor women in "advanced state of pregnancy," mothers of young children turned out of doors without protection, their husbands in the army or dead. "What has this helpless people done," he asked. It was the wrong argument to make to Sherman. "If they want peace," he said, "they and their relations must stop war." Sherman to Halleck, Sept. 4, 1864, in Simpson and Berlin, eds., *Sherman's Civil War*, p. 697.

96. Sherman to Brevet Major General Stephen G. Burbridge, June 21, 1864, in *O.R.*, ser. I, vol. 39, pt. 2, pp. 135–136, http://ehistory.osu.edu/books /official-records/078/0135; Sherman to Grant, Sept. 19, 1864, in *O.R.*, ser. I, vol. 39, pt. 2, p. 404, http://ehistory.osu.edu/books/official-records/078/0404; Sherman to Hood, Sept. 10, 1864, in *O.R.*, ser. I, vol. 39, pt. 2, p. 416, http:// ehistory.osu.edu/books/official-records/078/0416.

97. Sherman's march to the sea emerged quickly as a central element of the myth of the Lost Cause, not least as a result of the contributions of Confederate women writers and memorialists. Most scholars concur that the destruction was extensive but mostly confined to property, notwithstanding the rhetoric of rape so frequently used by Confederate women to describe events. Those accounts did not contend with the rape of African American women by armies on the move, an issue only now being taken up. For a selection of Confederate women's writings, see Katherine M. Jones, *When Sherman Came: Southern Women and the Great March* (New York: Bobbs-Merrill, 1964). For the secondary literature, see, for example, Grimsley, *Hard Hand of War;* Jacqueline Glass Campbell, *When Sherman Marched North from the Sea: Resistance on the Confederate Homefront* (Chapel Hill: University of North Carolina Press, 2003); and Lisa Tendrich Frank, "Bedrooms as Battlefields: The Role of Gender Politics in Sherman's March," in Whites and Long, eds., *Occupied Women*, pp. 33–48. On the march itself, see Joseph Glatthar, *The March to the Sea and Beyond: Sherman's Troops in the Savannah and Carolinas Campaigns* (New York: New York University Press, 1985).

98. An argument made by Kinsella, *Image before the Weapon.*

99. Francis Lieber, "Reflections on the Changes Which May Seem Necessary in the Present Constitution of the State of New York," in *Miscellaneous Writings of Francis Lieber*, vol. I, *Reminiscences, Addresses, and Essays*, ed. Daniel Coit Gilman (Philadelphia: J. B. Lippincott, 1881), pp. 181–219, 207, 209 (quotations). For more on Lieber's views on women's nature and his opposition to suffrage, see the draft fragments and notes in his papers at the Huntington Library: "Lecture on Woman Suffrage" and folder of clippings (which includes the text of a brilliant response by a woman published in *The Nation*), LI 114, FLP, HL.

100. I take this issue up fully in chapter 2. The literature on these subjects is now significant but for an introduction, see the following: On the dangers of the

Thirteenth Amendment for the rights of husbands, see Nancy Cott, *Public Vows,* chap. 4, and Amy Dru Stanley, "Instead of Waiting for the Thirteenth Amendment: The War Power, Slave Marriage, and Inviolate Human Rights," *American Historical Review* 115, no. 3 (June 2010): 732–765. On the long pro-slavery usage of marriage to legitimize slavery, see Stephanie McCurry, *Masters of Small Worlds: Yeoman Households, Gender Relations, and the Political Culture of the South Carolina Low Country* (New York: Oxford University Press, 1995). On the meaning of the war for women's suffrage, see especially Stansell, *Feminist Promise,* chap. 4, and Ellen Carol DuBois, *Feminism and Suffrage: The Emergence of an Independent Women's Movement in America, 1838–1869* (Ithaca, N.Y.: Cornell University Press, 1978).

2. The Story of the Black Soldier's Wife

1. *Congressional Globe,* 37th Congress, 2nd Session, 1862, p. 3198. For context, see Louis P. Masur, *Lincoln's Hundred Days: The Emancipation Proclamation and the War for the Union* (Cambridge, Mass.: Harvard University Press, 2012); Eric Foner, *The Fiery Trial: Abraham Lincoln and American Slavery* (New York: Norton, 2010); and *Slaves No More: Three Essays on Emancipation and the Civil War,* by Ira Berlin, Barbara J. Fields, Steven F. Miller, Joseph P. Reidy, and Leslie S. Rowland (New York: Cambridge University Press, 1992).

2. As a Republican senator from Vermont immediately pointed out during this debate. *Congressional Globe,* 37th Congress, 2nd Session, 1862, p. 3228. Enslaved people had no right to enter into the civil contract of marriage. Note also that slave men had no paternal right to their children. The maternal descent of slaves—or legal doctrine of *partus sequitur ventrem*—which held that the status of children born in the colonies to be bond or free according to the status of the mother. It had been a foundational legal basis of slavery since the seventeenth century. For one example, see Act XII, Laws of Virginia, Dec. 1662, in William Waller Hening, ed., *The Statutes at Large, Being a Collection of All the Laws of Virginia from the First Session of the Legislature, in the Year* 1619 (New York: William Waller Hening, 1823), 2:170.

3. Nancy F. Cott, *Public Vows: A History of Marriage and the Nation* (Cambridge, Mass.: Harvard University Press, 2000), especially pp. 77–104.

4. "Act to Establish a Bureau for the Relief of Freedmen and Refugees," in *U.S. Statutes at Large, Treaties, and Proclamations of the United States of America,* vol. 13 (Boston: Little, Brown, 1866), pp. 507–509, sec. 2.

5. The pattern is hardly limited to the United States but can be seen across a range of historical cases of the making of new polities in the modern period. For one exemplary history of the heteronormative family in French republican politics dating from the French Revolution, see Camille Robcis, *The Law of Kinship: Anthropology, Psychoanalysis, and the Family in Twentieth Century France* (Ithaca, N.Y.: Cornell University Press, 2013). Nancy Cott has made this point clearly about the United States in *Public Vows* although her analysis focuses primarily on the post–Civil War period and debates over the Thirteenth Amendment and Civil Rights Act. Tera W. Hunter's recent excellent book on black marriages in the nineteenth century offers a rich account of the Civil War history. See Hunter, *Bound in Wedlock: Slave and Free Black Marriage in the Nineteenth* Century (Cambridge, Mass.: Harvard University Press, 2017). My approach focuses on marriage and governance, and on the logic of the process of military emancipation *during* the war.

6. Vicksburg Marriage Register: Register of Marriages, 1863–1865, vols. 43–46, Registers of Marriages, ser. 2073, MS Asst. Comr., RG 105 (Records of the Bureau of Refugees, Freedmen, and Abandoned Lands), National Archives [FSSP A-9533]. The FSSP file number refers to copies of National Archives documents consulted at the Freedmen and Southern Society Project, University of Maryland, College Park. John Eaton, *Grant, Lincoln, and the Freedmen: Reminiscences of the Civil War* (London: Longmans, Green, 1907), p. 212. On the history of marriage and the complex forms of the family in the African American community, see especially Hunter, *Bound in Wedlock,* and Tony Kaye, *Joining Places: Slave Neighborhoods in the Old South* (Chapel Hill: University of North Carolina Press, 2007). Thavolia Glymph argues that the refugee camps and abandoned plantations to which women were consigned by federal policymakers and Union commanders were themselves sites of war, a different part of the war to make "a new world of freedom" that women were forced to fight. See Glymph, "Women at War: Race, Gender, and Power in the War Over Slavery" (unpublished manuscript in possession of the author), chap. 7, pp. 185–186, 193, 213, and throughout.

7. Ranajit Guha, "The Small Voices of History," in *Subaltern Studies*, vol. 9, ed. Shahid Amin and Dipesh Chakrabarty (Oxford: Oxford University Press, 1996), pp. 1–12.

8. For one distillation of this historiographical shift, see James M. McPherson, "Who Freed the Slaves?" *Reconstruction* 2, no. 3 (1994): 35–40, and Ira Berlin, "Emancipation and Its Meaning in American Life," *Reconstruction* 2, no. 3 (1994): 41–44.

9. Berlin et al., *Slaves No More*, pp. 189–190; *Free at Last: A Documentary History of Slavery, Freedom, and the Civil War*, ed. Ira Berlin, Barbara J. Fields, Steven F. Miller, Joseph P. Reidy, and Leslie S. Rowland (New York: New Press, 1992), p. 119. For the now canonical view, see Eric Foner, *Reconstruction: American's Unfinished Revolution, 1863–1878* (New York: Harper and Row, 1988), pp. 7–8. For one example of that narrative drive, see the chapter "A War for Freedom," in Berlin et al, eds., *Free at Last*, pp. 95–166. The authors of *Slaves No More* acknowledge that "military service created important differences in the way [black men and women] experienced the war and emancipation." Berlin et al., *Slaves No More*, p. 227. In the edited volumes, they provide some of the materials by which that difference might be analyzed. But in their analysis the women's story accrues as difference acknowledged and a series of exceptions noted. It is a position that becomes explicit in *Families and Freedom: A Documentary History of African-American Kinship in the Civil War Era*, ed. Ira Berlin and Leslie S. Rowland (New York: New Press, 1997), which takes an openly romantic view of the black family.

There have been critiques of the focus on black soldiers and soldiering going back to W. E. B. Du Bois, *Black Reconstruction in America* (1935; reprint, New York: Macmillan, 1992), p. 110, where he wrote, "How extraordinary that . . . in the minds of most people . . . only murder makes men." More recent critiques include Stephanie McCurry, *Confederate Reckoning: Power and Politics in the Civil War South* (Cambridge, Mass.: Harvard University Press, 2010); Thavolia Glymph, "W. E. B. Du Bois' Black Reconstruction: Past and Present," *South Atlantic Quarterly* 112, no. 3 (Summer 2013): 489–505; and Carole Emberton, "Only Murder Makes Men: Reconsidering the Black Military Experience," *Journal of the Civil War Era* 2, no. 3 (2012): 369–393.

10. For a preliminary statement of the critique and argument, see Stephanie McCurry, "War, Gender and Emancipation in the Civil War South," in *Lincoln's*

Proclamation: Emancipation Reconsidered, ed. William A. Blair and Karen Fisher Younger (Chapel Hill: University of North Carolina Press, 2009), pp. 120–150.

11. Thavolia Glymph, "Rose's War and the Gendered Politics of a Slave Insurgency in the Civil War," *Journal of the Civil War Era* 3, no. 4 (December 2013): 501–532. Glymph calls the women "insurrectionists." For the United States, see especially Elsa Barkley Brown, "Negotiating and Transforming the Black Public Sphere: African American Political Life in the Transition from Slavery to Freedom," in *The Black Public Sphere: A Public Culture Book,* ed. Black Public Sphere Collective (Chicago: University of Chicago Press, 1995), pp. 111–150; Leslie Schwalm, *A Hard Fight for We: Women's Transition from Slavery to Freedom in South Carolina* (Urbana: University of Illinois Press, 1998); Nora Lee Frankel, *Freedom's Women: Black Women and Families in Civil War Era Mississippi* (Bloomington: Indiana University Press, 1999); Nancy Bercaw, *Gendered Freedoms: Race, Rights, and the Politics of Household in the Delta, 1861–1875* (Gainesville: University Press of Florida, 2003); Susan E. O'Donovan, *Becoming Free in the Cotton South* (Cambridge, Mass.: Harvard University Press, 2007); Thavolia Glymph, *Out of the House of Bondage: The Transformation of the Plantation Household* (Cambridge: Cambridge University Press, 2008); and McCurry, *Confederate Reckoning.* On the Caribbean, see especially Pamela Scully and Diana Paton, eds., *Gender and Slave Emancipation in the Atlantic World* (Durham, N.C.: Duke University Press, 2005); Elizabeth Colwill, "Gender, Slavery, War and Violence in and beyond the Age of Revolutions," in *The Oxford Handbook of Gender, War and the Western World since 1600,* ed. Karen Hagemann et al. (New York: Oxford University Press, 2018), chap. 6; Mimi Sheller, *Citizenship from Below: Erotic Agency and Caribbean Freedom* (Durham, N.C.: Duke University Press, 2012); Natasha Lightfoot, *Troubling Freedom: Antigua and the Aftermath of British Emancipation* (Durham, N.C.: Duke University Press, 2015); and Marisa J. Fuentes, *Dispossessed Lives: Enslaved Women, Violence, and the Archive* (Philadelphia: University of Pennsylvania Press, 2016).

12. Emancipation Proclamation, Jan. 1, 1863, http://www.yale.edu/lawweb /avalon/emancipa.htm.

13. For an overview of most cases, see Robin Blackburn, *The Overthrow of Colonial Slavery, 1776–1848* (New York: Verso, 1988). On the American Revolution, see Benjamin Quarles, *The Negro in the American Revolution* (Chapel Hill: University of North Carolina Press, 1961); Sylvia Frey, *Water from the Rock: Black*

Resistance in a Revolutionary Age (Princeton, N.J.: Princeton University Press, 1991); Gary Nash, *Forgotten Fifth: African Americans in the Age of Revolution* (Cambridge, Mass.: Harvard University Press, 2006); and Phillip D. Morgan and Andrew Jackson O'Shaughnessy, "Arming Slaves in the American Revolution," in *Arming Slaves from Classical Times to the Modern Age*, ed. Christopher Leslie Brown and Philip D. Morgan (New Haven, Conn.: Yale University Press, 2006), pp. 180–208. On Haiti, see Carolyn Fick, *The Making of Haiti: The Saint Dominque Revolution from Below* (Knoxville: University of Tennessee Press, 1990); Laurent Dubois, *A Colony of Citizens: Revolution and Slave Emancipation in the French Caribbean, 1787–1804* (Chapel Hill: University of North Carolina Press, 2004); David Geggus, "The Arming of Slaves in the Haitian Revolution," in Brown and Morgan, eds., *Arming Slaves*, pp. 209–302; and Ada Ferrer, *Freedom's Mirror: Cuba and Haiti in the Age of Revolution* (Cambridge: Cambridge University Press, 2014). On Cuba, see Rebecca J. Scott, *Slave Emancipation in Cuba: The Transition to Free Labor, 1860–1899* (Princeton, N.J.: Princeton University Press, 1985), and Ada Ferrer, *Insurgent Cuba: Race, Nation, and Revolution, 1868–1898* (Chapel Hill: University of North Carolina Press, 1999). On Brazil, see Hendrik Kraay, "Slavery, Citizenship and Military Service in Brazil's Mobilization for the Paraguayan War," *Slavery and Abolition* 18, no. 3 (Dec. 1997): 228–256. For a view of emancipation in the United States that questions the idea of two emancipations, see Steven Hahn, *The Political Worlds of Slavery and Freedom* (Cambridge, Mass.: Harvard University Press, 2009).

14. Berlin et al., *Slaves No More*, pp. 5–6.

15. The still classic account is C. L. R. James, *The Black Jacobins: Toussaint Louverture and the San Domingo Revolution* (1938; reprint, New York: Random House, 1963). More recently, see Fick, *Making of Haiti*; Blackburn, *Overthrow of Colonial Slavery*; David Geggus, *Slavery, War, and Revolution* (Oxford: Clarendon Press, 1982); Geggus, *Haitian Revolutionary Studies* (Bloomington: Indiana University Press, 2002); Laurent Dubois, *Avengers of the New World: The Story of the Haitian Revolution* (Cambridge, Mass.: Harvard University Press, 2004); John D. Garrigus, *Before Haiti: Race and Citizenship in French Saint-Domingue* (New York: Palgrave Macmillan, 2006); and Ferrer, *Freedom's Mirror*. My own thinking has been shaped most directly by Elizabeth Colwill, "Fêtes de l'hymen, fêtes de la liberté: Marriage, Manhood, and Emancipation in Revolutionary Saint-Domingue," in *The World of*

the Haitian Revolution, ed. David Patrick Geggus and Norman Fiering (Bloomington: Indiana University Press, 2009), pp. 125–155; Colwill, "Gender, Slavery, War and Violence"; and Colwill, "Gendering the June Days: Race, Masculinity, and Slave Emancipation in Saint-Domingue, 1793," *Journal of Haitian Studies* 15 (Spring–Fall 2009): 103–124.

16. Geggus, *Haitian Revolutionary Studies*, pp. 99–118; Geggus, "The Arming of Slaves in the Haitian Revolution," pp. 209–232.

17. Blackburn, *Overthrow of Colonial Slavery*, p. 194.

18. Fick, *Making of Haiti*, pp. 115–116.

19. For the numbers, see Geggus, "The Arming of Slaves in the Haitian Revolution," pp. 222–223.

20. Blackburn, *Overthrow of Colonial Slavery*, p. 218; Colwill, "Fêtes de l'hymen"; Fick, *Making of Haiti*, p. 161.

21. Colwill, "Fêtes de l'hymen," pp. 12, 23.

22. Blackburn, *Overthrow of Colonial Slavery*, p. 218.

23. An argument made powerfully in another case by Ferrer, *Insurgent Cuba.*

24. A process painstakingly reconstructed by Colwill, "Fêtes de l'hymen"; Elizabeth Colwill, "Freedwomen's Familial Politics: Marriage, War and Rites of Registry in Post-Emancipation Saint-Domingue," in *Gender, War, and Politics: The Wars of Revolution and Liberation—Transatlantic Comparisons, 1775–1820*, ed. Karen Hagemann, Gisele Mettele, and Jane Randall (Basingstoke, U.K.: Palgrave Macmillan, 2010), pp. 103–124; and Dubois, *A Colony of Citizens*, especially pp. 249–276.

25. Colwill, "Gender, Slavery, War and Violence," p. 20.

26. Elizabeth Colwill is the only one of the historians cited above to analyze directly the role of marriage in republican emancipation policy in Saint-Domingue. But see also Fick, *Making of Haiti*, p. 163.

27. Fick, *The Making of Haiti*, p. 170; Blackburn, *Overthrow of Colonial Slavery*, p. 235.

28. Emancipation Proclamation.

29. McCurry, *Confederate Reckoning*, pp. 218–262.

30. Second Confiscation Act, July 17, 1862, *U.S. Statutes at Large, Treaties, and Proclamations of the United States of America*, vol. 12 (Boston: Little, Brown, 1863), pp. 589–592.

31. I do not take up the Confederate case here. For that, see McCurry, *Confederate Reckoning*, pp. 218–357.

32. Butler to Lieutenant General Winfield Scott, May 24, 25, 27, 1861; John B. Cary to Butler, Mar. 9, 1891, in Benjamin Butler, *Private and Official Correspondence of General Benjamin F. Butler during the Period of the Civil War* (Norwood, Mass.: Plimpton Press, 1917), 1:104–108, 112–114, 102–103. The key document (Butler to Scott, May 27, 1861) is reproduced in *Freedom: A Documentary History of Emancipation, 1861–1867*, ser. I, vol. I, *The Destruction of Slavery*, ed. Ira Berlin, Barbara J. Fields, Thavolia Glymph, Joseph P. Reidy, and Leslie S. Rowland (New York: Cambridge University Press, 1985), pp. 70–72 (hereafter Berlin et al., eds., *Destruction of Slavery*). See also testimony of Harry Jarvis in John Blassingame, ed., *Slave Testimony: Two Centuries of Letters, Speeches, Interviews and Autobiographies* (Baton Rouge: Louisiana State University Press, 1977), pp. 606–611, and Robert F. Engs, *Freedom's First Generation: Black Hampton, Virginia, 1861–1890* (Philadelphia: University of Pennsylvania Press, 1979).

33. Butler to Scott, May 25, 1861; Blair to Butler, May 29, 1861; Secretary of War Simon Cameron to Butler, May 30, 1861, in Butler, *Private and Official Correspondence*, 1:106, 112–114, 116–117, 119.

34. Butler to Scott, May 25, 1861; Butler to Colonel John W. Phelps, May 28, 1861, in ibid., 1:105–106, 114; Edward Pierce, "The Contrabands at Fortress Monroe," *Atlantic Monthly*, November 1861, pp. 626–640, 626 (quotation).

35. Butler to Scott, May 27, 1861, in Butler, *Private and Official Correspondence*, 1:113.

36. Pierce, "Contrabands at Fortress Monroe," pp. 636–637.

37. Ibid.; Butler to Cameron, July 30, 1861, in Butler, *Private and Official Correspondence*, 1:186–188. Butler appears to be referring to orders of Brigadier General Irvin McDowell, issued in July 1861; see Berlin et al., eds., *Destruction of Slavery*, pp. 342–343. On the effect of the slave trade on Virginia families, see Brenda Stevenson, *Life in Black and White: Family and Community in the Slave South* (New York: Oxford University Press, 1997), and on the slave trade and sexual violence more generally, see Walter Johnson, *Soul by Soul: Life Inside the Antebellum Slave Market* (Cambridge, Mass.: Harvard University Press, 1999), and Daina Ramey Berry, *The Price for Their Pound of Flesh: The Value of the Enslaved, from Womb to Grave, in the Building of a Nation* (Boston: Beacon Press, 2017). White abolitionists' preoccupa-

tion with the South's "white slaves" was a common theme in wartime accounts. On slave breeding, see Amy Dru Stanley, "Slave Breeding and Free Love: An Antebellum Argument over Slavery, Capitalism, and Personhood," in *Capitalism Takes Command,* ed. Michael Zakim and Gary Kornblith (Chicago: University of Chicago Press, 2012), pp. 119–144.

38. Butler to Cameron, July 30, 1861; Blair to Butler, May 29, 1861; Cameron to Butler, May 30, Aug. 8, 1861, in Butler, *Private and Official Correspondence,* I:186, 116, 119, 202–203. Chandra Manning has recently emphasized that the value of fugitive women's labor was well recognized by army officers. However, she tends to talk of contraband and laborers generally without regard to the difference gender made, and she does not address the illogic of the contraband policy itself. See Chandra Manning, *Troubled Refuge: Struggling for Freedom in the Civil War* (New York: Knopf, 2016), pp. 55, 189–190.

39. *U.S. Statutes at Large,* 12:319; Berlin et al., *Slaves No More,* p. 23.

40. For the numbers, see Berlin et al., eds., *Destruction of Slavery,* pp. 70–72, 304–306, 91; Manning, *Troubled Refuge,* pp. 66–67, 79, 114–117. Leslie Schwalm was the first to notice the gender problem. See Schwalm, *A Hard Fight for We,* p. 90. Other early accounts include Thavolia Glymph, "'This Species of Property': Female Slave Contrabands in the Civil War," in *A Woman's War: Southern Women, Civil War, and the Confederate Legacy,* ed. Edward D. C. Campbell, Jr., and Kym S. Rice (Richmond, Va.: Museum of the Confederacy, 1996), pp. 55–71. On military posts as refugee camps, see Manning, *Troubled Refuge,* p. 20. For the cultural history of the contraband camps and a digital map, see Abigail Cooper, "'Lord, Until I Find Reach My Home': Inside the Refugee Camps of the American Civil War" (Ph.D. diss., University of Pennsylvania, 2015).

41. Butler to Cameron, July 30, 1861, in Butler, *Private and Official Correspondence,* I:185–186; Pierce, "Contrabands at Fortress Monroe," pp. 635, 633, emphasis added; Willie Lee Rose, *Rehearsal for Reconstruction: The Port Royal Experiment* (1964; reprint, Athens: University of Georgia Press, 1999), pp. 21–22.

42. Berlin et al., eds., *Destruction of Slavery,* pp. 88–90; Manning, *Troubled Refuge,* p. 58.

43. For one account of the scale of the problem, see Eaton, *Grant, Lincoln.* The idea of the Civil War as involving a major humanitarian crisis is developed in a number of recent works. See Glymph, "Women at War," chap. 7; Manning,

Troubled Refuge; Jim Downs, *Sick from Freedom: African-American Illness and Suffering during the Civil War and Reconstruction* (New York: Oxford University Press, 2012); and Yael Sternhell, "Revisionism Reinvented: The Antiwar Turn in Civil War Scholarship," *Journal of the Civil War Era* 3, no. 2 (June 2013): 239–256.

44. Christopher Leslie Brown, *Moral Capital: Foundations of British Abolitionism* (Chapel Hill: University of North Carolina Press, 2007), pp. 206, 236; American Freedmen's Inquiry Commission, Preliminary Report, *Senate Executive Document No. 53,* 38th Congress, 1st Session (New York: n.p., 1863), pp. 1–24. On the problem of marriage and welfare in federal policy, see especially Amy Dru Stanley, *From Bondage to Contract: Wage Labor, Marriage and the Market in the Age of Slave Emancipation* (Cambridge: Cambridge University Press, 1998). On the problem of freedwomen and dependency, see Linda K. Kerber, *No Constitutional Right to Be Ladies: Women and the Obligations of Citizenship* (New York: Hill and Wang, 1998), pp. 47–80. For a review essay that lays out my views of marriage and citizenship in the Civil War era, see Stephanie McCurry, "Review Essay," *Signs: Journal of Women in Culture and Society* 30, no. 2 (Winter 2005): 1659–1670.

45. Hunter, *Bound in Wedlock,* pp. 134–135, chap. 4. The idea of government documents as an insurance policy comes from Colwill, "Freedwomen's Familial Politics."

46. Hunter, *Bound in Wedlock,* chap. 4, p. 7 (quotation); Rose, *Rehearsal for Reconstruction,* p. 236. On enslaved people's intimate relationships, from taking up to marriage, see also the pioneering analysis of Kaye, *Joining Places.* On the Civil War push for national marital conformity, see Cott, *Public Vows,* and Sarah Barringer Gordon, *The Mormon Question: Polygamy and Constitutional Conflict in Nineteenth Century America* (Chapel Hill: University of North Carolina Press, 2002).

47. Second Confiscation Act, July 17, 1862, *U.S. Statutes at Large,* 12:589–592, sec. 10 (quotation). On hard-war tactics, see Mark Grimsley, *The Hard Hand of War* (New York: Cambridge University Press, 1995). On Lincoln and the timing of the Preliminary Emancipation Proclamation, see Masur, *Lincoln's Hundred Days.* Masur's account stresses the importance of congressional action on confiscation and arming slaves to Lincoln's decision-making. On the Second Confiscation Act and Militia Act, see Berlin et al., *Slaves No More,* pp. 40–42, 193–199, and John Syrett, *The Civil War Confiscation Acts: Failing to Reconstruct the South* (New York: Fordham University Press, 2005).

48. Militia Act, July 17, 1862, *U.S. Statutes at Large*, 12:597–600.

49. On Hunter's effort see Hunter to Edwin Stanton, June 23, 1862, in *Freedom: A Documentary History of Emancipation, 1861–1867*, ser. 2, *The Black Military Experience*, ed. Ira Berlin, Joseph P. Reidy, and Leslie S. Rowland (New York: Cambridge University Press, 1982), pp. 51–53 (hereafter Berlin et al., eds., *Black Military Experience*). For other early attempts by Brigadier General J. W. Phelps and James H. Lane, see ibid., pp. 62–63, 68–69.

50. Amy Dru Stanley, "Instead of Waiting for the Thirteenth Amendment: The War Power, Slave Marriage, and Inviolate Human Rights," *American Historical Review* 115, no. 3 (June 2010): 732–765.

51. *Congressional Globe*, 37th Congress, 2nd Session, June 27, 1862, p. 2971; July 9, 1862, p. 3198; July11, 1862, p. 3265; July 9, 1862, p. 3205.

52. Ibid., July 9, 1862, p. 3198.

53. Ibid., July 10, 1862, p. 3228; July 9, 1862, p. 3199; July 11, 1862, p. 3251; July 15, 1862, p. 3338; July 15, 1862, p. 3339. Senator Edgar Cowan reminded King that when Britain used slaves in the Revolutionary War, the United States had charged that they violated the laws of war and "outraged the sense of the civilized world." Per usual, the concern was the protection of women and children: "Will he [the slave soldier] make war on women or children?" Ibid., July 11, 1862, p. 3251. On the laws of war and US interpretation of them, Cowan had a point. As John Fabian Witt has argued, the Lincoln government's emancipation policy overturned a position on slavery and the laws of war the US government had maintained since the founding. See Witt, *Lincoln's Code: The Laws of War in American History* (New York: Free Press, 2012).

54. *Congressional Globe*, 37th Congress, 2nd Session, 1862, pp. 3198, 3234–3235, 3338. John Sherman claimed compensation to loyal men would cost $1 billion. See ibid., p. 3338.

55. Second Confiscation Act, July 17, 1862, *U.S. Statutes at Large*, 12:589–592, secs. 9, 11; Militia Act, July 17, 1862, ibid., 12:597–600, sec. 13.

56. A point acknowledged but not developed in Berlin et al., *Slaves No More*, pp. 44–45.

57. Emancipation Proclamation; Witt, *Lincoln's Code*, pp. 197–219.

58. For an excellent overview of the process, see Berlin et al., *Slaves No More*, pp. 51, 200–201, 197 (quotation). For a detailed account of this process, see

Berlin et al., eds., *Black Military Experience*, pp. 1–45; for recruitment numbers, see table, p. 12. On the American Freedmen's Inquiry Commission, see American Freedmen's Inquiry Commission, Preliminary Report, June 30, 1863.

59. Grant quoted in Eaton, *Grant, Lincoln*, pp. 12–13.

60. Ibid., pp. 2, 111, 216–217. Numbers provided in ibid., pp. 69, 105, 123–124, 216–217.

61. American Freedmen's Inquiry Commission, Preliminary Report, pp. 2, 13, 4, 15.

62. Ann Laura Stoler, "Colonial Archives and the Arts of Governance," *Archival Science* 2 (2002): 87–109.

63. Eaton, *Grant, Lincoln*, pp. 216–217, 34–35, 212, 211, 214 (quotations).

64. Ibid., pp. 34–35, 36 (quotations).

65. Berlin et al., *Slaves No More*, p. 53. On the plantations under northern lessees, see Lawrence N. Powell, *New Masters: Northern Planters during the Civil War and Reconstruction* (New Haven, Conn.: Yale University Press, 1980). On the military sorting, see Bercaw, *Gendered Freedoms*, pp. 31–50. On Lorenzo Thomas and his policy, see Erik Mathisen, *The Loyal Republic: Traitors, Slaves and the Remaking of Citizenship in Civil War America* (Chapel Hill: University of North Carolina Press, 2018), chap. 4.

66. Major George L. Stearns to Edwin Stanton, August 17, 1863, in Berlin et al., eds., *Black Military Experience*, pp. 98–101, 100 (quotation); Eaton, *Grant, Lincoln*, pp. 66, 135; Governor David Tod to Langston, May 16, 1863; Delaney to Stanton, December 15, 1863, in Berlin et al., eds., *Black Military Experience*, pp. 92–93, 101–102.

67. Mathisen, *The Loyal Republic*, chap. 4, pp. 149, 148 (quotations).

68. Ibid., p. 145.

69. Bercaw, *Gendered Freedoms*, p. 44. Bercaw estimates that 69 percent of the laborers on leased plantations were women.

70. Glymph, "Women at War," chap. 7, pp. 185–186; Vicksburg Marriage Register: Register of Marriages, 1863–1865, vols. 43–46.

71. Glymph, "Women at War," chap. 7, pp. 181, 208, 184, 213, 185; American Freedmen's Inquiry Commission, Preliminary Report, p. 14; Bercaw, *Gendered Freedoms*, p. 36; Eaton, *Grant, Lincoln*, pp. 143–173. On northern lessees on Mississippi Valley plantations, see Powell, *New Masters*.

72. Berlin et al., eds., *Destruction of Slavery*, pp. 304–306, 306 (quotation).

73. Rose, *Rehearsal for Reconstruction*, pp. 247, 265–266; Bercaw, *Gendered Freedoms*, pp. 36–47; General Orders No 22, Head Quars 14th A Co, 20 Nov. 1864, vol. 6 / 8 14AC, pp. 86–87, General Orders & Circulars Issued, ser. 5701, 14th Army Corps, RG 393 Pt. 2 No. 371 (Records of the U.S. Army Continental Commands, 1821–1920), National Archives [FSSP C-8787].

74. Berlin et al., eds., *Black Military Experience*, table, p. 12; pp. 126–128, 127 (quotation).

75. For the numbers, see Berlin et al., *Slaves No More*, p. 203.

76. "The Negro Troops in the Southwest," *Harper's Weekly*, Nov. 14, 1863, pp. 721–722.

77. On marriage and federal policy in the Civil War, see Cott, *Public Vows*, pp. 77–104. On the marriage of slaves and freed people during the war, and for the debate over how common legal marriage was, see Herbert Gutman, *The Black Family in Slavery and Freedom, 1750–1925* (New York: Vintage Books, 1976), pp. 363–431; Frankel, *Freedom's Women*; Glymph, "'This Species of Property'"; Laura Edwards, "'The Marriage Covenant Is at the Foundation of All Our Rights': The Politics of Slave Marriages in North Carolina after Emancipation," *Law and History Review* 14 (Spring 1996): 81–124; Bercaw, *Gendered Freedoms*, pp. 19–50; and, most recently, Hunter, *Bound in Wedlock*.

78. See for example Adjutant Lorenzo Thomas, General Orders No. 15, issued at Natchez, Mar. 28, 1864, cited in Berlin et al., eds., *Black Military Experience*, p. 712. And for one record of local enforcement, see Special Orders No. 13, Officer of Superintendent and Provost Marshal of Freedmen, Natchez, Mississippi, Dec. 24, 1864, Freedmen's Bureau Letter Book and Order Book, 1864–1866, George D. Reynolds Papers, Missouri History Museum, Library and Research Center, St. Louis.

79. The coercive features were evident in Special Orders No. 13 cited above, which required freed people living together as man and wife to be lawfully married and which explicitly stated "all persons violating the above orders will when found guilty be severely punished." On the dignity conferred by marriage and the coercive context, see Hunter, *Bound in Wedlock*.

80. Chaplain C. W. Buckley to Lieut A. R. Mills, 1 Aug. 1864 B-1124 1864, Letters Received, ser. 12, RG 94 (Records of the Adjutant General's Office),

National Archives [FSSP K-541]; General Orders No. 46 (By Command of Major General Butler, Department of Virginia and North Carolina), Dec. 5, 1863; Ann Summer to Butler, Feb. 28, 1864, in Berlin et al., eds., *Black Military Experience*, pp. 7, 135–138, 135, 721 (quotations). On the politics of subsistence of soldier's wives in the Confederacy, see McCurry, *Confederate Reckoning*, chaps. 4–5. On Union soldiers' wives, see Judith Giesberg, *Army at Home: Women and the Civil War on the Northern Home Front* (Chapel Hill: University of North Carolina Press, 2009).

81. Harris to Ullman, Dec. 27, 1864; Davis to Brigadier General James Bowen, Aug. 21, 1863; Rice to "My Children," Sept. 3, 1864, in Berlin et al., eds., *Black Military Experience*, pp. 691–692, 157–158, 689–690.

82. Colonel F. W. Lister to Brigadier General W. D. Whipple, Dec. 14, 1865; Lieutenant John Foley to Lieutenant Colonel T. Harris, Jan. 11, 1865, in ibid., pp. 712–715, 714, 719 (quotations).

83. Colonel F. W. Lister to Brigadier General W. D. Whipple, Dec. 14, 1865; General Orders No. 41, Feb. 3, 1865, in ibid., pp. 712–715, 714 (quotation), 719, 709. The casting of African American marriages as illicit sexual relations was a strategy that endured into the postwar period. See Peggy Pascoe, *What Comes Naturally: Miscegenation Law and the Making of Race in America* (New York: Oxford University Press, 2009).

84. Circular, Office Superintendent and Provost Marshal of Freedmen, Natchez, Mississippi, Oct. 3, 1864, George D. Reynolds Papers, Missouri History Museum; Brig. Genl. John P. Hawkins to Lt. Col. H. C. Rodgers, 7 Sept. 1864, Letters & Orders Received by Forces under the Department of the Gulf, ser. 1753, Dept. of the Gulf, RG 393 Pt. 1 (Records of the U.S. Army Continental Commands, 1821–1920), National Archives [FSSP C-608]; Chaplain Jas. Peet to Brig. Gen'l. L. Thomas, 1 Nov. 1864, P-1205 1864, Letters Received, ser. 12, RG 94 (Records of the Adjutant General's Office), National Archives [FSSP K-549]; Endorsement by Col. Sam'l Thomas, 31 Jan. 1865, on letter of Chaplain G. H. Carruthers, 27 Jan. 1865, vol. 73, pp. 6–8, Register of Letters Received, ser. 2036, MS Asst. Supt. of Freedmen, RG 105 (Records of the Bureau of Refugees, Freedmen, and Abandoned Lands), National Archives [FSSP A-4020].

85. Col Geo. M. Ziegler to Col Sam'l Thomas, 9 Nov. 1865, Unregistered Letters Received, ser. 2348, Western Dist. Of MS Acting Asst. Comr., RG 105 (Records of the Bureau of Refugees, Freedmen, and Abandoned Lands), National Archives [FSSP A-9269]. On Natchez, see Justin Behrend, *Reconstructing Democracy: Grassroots Black Politics in the Deep South after the Civil War* (Athens, Ga.: University of Georgia Press, 2017). On ongoing issues of public health cast as vice, see Tera Hunter, *To Joy My Freedom: Southern Black Women's Lives and Labors after the Civil War* (Cambridge, Mass.: Harvard University Press, 1997).

86. Hanon to Thomas, Nov. 19, 1865, in Berlin et al., eds., *Black Military Experience*, p. 713. For one example of sexual predation, see Col. Richd Owen to Col. Scates, 9 May 1863, vol. 3 13AC, pp. 162–165, Letters Received, ser. 5536, 13th Army Corps, RG 393 Pt. 2 No. 352 (Records of U.S. Army Continental Commands, 1821–1920), National Archives [FSSP C-7624]. For a woman labeled a prostitute for accepting the protection of another man, see Affidavit of Harriet Ann Bridwell, Louisville, Ky., Apr. 3, 1865, in Berlin et al., eds., *Black Military Experience*, pp. 678–679. On marriage rules as a test designed for failure, see Hunter, *Bound in Wedlock*, and, more generally, Saidiya V. Hartman, *Scenes of Subjection: Terror, Slavery, and Self-Making in Nineteenth-Century America* (New York: Oxford University Press, 1997).

87. Colonel H. N. Frisbee to Thomas W. Conway, Oct. 2, 1865, in Berlin et al., eds., *Black Military Experience*, pp. 701–702, 701 (quotation); Frankel, *Freedom's Women*; Elizabeth Regosin and Donald Shaffer, *Voices of Emancipation: Understanding the Civil War and Reconstruction through the United States Pension Bureau Files* (New York: New York University Press, 2008).

88. "A Resolution to Encourage Enlistments and to Promote the Efficiency of the Military Service," March 3, 1865, in *Official Records*, ser. 3, vol. 4 (Washington, D.C.: Government Printing Office, 1900), pp. 1219, 1228. For the text of the act, see *U.S. Statutes at Large*, 13:571. Abraham Lincoln, Second Inaugural Address, March 4, 1865, http://avalon.law.yale.edu/19th_century/lincoln2.asp. On the debate over the Enlistment Act, see Stanley, "Instead of Waiting for the Thirteenth Amendment," pp. 732–765; Cott, *Public Vows*, pp. 77–104; and Berlin et al., eds., *Black Military Experience*, pp. 195–197. For the political history of the Thirteenth Amendment, see Michael Vorenberg, *Final Freedom: The Civil War, the*

Abolition of Slavery, and the Thirteenth Amendment (Cambridge: Cambridge University Press, 2001).

89. Berlin et al., *Slaves No More*, p. 203. On the slow destruction of slavery and military enlistment in Kentucky, see the excellent overviews in Berlin et al., eds., *Destruction of Slavery*, pp. 493–518; Berlin et al., eds., *Black Military Experience*, pp. 183–197; and Aaron Astor, *Rebels on the Border: Civil War, Emancipation, and the Reconstruction of Kentucky and Missouri* (Baton Rouge: Louisiana State University Press, 2012). Slavery also remained legal in Delaware until ratification of the Thirteenth Amendment, but the number of people still enslaved there was by that point very small. Berlin et al., *Slaves No More*, p. 203.

90. Berlin et al., eds., *Destruction of Slavery*, pp. 489, 610; "Wife of a Kentucky Black Soldier to Her Husband," in Berlin et al., eds., *Black Military Experience*, pp. 697–698. For a sample of black soldiers' letters and officers' letters, see Berlin et al., eds., *Black Military Experience*, pp. 692–694, 683–684.

91. "Affidavit of a Kentucky Black Soldier's Wife," Mar. 25, 1865, in Berlin et al., eds., *Black Military Experience*, pp. 694–695.

92. "Assistant Provost Marshal at Fulton, Missouri, to the Provost Marshal General of the Department of the Missouri," March 28, 1864, in ibid., p. 688; "Affidavit of a Kentucky Black Soldier's Wife," Mar. 25, 1865, in ibid., pp. 694–695.

93. Stanley, "Instead of Waiting for the Thirteenth Amendment," pp. 745, 755; Berlin et al., *Slaves No More*, pp. 70–73. For Wilson's vote in 1862, see *Congressional Globe*, 37th Congress, 2nd Session, 1862, p. 3339. A sample of the letters is included in Berlin et al., eds., *Destruction of Slavery*, pp. 479–489, and Berlin et al., eds., *Black Military Experience*, pp. 240–250.

94. Stanley, "Instead of Waiting for the Thirteenth Amendment," pp. 749, 750, 746, 747.

95. "A Resolution to Encourage Enlistments."

96. Military estimates range from 75,000–100,000 based on Kentucky enlistment of 25,000 formerly enslaved soldiers. Berlin et al., eds., *Black Military Experience*, pp. 191–197. Stanley says "upwards of 50,000." See Stanley, "Instead of Waiting for the Thirteenth Amendment," p. 732.

97. Stanley, "Instead of Waiting for the Thirteenth Amendment," p. 760.

98. "Commander of a Missouri Black Regiment to the Officers and Men of the Regiment," in Berlin et al., eds., *Black Military Experience*, pp. 782–785, 783 (quotation). For one excellent article on the implications, see Edwards, "'Marriage Is at the Foundation of All Our Rights.'"

99. Mary Astell, "Some Reflections on Marriage," quoted in Cott, *Public Vows*, p. 65; George Fitzhugh, *Sociology for the South; or, The Failure of Free Society* (Richmond, Va.: A. Morris, 1854), 205; Stanley, "Instead of Waiting for the Thirteen Amendment"; Stanley, *From Bondage and Contract*. On the proslavery uses, see my earlier work, particularly Stephanie McCurry, *Masters of Small Worlds: Yeoman Households, Gender Relations, and the Political Culture of the Antebellum South Carolina Low Country* (New York: Oxford University Press, 1995), and "The Two Faces of Republicanism: Gender and Proslavery Politics in Antebellum South Carolina," *Journal of American History* 78, no. 4 (March 1992): 1245–1262.

100. Thirteenth Amendment, sec. 1, https://www.avalon.law.yale.edu/18th _century/amend1.asp#13; Sumner quoted in Stanley, "Instead of Waiting for the Thirteenth Amendment," p. 7. On Lieber's version, see Vorenberg, *Final Freedom*, p. 67.

101. Sumner, Howard, and Charles White quoted in Cott, *Public Vows*, pp. 80, 79, and Sumner quoted in Stanley, "Instead of Waiting for the Thirteenth Amendment," p. 7. For Howard's vote in 1862, see *Congressional Globe*, 37th Congress, 2nd Session, 1862, pp. 3338, 3339; for his speech on the Thirteenth Amendment, see *Congressional Globe*, 38th Congress, 1st Session, April 8, 1864, p. 1488. Vorenberg, *Final Freedom*, p. 57. For the text of the French Declaration of the Rights of Man (1789), see http://avalon.law.yale.edu/18th_century/rightsof.asp.

102. On gender and constitutionalism, see particularly Reva B. Siegel, "Gender and the United States Constitution: Equal Protection, Privacy, and Federalism," in *The Gender of Constitutional Jurisprudence*, ed. Beverley Baines and Ruth Rubio-Marin (Cambridge: Cambridge University Press, 2005), pp. 306–333. On the losing feminist struggle over the Fourteenth and Fifteenth Amendments, see Ellen Carol DuBois, *Feminism and Suffrage* (Ithaca, N.Y.: Cornell University Press, 1999), and on the Civil War–era politics of the women's movement more generally, see Christine Stansell, *Feminist Promise* (New York: Modern Library, 2013).

103. The Nineteenth Amendment was passed in 1919 and ratified in 1920. On the suffrage movement and African American women's disfranchisement, see Rosalyn Terborg-Penn, *African-American Women in the Struggle for the Vote, 1850–1920* (Bloomington: Indiana University Press, 1998), and Glenda Gilmore, *Gender and Jim Crow: Women and the Politics of White Supremacy, 1896–1920* (Chapel Hill: University of North Carolina Press, 1996).

104. Representative Thomas D. Elliot of Massachusetts (1866) quoted in Cott, *Public Vows*, p. 94. The enforcement of the Thirteenth Amendment and the laws of marriage and family required to enforce it is the subject of an article I am currently working on. See Stephanie McCurry, "Reconstructing Belonging: The Thirteenth Amendment at Work in the World," in Margot Canaday, Nancy Cott, and Robert Self, eds., *The Intimate State* (forthcoming).

105. For examples in French colonial law in the nineteenth century, see Judith Surkis, "Sex, Law and Sovereignty," unpublished paper in possession of the author, and Emmanuelle Saada, *Empire's Children: Race, Filiation, and Citizenship in the French Colonies* (Chicago: University of Chicago Press, 2012). The idea of the postwar southern states as colonies of an imperial United States dates back to C. Vann Woodward, *Origins of the New South, 1877–1913* (1951; reprint, Baton Rouge: Louisiana State University Press, 1971).

106. "Nashville Blacks to the Union Convention of Tennessee," in Berlin et al., eds., *Black Military Experience*, pp. 811–816, 812 (quotation). This was, of course, a longstanding characteristic of republican government, including in the United States, and had shaped the gender of citizenship profoundly since 1787. On that long history, see especially Kerber, *No Constitutional Right to Be Ladies*.

3. Reconstructing a Life amid the Ruins

1. Even defeat has a gendered history. For one powerful account, see Atina Grossmann, *Jews, Germans and Allies: Close Encounters in Occupied Germany* (Princeton, N.J.: Princeton University Press, 2007), especially chap. 2: "Both that *Zusammenbruch* (collapse) and the moves toward reconstruction . . . were experienced in gendered terms" (48).

2. For a number of examples, see Baring Brothers Liverpool to Baring Brothers London, Mar. 31, Apr. 15, 16, May 3, 12, 1865, Baring Archive, HC 3.35, ING

Baring Brothers Archive, London; Sven Beckert, *Empire of Cotton: A Global History* (New York: Knopf, 2014), chaps. 9–10; and W. E. B. Du Bois, *Black Reconstruction in America: An Essay toward a History of the Part Which Black Folk Played in the Attempt to Reconstruct Democracy in America, 1860–1880* (1935; reprint, New York: Free Press, 1992).

3. Ella Gertrude Clanton Thomas, Diary, Ella Gertrude Clanton Thomas Papers (hereafter EGCT Papers), David M. Rubenstein Rare Book and Manuscript Library, Duke University, Durham, N.C. The published version is Virginia Ingraham Burr, ed., *The Secret Eye: The Journal of Ella Gertrude Clanton Thomas, 1848–1889* (Chapel Hill: University of North Carolina Press, 1990). The manuscript diary is much longer than the published one. I refer to the manuscript diary when the material quoted or cited is not reproduced in the published version. There is one biography of Thomas, Carolyn Newton Curry, *Suffer and Grow Strong: The Life of Ella Gertrude Clanton Thomas, 1834–1907* (Macon, Ga.: Mercer University Press, 2014), which relies heavily on the diary. There is also an excellent chapter on Thomas in Nell Irvin Painter, *Southern History across the Color Line* (Chapel Hill: University of North Carolina Press, 2002), chap. 2, "The Journal of Ella Gertrude Thomas: A Testament of Wealth, Loss, and Adultery," pp. 40–92. This essay was initially published as the introduction to the diary. See Painter, "The Journal of Ella Gertrude Clanton Thomas: An Educated White Woman in the Eras of Slavery, War, and Reconstruction," in Burr, ed., *Secret Eye*, pp. 1–67.

4. Burr, ed., *Secret Eye*, May 8, 1865, p. 264.

5. Tony Judt, *Postwar: A History of Europe since 1945* (New York: Penguin, 2005), p. 35.

6. Margaret Ann Morris Grimball, Diary, no. 975-z, Southern Historical Collection, Wilson Library, University of North Carolina at Chapel Hill (hereafter SHC). The term and important concept of "free homes" is taken from and brilliantly developed in Thavolia Glymph, *Out of the House of Bondage: The Transformation of the Plantation Household* (New York: Cambridge University Press, 2008), chap. 5.

7. Beckert, *Empire of Cotton*; Charles S. Maier, *Leviathan 2.0: Inventing Modern Statehood* (Cambridge, Mass.: Belknap Press of Harvard University Press, 2012); Vanessa Ogle, "Whose Time Is It? The Pluralization of Time and the Global

Condition, 1870s–1940s," *American Historical Review* 118, no. 5 (Dec. 2013): 1376–1402; Sebouh David Aslanian et al., *"AHR* Conversation: How Size Matters: The Question of Scale in History," *American Historical Review* 118, no. 5 (Dec. 2013): 1431–1472.

8. Du Bois, *Black Reconstruction in America,* pp. 15–16, 346–347.

9. Karen and Barbara Fields note the value of such a perspective as a check "on the elaboration of a collective picture so grand and encompassing that it blots out individual experience." Karen E. Fields and Barbara J. Fields, *Racecraft: The Soul of Inequality in American Life* (New York: Verso, 2012), pp. 78–79; Beckert, *Empire of Cotton;* Maier, *Leviathan 2.0.*

10. Eric Foner, *Reconstruction: America's Unfinished Revolution, 1863–1877* (New York: Harper and Row, 1988); Ira Berlin et al., *Slaves No More: Three Essays on Emancipation and the Civil War* (Cambridge: Cambridge University Press, 1992), and the other publications of the Freedmen and Southern Society Project, including *Freedom: A Documentary History of Emancipation, 1861–1867,* 6 vols. (New York: Cambridge University Press, 1982–2013), and *Free at Last: A Documentary History of Slavery, Freedom, and the Civil War* (New York: New Press, 1992); Steven Hahn, *A Nation under Our Feet: Black Political Struggles in the Rural South from Slavery to the Great Migration* (Cambridge, Mass.: Belknap Press of Harvard University Press, 2003). For a brief and useful account, see Ira Berlin et al., "The Terrain of Freedom: The Struggle over the Meaning of Free Labor in the U.S. South," *History Workshop Journal* 22 (Oct. 1986): 108–130.

11. For a fuller account of my views, see Stephanie McCurry, "Plunder of Black Life," review of Sven Beckert and Seth Rockman, eds., *Slavery's Capitalism: A New History of American Economic Development, Times Literary Supplement,* May 17, 2017. Other accounts include Walter Johnson, *River of Dark Dreams: Slavery and Empire in the Cotton Kingdom* (Cambridge, Mass.: Belknap Press of Harvard University Press, 2013); Edward E. Baptist, *The Half Has Never Been Told: Slavery and the Making of American Capitalism* (New York: Basic Books, 2016); and Calvin Schermerhorn, *The Business of Slavery and the Rise of American Capitalism, 1815–1860* (New Haven, Conn.: Yale University Press, 2015). For an excellent statement of the state of the field in economic history, see Peter Coclanis, "The American Civil War and Its Aftermath," in *Cambridge World History of Slavery,* vol. 4, ed. David Eltis et al. (Cambridge: Cambridge University Press, 2017), pp. 513–539.

12. On the Civil War history, see Yael Sternhell's review essay, "Revisionism Reinvented? The Antiwar Turn in Civil War Scholarship," *Journal of the Civil War Era* 3, no. 2 (June 2013): 239–256. Gregory P. Downs and Kate Masur question the utility of the concept in the introduction to *The World the Civil War Made*, ed. Gregory P. Downs and Kate Masur (Chapel Hill: University of North Carolina Press, 2015), p. 4. The unsettled state of the literature is evident in this anthology in the obvious contradiction between the introduction written by the editors and the afterword written by Steven Hahn; Hahn adheres fully to the (older) view of Reconstruction as a bourgeois revolution. See Hahn, "What Sort of World Did the Civil War Make?" pp. 337–356. On the violence of Reconstruction, see especially Richard Zucek, *State of Rebellion: Reconstruction in South Carolina* (Columbia: University of South Carolina Press, 1996); Carole Emberton, *Beyond Redemption: Race, Violence and the American South after the Civil War* (Chicago: Chicago University Press, 2013); and Douglas R. Egerton, *The Wars of Reconstruction: The Brief Violent History of America's Most Progressive Era* (New York: Bloomsbury, 2014). On the increasing weakness of the federal state and army of occupation, see Gregory P. Downs, *After Appomattox: Military Occupation and the Ends of War* (Cambridge, Mass.: Harvard University Press, 2015).

13. Ta-Nehisi Coates, "The Case for Reparations," *The Atlantic*, June 2014, https://www.theatlantic.com/magazine/archive/2014/06/the-case-for-reparations/361631/; Coates, *Between the World and Me* (New York: Spiegel and Grau, 2015), pp. 71, 111; Bryan Stevenson, *Just Mercy: A Story of Justice and Redemption* (New York: Spiegel and Grau, 2014), pp. 192–193; Jeffrey Toobin, "Justice Delayed," *New Yorker*, Aug. 22, 2016, pp. 40, 44; Michelle Alexander, *The New Jim Crow: Mass Incarceration in the Age of Colorblindness* (New York: New Press, 2010), pp. 14, 29–30. "It's a direct line from slavery to the treatment of black suspects today," Stevenson says. Notwithstanding his own untiring work, including in public history projects, he registers an increasing pessimism that spares neither present nor past.

14. I want to thank Anne Kerth, whose response to my paper at the Princeton Modern American History Workshop at Princeton in March 2018 sharpened my thinking immensely.

15. Burr, ed., *Secret Eye*, Nov. 21, 1864, p. 243; Amy Dru Stanley, "Instead of Waiting for the Thirteenth Amendment: The War Power, Slave Marriage, and

Inviolate Human Rights," *American Historical Review* 115, no. 3 (June 2010): 732–765; Nancy F. Cott, *Public Vows: A History of Marriage and the Nation* (Cambridge, Mass.: Harvard University Press, 2002).

16. Burr, ed., *Secret Eye*, Oct. 8, 1865, p. 276; June 26, 1869, p. 321. On the term "miscegenation," which was introduced by Democratic Party discourse in the leadup to the 1864 election, see Kate Masur, "'A Rare Example of Philological Vegetation': The Word 'Contraband' and the Meanings of Emancipation in the United States," *Journal of American History* 93 (Mar. 2007): 1050–1084.

17. Turner Clanton, Will, Probate Records, Richmond County, Georgia, FamilySearch.Org. She got $15,000 in his will. On her father's wealth when he died in 1864, see Curry, *Suffer and Grow Strong*, pp. 19–24, and Burr, ed., *Secret Eye*, Apr. 3, 1888, p. 443; Jan. 2, 1880, p. 392.

18. This story has been told before in pieces. Among the best accounts are Eugene D. Genovese, *Roll, Jordan, Roll: The World the Slaves Made* (New York: Vintage, 1974), and James L. Roark, *Masters without Slaves: Southern Planters in the Civil War and Reconstruction* (New York: Norton, 1977). The political history of the postwar planter class is very large but see the following in addition to Foner, *Reconstruction*: Dan T. Carter, *When the War Was Over: The Failure of Self Reconstruction in the South, 1865–1867* (Baton Rouge: Louisiana State University Press, 1985); Michael Perman, *Reunion without Compromise: The South and Reconstruction, 1865–1868* (Cambridge: Cambridge University Press, 1973); Steven Hahn, "Class and State in Post-Emancipation Societies: Southern Planters in Comparative Perspective," *American Historical Review* 95, no. 1 (Feb. 1990): 75–98; Bruce Levine, *The Fall of the House of Dixie: The Civil War and the Social Revolution That Transformed the South* (New York: Random House, 2013); and Lewis Nicholas Wynne, *The Continuity of Cotton: Planter Politics in Georgia, 1865–1892* (Macon, Ga.: Mercer University Press, 1986).

19. See Burr, ed., *Secret Eye*, Nov. 30, 1870, p. 342, for Thomas's comment, "I have never been so much opposed to having children as many women I know," and her discussion of limiting births. For the births and deaths of Thomas's children, see Burr, ed., *Secret Eye*, April 8, 1855, p. 119; Jan. 1, 1856, p. 141; Sept. 6, 1857, p. 155; Dec. 28, 1857, pp. 158–159; Nov. 14, 1858, pp. 162–164, 171; July 16, 1861, p. 186; July 24 [23], 1863, p. 214; Oct. 14, 1865, pp. 277–278, 288; Nov. 16, 1879, pp. 386, 374.

20. This point was made clear in Judt, *Postwar*.

21. Burr, ed., *Secret Eye*, Sept. 4 [3], 1864, p. 233; Diary, Dec. 12, 1864, EGCT Papers. For Thomas's pregnancy, see Burr, ed., *Secret Eye*, Feb. 12, 1865, p. 254; Oct. 14, 1865, pp. 277–278. The baby was born prematurely in July 1865, which Thomas attributed to the "constant strain upon my nervous system," and died a day later. This death is described in the Oct. 14, 1865, entry.

22. Burr, ed., *Secret Eye*, Dec. 12, 1864, p. 247; Thavolia Glymph, "Rose's War and the Gendered Politics of a Slave Insurgency in the Civil War," *Journal of the Civil War Era* 3, no. 4 (Dec. 2013): 501–532.

23. Diary, Dec. 12, 1864, EGCT Papers.

24. Genovese, *Roll, Jordan, Roll*, p. 97.

25. Thomas, Diary, Dec. 12, 1865, EGCT Papers. For one example of a slaveholder's obsessive accounting of "his people," see John Berkley Grimball, "List of the Negroes, Belonging to J. B. Grimball Who Left ... on the Night of the 2nd March 1862," Slave Material, 1828–1861, ser. 2, folder 81, Grimball Family Papers, SHC, and John Berkley Grimball, Diaries, Mar. 5, 8, 1862, ser. 1, vol. 15, John Berkley Grimball Papers, SHC. Grimball's wife said he was entirely unstrung by it.

26. That fundamental division was firmly on display upon entry of the Union Army to Augusta. After years of hiding their joy at Union military success, African Americans now expressed it on the streets. See Burr, ed., *Secret Eye*, May 7, 1865, p. 263.

27. Ibid., Sept. 17, 1864, p. 236. Thomas wrote that she would not like to give up "all we own for the sake of a principle, but I do think that if we had the same invested in something else as means of support I would willingly ... have the responsibility of them taken off my shoulders." For other examples of Thomas's reflections on the "demoralizing influence" of slavery, see ibid., Jan. 2, 1859, p. 168; Sept. 23, 1864, pp. 238–239.

28. Thirteenth Amendment, *U.S. Statutes at Large, Treaties, and Proclamations of the United States of America*, vol. 13 (Boston: Little, Brown, 1866), pp. 774–775; Andrew Johnson, "Amnesty Proclamation," May 29, 1865, in *The Papers of Andrew Johnson*, vol. 8, ed. Leroy P. Graf and Ralph W. Haskins (Knoxville: University of Tennessee Press, 1989), pp. 128–131; *Freedom: A Documentary History of Emancipation, 1861–1867*, ser. 3, vol. 1, *Land and Labor, 1865*, ed. Steven Hahn, Steven F. Miller,

Susan E. O'Donovan, John C. Rodrigue, and Leslie S. Rowland (Chapel Hill: University of North Carolina Press, 2008), p. 392 (quotation) (hereafter *Land and Labor, 1865*). Estimate of contemporary household assets figure from Chris Hayes, "The New Abolitionism," *The Nation*, April 22, 2014, https://www .thenation.com/article/new-abolitionism/. In 1866, the state of Georgia declared its losses, "the accumulated capital of nearly a century, represented by slave labor, amounting to nearly three hundred millions of dollars." See "An Act for the Relief of the People of Georgia, and to Prevent the Levy and Sale on Property," no. 255, Mar. 6, 1866, in *Acts of the General Assembly of the State of Georgia* (Milledgeville, Ga.: Boughton, Nisbet, Barnes and Moore, 1866), pp. 241–243.

29. Coclanis, "The American Civil War and Its Aftermath."

30. Burr ed., *Secret Eye*, Oct. 8, 1865, p. 276; May 1, 1865, p. 262; May 2, 1865, p. 262; Sept. 22, 1864, p. 237.

31. The Fourteenth Amendment put an end to such claims. Fourteenth Amendment, *U.S. Statutes at Large*, 39th Congress, 1st session, p. 358, https:// memory.loc.gov/cgi-bin/ampage?collId=llsl&fileName=014/llsl014.db&recNum =389. On ex-Confederate states more broadly, see Perman, *Reunion without Compromise.*

32. Thomas, Diary, May 7, 8, 17, 26, 27, 1865, EGCT Papers; Burr, ed., *Secret Eye*, July 16, 1861, p. 187; May 2, 1865, p. 263; July 30, 1870, p. 333; July 31, 1863, p. 218; Sept. 23, 1864, p. 238. The big task was "the making of free black homes." On that, see Glymph, *Out of the House of Bondage*, p. 245.

33. This is a process analyzed brilliantly in Glymph, *Out of the House of Bondage*, chaps. 4–5.

34. Burr, ed., *Secret Eye*, May 2, 1865, p. 263; March 29, 1865, p. 259; May 29, 1865, pp. 271–274.

35. Burr, ed., *Secret Eye*, May 27, 1865, pp. 271–272; Thomas, Diary, May 26, 28, 1865, EGCT Papers. This resolve never again to hire black servants was a common (and quickly abandoned) sentiment.

36. On the transformation of domestic service, see Tera W. Hunter, *To 'Joy My Freedom: Southern Black Women's Lives and Labors after the Civil War* (Cambridge, Mass.: Harvard University Press, 1997), and Glymph, *Out of the House of Bondage.*

37. In 1870, left without a baby nurse, she bathed the children herself for the first time; in May 1871, she complained bitterly about having to stay home from a club meeting because her "hired girl had a previous engagement and my pleasure must give way to accommodate her." Thomas, Diary, Feb. 7, 1870; May 4, 1871, EGCT Papers.

38. The phrase "masters without slaves" is from Roark, *Masters without Slaves.* For a classic statement of the concept of paternalism, see Genovese, *Roll, Jordan, Roll.* On familialism and proslavery ideology more broadly, see Stephanie McCurry, "The Two Faces of Republicanism: Gender and Proslavery Politics in Antebellum South Carolina," *Journal of American History* 78, no. 4 (Mar. 1992): 1245–1262.

For one interesting article about the continuation of proslavery religious beliefs after the war, see Luke E. Harlow, "The Long Life of Proslavery Religion," in Downs and Masur, eds., *World the Civil War Made,* pp. 132–158. Unfortunately, it deals mostly with theology and not the experiences of lay people.

39. Robert Habersham and other planters to O. O. Howard, reprinted as "A Meeting of Planters Held in Savannah, Georgia, June 6, 1865," in Paul Alan Cimbala, *The Freedmen's Bureau: Reconstructing the American South after the Civil War* (Malabar, Fla.: Krieger, 2005), pp. 117–119.

40. Sallie Crane, *The American Slave: A Composite Autobiography,* in George P. Rawick, ed., *Arkansas Narratives,* parts 1 and 2, vol. 8 (Westport, Conn.: Greenwood Press, 1972), p. 50; Saidiya Hartman, *Lose Your Mother: A Journey along the Atlantic Slave Route* (New York: Farrar, Straus and Giroux, 2007), p. 133; Heather Andrea Williams, *Help Me to Find My People: The African American Search for Family Lost in Slavery* (Chapel Hill: University of North Carolina Press, 2012), p. 172. Williams says that "most people never found their relatives."

41. Abigail Cooper, "'Lord, Until I Reach My Home': Inside the Refugee Camps of the American Civil War" (Ph.D. diss., University of Pennsylvania, 2015), and Abigail Cooper. "'Away I Goin' to Find My Mamma': Self-Emancipation, Migration, and Kinship in Refugee Camps in the Civil War Era," *Journal of African American History* 102, no. 4 (2017): 444–467; Sigismunda Stribling Kimball, Diary, Accession no. 2534, Special Collections, University of Virginia Library, Charlottesville; the moving account of Williams, *Help Me to Find*

My People; Sydney Nathans, *To Free a Family: The Journey of Mary Walker* (Cambridge, Mass.: Harvard University Press, 2012).

42. Burr, ed., *Secret Eye*, Nov. 1859, pp. 157–158. Gertrude Thomas urged that Isabella be sold notwithstanding her claims of attachment: "To this girl," she wrote, "I have a feeling amounting nearer to attachment than to any servant I ever met with in my life." Thomas remembered her without guilt more than twenty years later: "I wonder what ever became of Issabela. She was afterwards sold and I have never seen her since—she must be living somewhere in the world, and perhaps may be suffering but I scarcely think so. I hope not. August 1879."

43. Thomas, Diary, May [17], 27, 1865, EGCT Papers; Burr, ed., *Secret Eye*, May [17], 1865, pp. 267–268; May 27, 1865, p. 270; May 29, 1865, p. 274.

44. On apprenticeship laws and the binding out of children to old owners, see Foner, *Reconstruction*, pp. 201–202, and Barbara Jeanne Fields, *Slavery and Freedom on the Middle Ground: Maryland in the Nineteenth Century* (New Haven, Conn.: Yale University Press, 1985). For freed people's struggles to claim their children and fight apprenticeship laws that emerged to prevent them, see the excellent article by Laura F. Edwards, "'The Marriage Covenant Is at the Foundation of All Our Rights': The Politics of Slave Marriages in North Carolina after Emancipation," *Law and History Review* 14, no. 1 (Spring 1996): 81–124.

45. Burr, ed., *Secret Eye*, May 17, 1865, p. 268; Thomas, Diary, Nov. 2, 1868, EGCT Papers.

46. On expropriated and coerced emotional and maternal labor and the myth of mammy, see Micki McElya, *Clinging to Mammy: The Faithful Slave in Twentieth-Century America* (Cambridge, Mass.: Harvard University Press, 2007), p. 57. On black women's demands for justice against sexual violence, see especially Crystal N. Feimster, "'What If I Am a Woman': Black Women's Campaign for Sexual Justice and Citizenship," in Downs and Masur, eds., *World the Civil War Made*, pp. 249–268.

47. Burr, ed., *Secret Eye*, May 4, 1871, p. 370.

48. See Glymph, *Out of the House of Bondage*, 148, on freed people's efforts to take possession of their bodies, lives, and loved ones in 1865.

49. "An Act to Define the Term 'Persons of Color,'" no. 250, Mar. 17, 1866; "An Act to Prescribe and Regulate the Relation of Husband and Wife between Persons of Color," no. 252, Mar. 9, 1866; "An Act to Prescribe and Regulate the

Relation of Parent and Child among Persons of Color, in This State and for Other Purposes," no. 253, Mar. 9, 1866; "An Act to Alter and Amend the Laws of This State in Relation to Apprentices," no. 3, Mar. 17, 1866, in *Acts of the General Assembly of the State of Georgia*, pp. 239, 240, 6–8.

50. Captain John Emory Bryant's Labor Regulations, June 12, 1865, in Cimbala, *Freedmen's Bureau*, pp. 149–152. The bureau issued circulars such as this laying out guidelines about the binding out of children, insisting on the rights of parents and attempting to exercise oversight, especially in cases involving former owners. For another example, see Circular No. 3, Bureau of Ref. Freedmen and A.L., Office Act. Asst. Com. for State of Georgia, 14 Oct. 1865, vol. 26, pp. 328–330, General Orders, Special Orders, & Circulars Issued, ser. 636, GA Acting Asst. Comr., RG 105 (Records of the Bureau of Refugees, Freedmen, and Abandoned Lands), National Archives [FSSP A-10916].

51. Capt. Geo. R. Walbridge to Col. C. C. Sibley, 19 Feb. 1867, T. R. Littlefield to Lieut Wm F. Martin, 23 Jan. 1867, all filed with M-16 1866, Letters Received, ser. 631, GA Asst. Comr., RG 105 (Records of the Bureau of Refugees, Freedmen, and Abandoned Lands), National Archives [FSSP A-289]; Lt. Wm F. Martins to Hon Simeon Wallace, 18 Feb. 1867, enclosing Capt Geo R Walbridge to Lieut Wm F Martin, 10 Feb. 1867, M-50 1867, Letters Received, ser. 631, GA Asst. Comr., RG 105 (Records of the Bureau of Refugees, Freedmen, and Abandoned Lands), National Archives [FSSP A-296].

52. Laurent DuBois, *A Colony of Citizens: Revolution and Slave Emancipation in the French Caribbean* (Chapel Hill: University of North Carolina Press, 2004); Elizabeth Colwill, "Freedwomen's Familial Politics: Marriage, War and Rites of Registry in Post-Emancipation Saint-Domingue," in *Gender, War, and Politics: The Wars of Revolution and Liberation—Transatlantic Comparisons, 1775–1820*, ed. Karen Hagemann, Gisele Mettele, and Jane Randall (Basingstoke, U.K.: Palgrave Macmillan, 2010), pp. 103–124; Sarah Levine-Gronningsater, "Delivering Freedom: Gradual Emancipation, Black Legal Culture, and the Origins of Sectional Crisis in New York, 1759–1870" (Ph.D. diss., University of Chicago, 2014).

53. George W. Palmer to Capt Sherwood, 10 July 1866, Albert Bethel to Mr G. Palmer, 11 Apr. 1866, copy of endorsement by Brig Genl Davis Tillson, 10 April 1866, all filed as G-197 1866, Registered Letters Received, ser. 3798,

VA Asst. Comr., RG 105 (Records of the Bureau of Refugees, Freedmen, and Abandoned Lands), National Archives [FSSP A-5072]; Albert Bethel to Capt White, 20 Nov. 1866, Unregistered Letters Received, ser. 759, Augusta GA Subasst. Comr., RG 105 (Records of the Bureau of Refugees, Freedmen, and Abandoned Lands), National Archives [FSSP A-5072].

54. Jas. W. Rhew to Mary, 15 July 1866, filed with W-522 1867, Letters Received, ser. 631, GA Asst. Comr., RG 105 (Bureau of Refugees, Freedmen, and Abandoned Lands), National Archives [FSSP A-180].

55. Thomas, Diary, May 7, 1869, EGCT Papers; Lt. Wm F. Martins to Hon Simeon Wallace, 18 Feb. 1867, enclosing Capt Geo R Walbridge to Lieut Wm F Martin, 10 Feb. 1867, M-50 1867, Letters Received, ser. 631, GA Asst. Comr., RG 105 (Records of the Bureau of Refugees, Freedmen, and Abandoned Lands), National Archives [FSSP A-296]; Lt. Wm F. Martins to Captain Eugene Pickett, 26 Dec. 1866, Unregistered Letters Received, ser. 632, GA Asst. Comr., RG 105 (Records of the Bureau of Refugees, Freedmen, and Abandoned Lands), National Archives [FSSP A-5430]; Lt. Wm F. Martins to Captain W. W. Deane, 19 Aug. 1866, Unregistered Letters Received, ser. 632, GA Asst. Comr., RG 105 (Records of the Bureau of Refugees, Freedmen, and Abandoned Lands), National Archives [FSSP A-5430]. Paul Cimbala also notes that bureau officials like Tillson never grasped freed people's conception of family connections and the rights associated with them, including the custody claims of people / kinfolk other than parents. Cimbala, *Freedmen's Bureau*, p. 93.

56. Thomas, Diary, May 7, 1869; May 29, 17, 1865, EGCT Papers.

57. "Secret" as in Burr's "secret eye"—the secret at the heart of the diary. The literature on the sexual exploitation of enslaved women is considerable. For a recent contribution, see Feimster, "'What If I Am a Woman.'"

58. Burr, ed., *Secret Eye*, Jan. 3, 1865, pp. 252–254. On this event, see Stephanie McCurry, "Slavery, Sex, and Sin," *America's Civil War* 26, no. 5 (Nov. 2013): 22–23; Painter, *Southern History across the Color Line*, pp. 70–71; and Painter, "Journal of Ella Gertrude Clanton Thomas," p. 41.

59. See Peggy Pascoe, *What Comes Naturally: Miscegenation Law and the Making of Race in America* (New York: Oxford University Press, 2009), pp. 27–30.

60. For the episode with Lurany, see Burr, ed., *Secret Eye,* Jan. 2, 1859, pp. 167–169. For Thomas's observations about women "more sinned against than sinning," see ibid., Aug. 18, 1856, p. 152. On June 2, 1855, Thomas confessed to things that troubled her but could not be confided even to her diary. Still, she wanted to mark for future reference the "day that it happened . . . one of the most exciting conversations I have ever held. A conversation which in a moment, in flash of the eye will change the gay, thoughtless girl into a woman with all a woman's feelings." Ibid., June 2, 1855, pp. 128–129. On her husband, see ibid., [May] 12, 1856, pp. 147–148, where she expressed the view that there were "noble exceptions" to men's "general depravity," among whom "I class my own husband. I staked my own reputation upon his, and [in] that, perhaps acted rashly but I do not think I did." Highly ambivalent to say the least.

61. Thomas, Diary, Apr. 15, July 4, Aug. 27, 1864, EGCT Papers. The July entry discusses how all households have skeletons in their closets and expresses a desire for a diary with a lock so she could confide "thoughts, doubts, suggestions which present themselves to my mind."

62. Burr, ed., *Secret Eye,* Aug. 27, 1864, pp. 231–232. On the erasure, see ibid., p. 232n24. For Painter's reading, see Painter, *Southern History across the Color Line,* pp. 61–62. In that same entry, Thomas used the exact image she would reach for a few months later in writing her unhappy letter to General Sherman's wife: "It is a bitter cup which my heavenly Father . . . [allowed my] earthly father to press to my lips," she wrote. "I would not drink it, I rebelled. I . . . doubting everything. I was cold and indifferent to spiritual things. I had no faith in God or man."

63. Turner Clanton, Will.

64. This remains an area of unnecessary confusion among historians. Burr and Curry consulted the will but obfuscate for unclear reasons. Painter does not cite the will and may not have consulted it. Burr implies that what Thomas learned in the will was about the extent of her husband's indebtedness to the estate. See Burr, ed., *Secret Eye,* 232n25. Curry says that Gertrude Thomas "never speculated in the diary about who might have been the father of Lurany's children" and distances herself from Painter's conclusion. Curry, *Suffer and Grow Strong,* pp. 66, 123–124, 225n232, 235. Nell Irvin Painter speculates in the absence of evidence that Turner Clanton had "willed to his heirs as property, his own children." See Painter, "Journal of Ella Gertrude Clanton Thomas," p. 30. There is no citation

to the will either there or in the related essay on Thomas in Painter, *Southern History across the Color Line*, pp. 40–92.

65. Turner Clanton, Will. In 1869, Gertrude Thomas had a nightmare about Lurany, "one of our servants . . . in the spirit world." Thomas, Diary, Feb. 21, 1869, EGCT Papers.

66. Du Bois, *Black Reconstruction in America*, pp. 35–36, chap. 3; 1860 US Census, Slave Schedule, Georgia, Richmond County, Augusta City Ward, James J. Thomas, pp. 27–28, Ancestry.com. Nell Irvin Painter makes a much more pointed case about Jefferson Thomas's adultery and mixed-race children. Painter, *Southern History across the Color Line*, pp. 37, 41, 71, 87, 88.

67. Alexis Broderick Neumann analyzes the problem of incest for Thomas, in the Harper's photographs, and in the paternity cases at length in her dissertation, "American Incest: Kinship, Sex, and Commerce in Slavery and Reconstruction" (Ph.D. diss., University of Pennsylvania, 2018). Martha Hodes points out that it was "the problem of the child that brought the illicit liaison into the public realm beyond the confines of gossip and scandal." See Hodes, *White Women, Black Men: Illicit Sex in the 19th-Century South* (New Haven, Conn.: Yale University Press, 1997), p. 48. I explore the paternity cases in McCurry, "Reconstructing Belonging."

68. Some of the best scholarship on this tendency is about World War II. It includes Helen M. Kinsella, *The Image before the Weapon: A Critical History of the Distinction between Combatant and Civilian* (Ithaca, N.Y.: Cornell University Press, 2011); Grossmann, *Jews, Germans and Allies*; Margaret Randolph Higonnet et al., eds., *Behind the Lines: Gender and the Two World Wars* (New Haven, Conn.: Yale University Press, 1987); and Elaine Tyler May, *Homeward Bound: American Families in the Cold War Era* (New York: Basic Books, 1988). See also Elizabeth D. Leonard, *All the Daring of the Soldier: Women of the Civil War Armies* (New York: Norton, 1999).

69. On Thomas's membership in the Ladies' Memorial Association, see Burr, ed., *Secret Eye*, Feb. 3, 1880, pp. 396, 448; Painter, "Journal of Ella Gertrude Clanton Thomas," pp. 16–17; and Curry, *Suffer and Grow Strong*, pp. 169, 193. See Burr, ed., *Secret Eye*, May 1865, p. 261, for Thomas's observation that "rebel is a sacred word now."

70. This is a different emphasis than in Drew Gilpin Faust, *Mothers of Invention: Women of the Slaveholding South in the American Civil War* (Chapel Hill: University of North Carolina Press, 1996).

71. Burr, ed., *Secret Eye,* Jan. 3, 1865, p. 253; Feb. 12, 1865, p. 254; Sept. 20, 1866, p. 285. When Gertrude Thomas heard soon after she wrote the letter that Mrs. Sherman had lost a baby, she was glad she had refrained: by that point, she had learned that she was pregnant again herself.

72. Ibid., May 1, 1865, p. 261.

73. Lieber called it "the massacre in Washington." Lieber to General Henry Halleck, Apr. 15, 22, 1865; Lieber to Charles Sumner, April 15, 1865, Lieber Papers, Huntington Library, San Marino, Calif. (hereafter FLP, HL).

74. Thomas, Diary, May 8, 1865, EGCT Papers; Andrew Johnson, speech at Baltimore, March 20, 1863, in *The Papers of Andrew Johnson,* vol. 6, *1862–1864,* ed. Leroy P. Graf and Ralph W. Haskins (Knoxville: University of Tennessee Press, 1983), p. 177; Perman, *Reunion without Compromise,* pp. 44, 57. See also Carter, *When the War Was Over,* on the failure of "self-reconstruction."

75. Thomas, Diary, May 1, 8, 1865, EGCT Papers; Downs, *After Appomattox.* Johnson did not declare an official end to the war until August 1866.

76. Burr, ed., *Secret Eye,* May 8, 1865, p. 264; Oct. 22, 1868, p. 293; Johnson, "Amnesty Proclamation"; Thomas, Diary, Oct. 8, May 1, 1865, EGCT Papers. On Johnson's policies in spring and summer 1865, see Eric L. McKitrick, *Andrew Johnson and Reconstruction* (1960; reprint, New York: Oxford University Press, 1988); Perman, *Reunion without Compromise;* and William A. Blair, *With Malice toward Some: Treason and Loyalty in the Civil War Era* (Chapel Hill: University of North Carolina Press, 2014).

77. Lord Edward Henry Stanley quoted in Brooks T. Swett, "Reconstruction Refracted: British Statesmen and American Democratic Politics, 1865–1868," unpublished paper in author's possession. On the extreme contingency of the period, see Roark, *Masters without Slaves,* p. 206 and throughout, and Carter, *When the War Was Over,* chap. 1. On the redefinition of property, including new laws creating substrata mining rights, see Emma Teitelman, "Governing the Peripheries: The Social Reconstruction of the South and West after the American Civil War" (Ph.D. diss., University of Pennsylvania, 2018), chap. 4.

78. Jerome Blum, *The End of the Old Order in Rural Europe* (Princeton, N.J.: Princeton University Press, 1978); Barrington Moore, Jr., *Social Origins of Dictatorship and Democracy: Lord and Peasant in the Making of the Modern World*, trans. Patrick Camiller (Boston: Beacon Press, 1966). Jürgen Osterhammel discusses the "process of peasant emancipation" in *The Transformation of the World: A Global History of the Nineteenth Century* (Princeton, N.J.: Princeton University Press, 2009), pp. 703–706.

79. See Du Bois, *Black Reconstruction in America*; Foner, *Reconstruction*; and Hahn, *A Nation under Our Feet*. On Georgia, see Paul Cimbala, *Under the Guardianship of the Nation: The Freedmen's Bureau and the Reconstruction of Georgia, 1865–1870* (Athens: University of Georgia Press, 1997). Allen W. Trelease, *White Terror: The Ku Klux Klan Conspiracy and Southern Reconstruction* (New York: Harper and Row, 1971), remains an important account.

80. Hahn, "Class and State in Post-Emancipation Societies." The debate on the continuity of planters as a class is huge, but key entries include C. Vann Woodward, *Origins of the New South* (1951; reprint, Baton Rouge: Louisiana State University Press, 1971), and Jonathan M. Wiener, *Social Origins of the New South: Alabama, 1860–1885* (Baton Rouge: Louisiana State University Press, 1978). On the persistence of the planter class in Georgia, see the division of opinion between Wynne, *Continuity of Cotton*, and Numan V. Bartley, *The Creation of Modern Georgia* (Athens: University of Georgia Press, 1983).

81. Coclanis, "The American Civil War and Its Aftermath," notes the greater emphasis on uncertainty in recent economic history literature but makes clear that the "basic outlines" of postwar economic history (especially on matters of land, labor, and credit) remain much as they were left in the 1980s by Roger L. Ransom and Richard Sutch, *One Kind of Freedom: The Economic Consequences of Emancipation* (Cambridge: Cambridge University Press, 1977), and Harold Woodman, *King Cotton and His Retainers: Financing and Marketing the Cotton Crop of the South, 1800–1925* (Lexington: University of Kentucky Press, 1968).

82. Special Field Order No. 15, in *Freedom: A Documentary History of Emancipation, 1861–1867*, ser. 1, vol. 3, *The Wartime Genesis of Free Labor: The Lower South*, ed. Ira Berlin, Thavolia Glymph, Steven F. Miller, Joseph P. Reidy, Leslie S. Rowland, and Julie Saville (New York: Cambridge University Press, 1990), doc. 59,

pp. 338–340. The estimate of land in bureau hands is from Claude F. Oubre, *Forty Acres and a Mule: The Freedmen's Bureau and Black Land Ownership* (Baton Rouge: Louisiana State University, 1978), p. 37. On the land question the literature is huge, but see Hahn et al., eds., *Land and Labor, 1865*, chap. 4; Foner, *Reconstruction*, chaps. 2–4; Julie Saville, *The Work of Reconstruction: From Slave to Wage Laborer in South Carolina, 1860–1870* (Cambridge: Cambridge University Press, 1994), chap. 3; and Cimbala, *Under the Guardianship of the Nation*, chap. 7.

83. John Berkley Grimball, Diary, Nov. 15, 18, 1865, Jan. 25, 1866, Apr. 3, 1867; Foner, *Reconstruction*, pp. 68, 235–237, 245–246, 309–310, 316; Hahn et al., eds., *Land and Labor, 1865*, chap. 4.

84. In September 1865, President Johnson ordered Freedmen's Bureau commissioner Oliver O. Howard to return land to pardoned owners. See Circular No. 15, in Hahn et al., eds., *Land and Labor, 1865*, doc. 103, pp. 431–433. On congressional debates, see Foner, *Reconstruction*, chap. 6, and Cimbala, *Under the Guardianship of the Nation*, chap. 7.

85. Thomas, Diary, Oct. 9, 1866, EGCT Papers.

86. Lieber to Henry Halleck, May 19, 1866, box 28, FLP, HL. The key directive was Circular No. 15, issued in September 1865. See Circular No. 15, in Hahn et al., eds., *Land and Labor, 1865*, doc. 103, pp. 431–433. For numbers of pardons, see Foner, *Reconstruction*, pp. 190–191. On pardons, see McKitrick, *Andrew Johnson and Reconstruction*, pp. 145–150, and Perman, *Reunion without Compromise*, pp. 122–131.

87. I could find no pardon application for J. Jefferson Thomas or Gertrude Thomas in the records, although I did find one for his brother J. Pinckney Thomas. Jefferson Thomas appears on a list of registered voters in 1867, which confirms that he had received a pardon. "Returns of Qualified Voters under the Reconstruction Act of 1867, Richmond County, Georgia Governor's Office, Georgia Archives," Ancestry.com.

88. John Berkley Grimball, Diary, Dec. 27, 1865; J. B. Grimball to John Grimball, Jan. 9, 1866, box 1, folder 6, Grimball Family Papers, South Carolina Historical Society (SCHS), Charleston.

89. *Acts of the General Assembly of the State of Georgia*, no. 255, pp. 241–243. On land values, see Ransom and Sutch, *One Kind of Freedom*, p. 51; Wynne, *Continuity of Cotton*, p. 19; and Hahn, *The Roots of Southern Populism: Yeoman Farmers and the*

Transformation of the Georgia Upcountry, 1850–1890 (New York: Oxford University Press, 1983), p. 138.

90. Burr, ed., *Secret Eye*, Apr. 11 [10], 1855, p. 122.

91. Jones and Cheves quoted in Cimbala, *Under the Guardianship of the Nation*, pp. 133, 184; J. B. Grimball to John Grimball, Feb. 5, Oct. 30, 1866, box 1, folder 6, Grimball Family Papers, SCHS. On freed people's vision of an independent future, see especially Saville, *Work of Reconstruction*; Foner, *Reconstruction*; and Steven Hahn, "'Extravagant Expectations of Freedom': Rumour, Political Struggle, and the Christmas Insurrection Scare of 1865 in the American South," *Past and Present* 157, no. 1 (Nov. 1997): 122–158. Paul Cimbala describes the communal approach to labor and aspirations to economic independence in woodworking, hunting, and fishing economies adopted by freed people on islands in Sherman's Reserve. Cimbala, *Under the Guardianship of the Nation*, chap. 7.

92. For Bryant's reputation as a radical on Reconstruction matters, see Cimbala, *Freedmen's Bureau*, p. 149; however, Cimbala also calls him "Saxton's more moderate Augusta agent." See *Under the Guardianship of the Nation*, p. 51. On Bryant, see Ruth Currie-McDaniel, *Carpetbagger of Conscience: A Biography of John Emory Bryant* (Athens: University of Georgia Press, 1987).

93. Bryant's Circular, dated June 12, 1865, and first published in the Macon *Daily Telegraph*, is reproduced in Cimbala, *Freedmen's Bureau*, pp. 149–152. On contract freedom, see Amy Dru Stanley, *From Bondage to Contract: Wage Labor, Marriage, and the Market in the Age of Slave Emancipation* (Cambridge: Cambridge University Press, 1998), and on free-labor ideology and its contradictions, see especially Foner, *Reconstruction*, chap. 4, and Cimbala, *Freedmen's Bureau*, p. 13.

94. Bryant's Circular; Cimbala, *Freedmen's Bureau*, pp. 64–67.

95. Cimbala, *Under the Guardianship of the Nation*, p. 4.

96. Summary of letter from Thomas J. Jefferson, 11 Jan. 1866, vol. 1, p. 474, Registers of Letters Received, ser. 630, GA Acting Asst. Comr., RG 105 (Bureau of Refugees, Freedmen, and Abandoned Lands), National Archives [FSSP A-5061]; Endorsement by J. E. Bryant, 18 Jan. 1866, on communication from Jacob. R. Davis, vol. 20, pp. 67–68, Endorsements Sent, ser. 628, GA Acting Asst. Comr., RG 105 (Bureau of Refugees, Freedmen, and Abandoned Lands), National Archives [FSSP A-5061]; J E Bryant to Bvt Maj S. Willard Saxton, 4 Aug. 1865 B-6 1865, Registered Letters Received, ser. 2922, SC Asst. Comr.,

RG 105 (Bureau of Refugees, Freedmen, and Abandoned Lands), National Archives, [FSSP A-5289]. The term "swindled" was used in Jacob R. Davis to [W. L. White], 30 Nov. 1866, vol. 146, p. 37, Registers of Letters Received, ser. 756, August GA Subasst. Comr., RG 105 (Bureau of Refugees, Freedmen, and Abandoned Lands), National Archives, [FSSP A-5728]. Bryant's court was shut down by orders of Commissioner O. O. Howard; see Cimbala, *Under the Guardianship of the Nation*, and Currie-McDaniel, *Carpetbagger of Conscience*, p. 53. On the bureau's ad hoc courts, see Cimbala, *Under the Guardianship of the Nation*, p. 27.

97. Affidavit of Milly Hopkins, 5 Sept. 1865, and affidavit of Reef Velard, 17 Nov. 1865, both in Affidavits and Other Papers Relating to Freedmen's Complaints, ser. 764, Augusta GA Subasst. Comr., RG 105 (Bureau of Refugees, Freedmen, and Abandoned Lands), National Archives [FSSP A-5735]; A C Walker to Gen D Tilson, 24 Nov. 1865, Unregistered Letters Received, ser. 632, GA Asst. Comr., RG 105 (Bureau of Refugees, Freedmen, and Abandoned Lands), National Archives [FSSP A-5283].

98. Affidavit of Elick, 23 Dec. 1865, and affidavit of Isarael Kelley, 6 Jan. 1866, both in Affidavits and Other Papers Relating to Freedmen's Complaints, ser. 764, Augusta GA Subasst. Comr., RG 105 (Bureau of Refugees, Freedmen, and Abandoned Lands), National Archives [FSSP A-5735]; Affidavit of Mary Ann Walker, 14 Mar. 1866, filed with miscellaneous papers, Affidavits and Other Papers Relating to Freedmen's Complaints, ser. 764, Augusta GA Subasst. Comr., RG 105 (Bureau of Refugees, Freedmen, and Abandoned Lands), National Archives [FSSP A-5046]; Affidavit of Giles Drake, 18 Dec. 1865, Affidavits and Other Papers Relating to Freedmen's Complaints, ser. 764, Augusta GA Subasst. Comr., RG 105 (Bureau of Refugees, Freedmen, and Abandoned Lands), National Archives, [FSSP A-5739]. For the threats on Bryant and the broader context, see Cimbala, *Under the Guardianship of the Nation*, p. 75, chap. 6.

99. Brig. Gen. Davis Tillson to General O. O. Howard, 19 Mar. 1866, F-35, Letters Received, ser. 1711, Dept. of GA, RG 393 Pt. I (Records of U.S. Army Continental Commands), National Archives [FSSP C-4008]; Tillson quoted in Cimbala, *Freedmen's Bureau*, pp. 17, 92. Tillson's request coincided with the drawdown of the armed forces in the occupied South. Gregory Downs notes that "the most striking changes were in Georgia," where the number of military posts

fell from seventy-five in September 1865 to fourteen in January 1866. See Downs, *After Appomattox*, p. 107.

100. It was a common necessity in a place with few bailiffs and local law officers so unreconstructed the bureau could not call on them. On using freed people as "bailiffs," see Cimbala, *Under the Guardianship of the Nation*, p. 66.

101. Thomas, Diary, July 22, Oct. 8, 1865; Sept. 20, 1866, EGCT Papers.

102. Burr, ed., *Secret Eye*, Dec. 31, 1865, pp. 278–279.

103. According to Lawrence Powell, the average per capita circulation of currency was $1.70 in the South and $33.30 in New England. See Powell, *New Masters: Northern Planters during the Civil War and Reconstruction* (New York: Fordham University Press, 1998), p. 37. On the rising value of debt, see Richard Bensell, *The Political Economy of American Industrialization* (Cambridge: Cambridge University Press, 2000). On the new credit relations and arrangements, see Ransom and Sutch, *One Kind of Freedom*; Woodman, *King Cotton and His Retainers*; Woodman, "The Decline of Cotton Factorage after the Civil War," *American Historical Review* 71, no. 4 (July 1966): 1219–1220; and Woodman, *New South, New Law: The Legal Foundations of Credit and Labor Relations in the Postbellum Agricultural South* (Baton Rouge: Louisiana State University Press, 1995).

104. On the organization to promote labor immigration, see *Daily Constitutionalist* (Augusta, Ga.), Apr. 4, 1866. On the formation of the Agricultural Society, see *Augusta [Ga.] Chronicle*, Sept. 19, 1866. For an advertisement of Belmont for rent, see *Daily Constitutionalist*, Jan. 22, 1867. On the founding of Mosher, Thomas & Straub, see Burr, ed., *Secret Eye*, October 12, 1866, p. 287, and advertisements for the company in *Augusta Chronicle*, Apr. 12, 1866. On the dissolution of the partnership, see *Daily Constitutionalist*, May 7, 1869. On planters seeking alternative sources of labor, including abroad, see Roark, *Masters without Slaves*, pp. 165–168. On land-holding patterns and the move to sharecropping in Georgia, see Wynne, *Continuity of Cotton*, pp. 17–28, and Cimbala, *Under the Guardianship of the Nation*, p. 153.

105. Voter Counts: District No. 17 (Burke County), 813 White, 2,508 "Colored" voters; District No. 29 (Columbia County), 603 White 1,780 "Colored." The figures reported for the Georgia Third Military District are white, 95, 214, and "Colored," 93, 433. See Third Military District, Letters Received, box 5, 5782 [series] 1867–1868, Nov. 19, 1867, RG 393, Pt. I (Records of U.S. Army Continental Commands, 1821–1920) National Archives [FSSP

SS-693]. Bartley reports slightly different numbers of voters registered. Bartley, *Creation of Modern Georgia*, p. 48.

106. Before Congress passed the Military Reconstruction Acts, Georgia freed people petitioned Congress for the right to vote. See Petition of colored people in Geo for elective franchise, mid-Dec. 1865, 39A-H14.2, House Committee on the Judiciary, Petitions & Memorials, ser. 493, 39th Congress, RG 233 (Records of the United States House of Representatives), National Archives [FSSP D-26]. On Sam Drayton, see "List of Reliable Freedmen of Augusta GA," n.d. [Oct. 1865–Apr. 1867], Register of Complaints, ser. 763, vol. 167, Augusta GA Subasst. Comr., RG 105 (Bureau of Refugees, Freedmen, and Abandoned Lands), National Archives. In 1855, Gertrude Thomas had described Drayton as "one of the most intelligent Negroes I have ever met with" and noted his "decidedly fine command of language." Burr, ed., *Secret Eye*, April 11 [10], 1855, p. 121.

107. On freed people's participation in political clubs and formation of militias in Georgia, see Cimbala, *Under the Guardianship of the Nation*, pp. 113, 209; Bartley, *Creation of Modern Georgia*, p. 51; and Wm. Hale to Lieut. W F Martin, 20 Mar. 1867, H-73 1867, Letters Received, ser. 758, Augusta GA Subasst. Comr., RG 105 (Bureau of Refugees, Freedmen, and Abandoned Lands), National Archives [FSSP A-236]. The case went to the attorney general. George M. Hood to Hon Henry Stanbery, 20 June 1867, Letters Received: GA Private Citizens, Attorney General's Records, RG 60 (General Records of the Department of Justice), National Archives [FSSP W-11].

108. Mayor John Foster to Capt Dean, 29 Aug. 1866, Unregistered Letters Received, ser. 632, GA Asst. Comr., RG 104 (Records of the Bureau of Refugees, Freedmen, and Abandoned Lands), National Archives [FSSP A-5380]; General Tillson made a public statement in December 1865 that "All Men, without distinction of color, have the right to keep arms to defend their homes, families or themselves." Cimbala, *Freedmen's Bureau*, p. 92. Evidence that black militia companies were subsequently disarmed includes a Captain Lanum and four others, Petition from a company of colored militia to General Pope, 7 June 1867, H-26 1867, Letters Received, ser. 5738, 3rd Military Dist., RG 393 Pt. I (Records of U.S. Army Continental Commands, 1821–1920), National Archives [FSSP SS-508]. On Camilla, see the report of Capt. Wm Mills to Bvt Brig Genl R. C. Drum, 29 Sept. 1868, Miscellaneous Records, ser. 5757, 3rd Military

Dist., RG 393 Pt. I (Records of U.S. Army Continental Commands, 1821–1920), National Archives [FSSP SS-580]; Foner, *Reconstruction*, p. 342; Cimbala, *Under the Guardianship of the Nation*, p. 204; Trelease, *White Terror*, p. 117; and Lee W. Formwalt, "The Camilla Massacre of 1868: Racial Violence as Political Propaganda," *Georgia Historical Quarterly* 71, no. 3 (Fall 1987): 399–426.

109. Bartley, *Creation of Modern Georgia*, chaps. 3–4. The first election, in October 1867, was for representatives to a state constitutional convention, and the second, in April 1868, was to ratify the constitution and elect a governor and state legislators. On the Reconstruction government and constitutions in Georgia, see Du Bois, *Black Reconstruction in America*, pp. 487–525.

110. Foster Blodgett to Colonel J. F. Meline, Apr. 26, 1868, Letters Received, 3rd Military District, RG 393 Pt. I (Records of U.S. Army Continental Commands, 1821–1920), National Archives [FSSP SS-705].

111. Trelease, *White Terror*, pp. 118, 419–420. On political violence in Georgia, see also Downs, *After Appomattox*, and Emberton, *Beyond Redemption.*

112. Burr, ed., *Secret Eye*, Nov. 1, 1868, pp. 293–296.

113. Ibid.; Trelease, *White Terror*, p. 118; Thomas, Diary, Nov. 2, 1868, EGCT Papers.

114. Thomas, Diary, Nov. 3, 1868, EGCT Papers.

115. Compare the published diary entries in Burr, ed., *Secret Eye*, Nov. 2, 1868, pp. 296–298, and Nov. 3, 1868, pp. 298–300, with the fuller entries in Thomas, Diary, EGCT Papers. For the rumors about her brother's membership in the Klan, see Thomas, Diary, Dec. 30, 1870, EGCT Papers, and compare to the published version, which omits that section of the entry, in Burr, ed., *Secret Eye*, Dec. 30, 1870, pp. 354–356.

116. Trelease, *White Terror*, pp. xlvii, 73, 68, 117–118.

117. Burr, ed., *Secret Eye*, Nov. 1, 1868, p. 296; Nov. 3, 1868, pp. 298–300; Trelease, *White Terror*, pp. 118–119. Also see Wynne, *Continuity of Cotton*, p. 53, and Bartley, *Creation of Modern Georgia*, p. 59.

118. Burr, ed., *Secret Eye*, Nov. 1, 1868, p. 296; Oct. 8, 1865, pp. 276–277; Nov. 3, 1868, p. 298.

119. Diary, Nov. 2, 1868, EGCT Papers, Duke University. Note that this was the entry from Nov. 2 that Burr included in the published diary. See Burr, ed., *Secret Eye*, Nov. 2, 1868, pp. 296–298.

120. On political powerlessness, see Hahn, "Class and State in Post-Emancipation Societies." On the global reordering of capital flows, see Woodman, *King Cotton and His Retainers.*

121. Thomas, Diary, Aug. 1, 1870; Dec. 4, 1868; Dec. 5, Nov. 29, 1870, EGCT Papers.

122. Ibid., Aug. 1, 1870. This was of course true for black women as well. The terms of emancipation addressed in Chapter 2 only begin to suggest the importance of gender for freedwomen in the postwar order.

123. Ibid., Dec. 21, 4, 1868; Mar. 9, 1871; Curry, *Suffer and Grow Strong*, pp. 125–126, 130–131, 135–136, 141–142, 190–191.

124. Here I am building on ideas in Grossmann, *Jews, Germans, and Allies*, chap. 5.

125. Burr, ed., *Secret Eye*, Nov. 29 [30], 1868, pp. 299–300. For public notices of bankruptcy and sheriff's sale, see *Daily Constitutionalist*, May 7, 1869, and *Augusta Chronicle*, July 7, 1879.

126. *Acts of the General Assembly of the State of Georgia*, pp. 146–147; Constitution of 1868, art. 7, secs. 1–2, in John L. Conley, *The Constitution of the State of Georgia* (Atlanta: New Era Steam, 1870), p. 41. For the ensuing legal struggle over these stay laws, see Henri H. Freeman, "Some Aspects of Debtor Relief in Georgia during Reconstruction" (M.A. thesis, Emory University, 1951), and Joseph A. Ranney, *In the Wake of Slavery: Civil War, Civil Rights, and the Reconstruction of Southern Law* (Westport, Conn.: Greenwood, 2006), pp. 92–97.

127. Burr, ed., *Secret Eye*, June 19, 1869, p. 319.

128. The laws passed, Suzanne D. Lebsock insisted, *because* "they had nothing to do with feminism." Lebsock, "Radical Reconstruction and the Property Rights of Southern Women," *Journal of Southern History* 43, no. 2 (May 1977): 195–216, especially 209, 201, 197 (quotations). See also Carole Shammas, "Re-Assessing the Married Women's Property Acts," *Journal of Women's History* 6, no. 1 (Spring 1994): 10. For a very smart analysis of an earlier married women's property act (in Florida) designed to undergird a colonial settler society and displace Native peoples from control of their land, see Laurel Clark Shire, *The Threshold of Manifest Destiny: Gender and National Expansion in Florida* (Philadelphia: University of Pennsylvania Press, 2016), and Shire, "The Rights of a Florida Wife: Slavery, U.S. Expansion and Married Women's Property Law," *Journal of Women's History* 2, no 2 (Summer 2007): 39–63.

129. Burr, ed., *Secret Eye,* Dec. 14, 1870, p. 351; Jan. 10, 1870, p. 327; Thomas, Diary, "Wednesday Night" December 1870, EGCT Papers.

130. Reva B. Siegel, "The Modernization of Marital Status Law: Adjudicating Wives' Rights to Earnings, 1860–1930," *Georgetown Law Journal* 82, no. 7 (Sept. 1994): 2127–2130 and throughout.

131. See Burr, ed., *Secret Eye,* Aug. 1, 1870, pp. 333–334, and Thomas, Diary, Mar. 18, 1871, EGCT Papers, for two of many examples of Thomas's changed opinion of her husband.

132. Thomas, Diary, Dec. 4, 1868; May 3, 14, 1869 (China business), Nov. 1, 1870 (sheriff's sale announcement); cover of vol. 1870–1871; Nov. 29, 1870; Jan. 8, 1871 (Burke plantations); Dec. 5, 1870; Feb. 17, 1871; Mar. 6, 1870 (town home); Feb. 8, 1879 (Columbia plantation); May 3, 1879; Aug. 1, 1870; Jan. 9, 1870; Dec. 12, 1879, EGCT Papers.

133. Ibid., May 28, 1871; Burr, ed., *Secret Eye,* Dec. 31, 1878, p. 377. For Burr's discussion of the gap in the diary, see Burr, ed., *Secret Eye,* p. 374. For rumors that Thomas's daughter Cora destroyed it, see Curry, *Suffer and Grow Strong,* pp. 135, 226n253.

134. On the farm, see Burr, ed., *Secret Eye,* Jan. 4, 1879, pp. 378–379. On what her wages were used for, including taxes and Jefferson Thomas's payment of "the hands," see ibid., May 7, 1870, pp. 382–383; June 23, 1880, pp. 404–406.

135. Ibid., May 15, 1880, pp. 402–403; June 23, 1880, p. 405; Jan. 2, 1880, p. 392.

136. Ibid., Oct.1, 1880, pp. 410–412; Oct. 6, 1882, p. 430; Jan. 5, 1881, pp. 417–420; Feb. 8, 1879, pp. 379–381. On the move to Atlanta, see Burr, ed., *Secret Eye,* pp. 451–452, and Curry, *Suffer and Grow Strong,* p. 174.

137. Woodman, *King Cotton and His Retainers,* pp. 245–333, 297, 311 (quotations). On the new bourgeois merchant-planter class, see Woodward, *Origins of the New South.* For a new, quite idiosyncratic critique of Woodman and analysis of merchant capital in the postwar South, see Scott P. Marler, *The Merchants' Capital: New Orleans and the Political Economy of the Nineteenth-Century South* (New York: Cambridge University Press, 2013).

138. Burr, ed., *Secret Eye,* June 23, 1880, p. 405; Feb. 8, 1879, p. 380; Du Bois, *Black Reconstruction in America,* p. 54. Thomas routinely paid 20 percent on his loans from Stark. See Burr, ed., *Secret Eye,* Dec. 12, 1870, p. 348.

139. Curry, *Suffer and Grow Strong*, pp. 190–192.

140. Burr, ed., *Secret Eye*, Oct. 12, 1866, p. 287; Dec. 14, 1870, pp. 351–352; May 4, 1869, pp. 311–312; Nov. 29, 1870, pp. 341–342.

141. Ibid., Feb 3, 1880, pp. 395–396; June 28, 1880, p. 406.

142. Thomas, Diary, Jan. 10, 1870; May 3, 1869; Nov. 29, 1870; Apr. 2, 1871; Dec. 5, 1870; Mar. 18, 1871, EGCT Papers.

143. Ibid., "Wednesday Night" December 1870; Dec. 14, Jan. 10, 1870, EGCT Papers.

144. Burr, ed., *Secret Eye*, June 19, 1869, pp. 317–319; Jan. 10, 1870, p. 326; Dec. 5, 1870, pp. 343–347.

145. Thomas, Diary, Jan. 10, Dec. 4, 1870; June 19, Feb. 7, May 3, 1869; Jan. 9, 1870, EGCT Papers.

146. Burr, ed., *Secret Eye*, Nov. 2, 1868, pp. 297–298; Jan. 1, 1879, p. 378; Sept. 5, 1882, pp. 424, 449–450, 452–454; Painter, *Southern History across the Color Line*, pp. 40, 52–53, 63–69, 205n1, 217n171; Curry, *Suffer and Grow Strong*, chap. 10. On the women's suffrage movement in the South, see Marjorie Spruill Wheeler, *New Women of the New South: The Leaders of the Woman Suffrage Movement in the Southern States* (New York: Oxford University Press, 1993). On racism and the white women's movement, see Louise Newman, *White Women's Rights: The Racial Origins of Feminism in the United States* (New York: Oxford University Press, 1999).

147. Burr, ed., *Secret Eye*, Dec. 5, 1870, p. 345.

148. Ibid., Dec. 21, 1868, p. 302; June 19, 1869, pp. 317–318; Dec. 12, 1879, pp. 387–388. On privy exams, see Stacy Lorraine Braukman and Michael A. Ross, "Married Women's Property and Male Coercion: United States' Courts and the Privy Examination, 1864–1887," *Journal of Women's History* 12, no. 2 (Summer 2000): 57–80.

149. Meta Morris Grimball, Diary, Feb. 20, 1866, Mar. 21, 1867, SHC; John Berkley Grimball, Diary, Nov. 27, Dec 31, 1866, SHC; John Berkley Grimball and Margaret Ann Grimball, deed of trust with Berkley Grimball and John Grimball, Apr. 11, 1867, box 1; John Berkley Grimball to John Grimball, Oct. 30, 1866, box 1; Berkley Grimball to John Grimball, Feb. 11, 1862, box 2, Grimball Family Papers, SCHS.

150. Curry, *Suffer and Grow Strong*, p. 131.

151. Burr, ed., *Secret Eye*, Feb. 12, 1865, pp. 254–256; Oct. 14, 1865, pp. 277–278, 288; Nov. 30, 1870, pp. 342–343; Curry, *Suffer and Grow Strong*, pp. 101, 133, 137.

152. As explained in Grossmann, *Jews, Germans and Allies*, chap. 5.

153. Burr, ed., *Secret Eye*, Nov. 16, 1879, p. 386; Dec. 17, 1879, p. 389; Dec. 18, 1879, p. 390; Feb. 2, 1880, p. 394; Sept. 22, 1882, p. 425; May 19, 1880, p. 404; Jan. 2, 1880, p. 392; May 4, 1869, p. 311; Thomas, Diary, Sept. 2, 1880, EGCT Papers.

154. Burr, ed., *Secret Eye*, Jan. 10, 1870, pp. 326–328; Thomas, Diary, Mar. 9, 1871, EGCT Papers.

155. Burr, ed., *Secret Eye*, June 26, 1869, pp. 320–322. On reconstructing ideas of race, among a large literature, see for example Hannah Rosen, "The Rhetoric of Miscegenation and the Reconstruction of Race: Debating Marriage, Sex, and Citizenship in Postemancipation Arkansas," in *Gender and Slave Emancipation in the Atlantic World*, ed. Pamela Scully and Diana Paton (Durham, N.C.: Duke University Press, 2005), pp. 289–309, and Rosen, *Terror in the Heart of Freedom: Citizenship, Sexual Violence, and the Meaning of Race in the Postemancipation South* (Chapel Hill: University of North Carolina Press, 2009).

156. Du Bois, *Black Reconstruction in America*, p. 320.

157. Fields and Fields, *Racecraft*, especially chaps. 1, 4, p. 11 (quotation). Kidada Williams has recently pointed out that the archive itself has been shaped by the explicitly political focus of the charge issued in congressional investigations into the Ku Klux Klan and political violence against African American voters. See Kidada E. Williams, *They Left Great Marks on Me: African American Testimonies of Racial Violence from Emancipation to World War I* (New York: New York University Press, 2012), and Williams, "The Wounds That Cried Out: Reckoning with African Americans' Testimonies of Trauma and Suffering from Night Riding," in Downs and Masur, eds., *The World the Civil War Made*, pp. 159–182. For the widespread emphasis on the political causes of racial violence, see Rosen, *Terror in the Heart of Freedom;* Martha Hodes, "Sexualization of Reconstruction Politics: White Women and Black Men in the South after the Civil War," *Journal of the History of Sexuality* 3 (1993): 402–417; Foner, *Reconstruction;* Hahn, *A Nation under Our Feet;* and Trelease, *White Terror.*

158. Burr, ed., *Secret Eye*, Mar. 7, 1869, p. 309; Jan.10, 1870, p. 328; Nov. 30, 1870, p. 343; Dec. 17, 1879, p. 388n7; Oct. 3, 1882, p. 429.

159. Ibid., May 4, 1869, pp. 311–312; Nov. 13, 1870, pp. 339–340; Apr. 10, 1871, pp. 366–367; Nov. 30, 1870, pp. 342–343; Thomas, Diary, Dec. 19, 1870, EGCT Papers. Turner rode with spurs "formed of a portion of the band around the first shot which was fired at Fort Sumter." Burr, ed., *Secret Eye*, Nov. 13, 1870, p. 339. On rituals of subordination and deference, see Fields and Fields, *Racecraft*, p. 35.

160. Burr, ed., *Secret Eye*, June 26, 1869, pp. 320–321.

161. Thomas, Diary, June 26, 1869, EGCT Papers. Note the double meaning of "bright" in this entry, both as a racial category referring to light-skinned people of African descent and as a synonym for intelligence. On "bright" as a phenotype deployed in advertisements for slave sales, see Walter Johnson, *Soul by Soul: Life Inside the Antebellum Slave Market* (Cambridge, Mass.: Harvard University Press, 1999), pp. 113, 139, 157, 159.

162. Thomas, Diary, May 7, 14, 1869; July 30, 1870, EGCT Papers; Burr, ed., *Secret Eye*, June 19, 1869, pp. 318–319; Jan. 13, 1869, pp. 328–329.

163. Pascoe, *What Comes Naturally*, pp. 1–2, 17–74, 2, 45 (quotations). It is interesting to note that Pascoe misses the fear of past sexual mixing that hung over marriage law in the postwar South and which explains the analogy between miscegenation and incest evident in the law. See ibid., p. 72. For the Georgia Constitution of 1865, see *Journal of the Proceedings of the Convention of the People of Georgia, Held in Milledgeville in October and November 1865, Together with the Ordinances and Resolutions Adopted* (Milledgeville, Ga.: R. M. Orme and Sons, 1865), art. V, sec. 9, p. 226. For the constitution of 1868, see *Journal of the Proceedings of the Constitutional Convention of the People of Georgia* (Augusta, Ga.: E. H. Pughe, 1868). For the laws relating to marriage and divorce passed by the Georgia legislature in 1866, see Circular No. 5, Bureau of Ref. Freedmen and A.L., Office Act. Asst. Com. For State of Georgia, 7 April 1866, vol. 26, pp. 338–342, General Orders, Special Orders, & Circulars Issued, ser. 636, GA Acting Asst. Comr., RG 105 (Records of the Bureau of Refugees, Freedmen, And Abandoned Lands), National Archives [FSSP A-10919]. On the progressive constitutions of the Republican regimes, see Du Bois, *Black Reconstruction in America*, chaps. 10–13.

164. Thomas, Diary, July 30, 1870; May 7, 1869, EGCT Papers.

165. Painter, *Southern History across the Color Line*, p. 73.

166. Thomas, Diary, May 7, 1869, EGCT Papers. There are many other examples of her focus on black women's sexuality, but see, for example, Burr, ed., *Secret Eye*, Jan. 3, 1865, p. 253 (about a "good looking mulatto girl" traveling with General Kilpatrick and "lolling indolently in a rocking chair").

167. Thomas, Diary, June 26, 1869, EGCT Papers.

168. Ibid., May 7, June 26, 1869; Burr, ed., *Secret Eye*, [May] 12, 1856, pp. 147–148 ("depravity of man"). Painter reads the entry literally, as an example of the "leakages" and "deception clues" that indicate the secrets of the diary and Thomas's knowledge of "her husband's outside child." Jefferson Thomas, Painter concludes, had been involved in a relationship with a formerly enslaved woman dating back to the 1850s; Gertrude lived in an essentially "polygamous" marriage, and, in 1869, her son thus in fact labored beside his half-brother in the fields. Painter admits the evidence is far from conclusive. See Painter, *Southern History across the Color Line*, pp. 77–79, 82–89, 78, 83, 88 (quotations), and Curry, *Suffer and Grow Strong*, pp. 206–207. The editor of Thomas's diary, Virginia Burr, adheres to the same view as Curry.

169. See Sarah Haley, *No Mercy Here: Gender, Punishment and the Making of Jim Crow Modernity* (Chapel Hill: University of North Carolina Press, 2016). The black female body with which Thomas is obsessed is not the monstrous one on which Haley mostly focuses, but the seductive "mulatto" one that also fits in a long, dangerous history. On gender, sexuality, and the Jim Crow order, see also Glenda Gilmore, *Gender and Jim Crow: Women and the Politics of White Supremacy in North Carolina* (Chapel Hill: University of North Carolina Press, 1996), and Crystal N. Feimster, *Southern Horrors: Women and the Politics of Rape and Lynching* (Cambridge, Mass.: Harvard University Press, 2009).

170. Recent work on women in Reconstruction focuses more on black women as victims of sexual violence and on their efforts to achieve justice than on white women as perpetrators. See Rosen, *Terror in the Heart of Freedom*; Williams, *They Left Great Marks on Me*; and Feimster, "'What If I Am a Woman.'" A recent book on the Reconstruction Klan lacks even an index entry for "women." See Elaine Franz Parsons, *Ku-Klux: The Birth of the Klan during Reconstruction* (Chapel Hill: University of North Carolina Press, 2015).

171. Burr, ed., *Secret Eye*, pp. 448–453.

172. On this, see above all Saidiya Hartman, *Scenes of Subjection: Terror, Slavery, and Self-Making in Nineteenth-Century America* (New York: Oxford University Press, 1997).

173. In this context I think above all of Robert Paxton, *Vichy France: Old Guard and New Order, 1940–1944* (New York: Knopf, 1972).

Epilogue

1. Svetlana Alexievich, *The Unwomanly Face of War: An Oral History of Women in World War II*, trans. R. Pevear and L. Volokhonsky (New York: Random House, 2017), p. xxi.

2. Mary Beard, *Women and Power: A Manifesto* (New York: Liveright, 2017), p. **33**; Ranajit Guha, "The Small Voices of History," in *Subaltern Studies*, vol. 9, ed. Shahid Amin and Dipesh Chakrabarty (Oxford: Oxford University Press, 1996), p. 12. On silencing, see Michel-Rolph Trouillot, *Silencing the Past: Power and the Production of History* (Boston: Beacon Press, 1995).

3. On Lieber's postwar career, see Yael Sternhell, "The Afterlife of a Confederate Archive: Civil War Documents and the Making of Sectional Reconciliation," *Journal of American History* 102 (March 2016): 1025–1050, and John Fabian Witt, *Lincoln's Code: The Laws of War in American History* (New York: Free Press, 2012), pp. 285–324.

4. Francis Lieber, "Reflections on the Changes Which May Seem Necessary in the Present Constitution of the State of New York," in *The Miscellaneous Writings of Francis Lieber*, vol. 2, *Contributions to Political Science, Including Lectures on the Constitution of the United States and Other Papers*, ed. Daniel Coit Gilman (Philadelphia: J. B. Lippincott, 1881), p. 208.

5. Elizabeth Cady Stanton, *Address in Favor of Universal Suffrage, for the Election of Delegates to the Constitutional Convention, before the Judiciary Committees of the Legislature of New York, in the Assembly Chamber, January 23, 1867, in Behalf of the American Equal Rights Association* (Albany: Weed, Parsons, 1867), pp. 18, 11. I borrow the phrase from Nicole Gullace, *Blood of Our Sons: Men, Women and the Renegotiation of British Citizenship during the Great War* (New York: Palgrave Macmillan, 2002).

6. Lieber, "Reflections on the Changes Which May Seem Necessary," pp. 207–209; Frank Friedel, *Francis Lieber: Nineteenth-Century Liberal* (Baton Rouge: Louisiana State University Press, 1947), p. 385.

7. Lieber, "Reflections on the Changes Which May Seem Necessary," pp. 181–219, 208–209, 207 (quotations). There is a draft of this lecture in his files at the Huntington Library. See draft, notes, and newspaper clippings in folder labeled "Woman and Woman Suffrage, 1837–1869," Francis Lieber Papers, LI 114, Huntington Library, San Marino, Calif. (hereafter FLP, HL).

8. "A Woman in Reply to Dr. Lieber," *The Nation,* July 11, 1867, pp. 35–36; "Reasons Why Women Should Vote," *The Nation,* Nov. 21, 1867, pp. 35–36, 416–418, 417 (quotation). The woman was identified as the daughter of Massachusetts representative William Hooper; see Friedel, *Francis Lieber,* p. 386.

9. Lieber, "Woman and Woman Suffrage" folder, FLP, HL. On "women in need of protection," see Laura McLeod, "The Women, Peace and Security Resolutions: UNSCR 1325 to 2122," in *Handbook on Gender in World Politics,* ed. Jill Stearns and Daniela Tepe (Northampton, Mass.: Edward Elgar, 2016), pp. 271–279, 276 (quotation). On the Fourth Geneva Convention and the Protocol Additional of 1977, see Helen M. Kinsella, *The Image before the Weapon: A Critical History of the Distinction between Combatant and Civilian* (Ithaca, N.Y.: Cornell University Press, 2011), pp. 142–145, 104, 142, 145 (quotations).

10. United Nations Security Council, Resolution 1325 (2000), on "Women, Peace and Security," October 31, 2000, http://www.un.org/womenwatch/osagi /wps/; US Institute of Peace, statement of Kathleen Kuehnast, International Women's Day, 2018, https?/www.usip.org/blo g/2018/03 / making-women-visible. For an annotated version of Resolution 1325, see http://www.peacewomen.org /assets/file/BasicWPSDocs/annotated_1325.pdf.

11. Carol Cohn, Helen Kinsella, and Sheri Gibbings, "Women, Peace and Security: Resolution 1325," *International Feminist Journal of Politics* 6, no. 1 (March 2004): 130–140, 139 (quotation); McLeod, "The Women, Peace and Security Resolutions," pp. 278, 276; Helen M. Kinsella, "'With All the Respect Due to Their Sex': Gender and International Humanitarian Law," in Stearns and Tepe, eds., *Handbook on Gender in World Politics,* pp. 171–178, 176 (quotation); Kathleen Kuehnast, Chantal de Jonge Oudraat, and Helga Hernes, eds., *Women and War: Power and Protection in the 21st Century* (Washington, D.C.: US Institute of Peace Press, 2011).

12. Vasily Grossman, *Life and Fate,* trans. R. Chandler (New York: New York Review of Books, 1985); Alexievich, *Unwomanly Face of War.* For numbers on

women's service in World War II, see Kinsella, *Image before the Weapon*, p. 121. On Algeria, see Gerald Horne, *A Savage War of Peace: Algeria, 1954–1962* (New York: Viking Press, 1977), and the memoir by Zohra Drif, *Inside the Battle of Algiers: Memoir of a Woman Freedom Fighter* (Charlottesville, Va.: Just World Books, 2017).

13. Paul Preston, *The Spanish Holocaust: Inquisition and Extermination in Twentieth-Century Spain* (London: Harper Press, 2012); Attina Grossman, *Jews, Germans, and Allies: Close Encounters in Occupied Germany* (Princeton, N.J.: Princeton University Press, 2007); Alexandra Stiglmayer, *Mass Rape: The War against Women in Bosnia-Herzegovina* (Lincoln: University of Nebraska Press, 1994).

Acknowledgments

2018 was a trying year for feminists like myself. But it also offered up gifts, including a powerful reminder of the value of what we do as women in the world. It made me grateful beyond measure for the support and companionship of other women in the common political and scholarly endeavor of writing history. This is a small and imperfect book, a down payment on something far bigger, but writing it engaged all of my energies. More than the other books that I have written, it invited me—seemed to require me—to connect to my own past and to recognize the indelible impact of early events on me as a person and an intellectual. *Women's War* is about the American Civil War but I hope readers will see that I was aiming at something more, about the value of women's experience of history, and about our obligations in writing history, including, and perhaps especially, the history of wars.

The chapters of this book developed in conversation with many people, and it is my pleasure to acknowledge them here. I presented early versions of all three chapters as the 2015 Joanne Goodman Lectures at Western University, my alma mater. It was a very moving occasion for me. My teachers at Western launched me on this path and were there in the audience to hear me give the lectures. I would like to thank Craig Simpson and Neville Thompson for their friendship and lifelong support. Shelley McKellar ran the lectures that year and was a wonderful host. I would also like to thank Rande Kostal of Western University's law school, an old friend from undergraduate days, who encouraged me to publish my lecture on the Lieber code in a legal history journal and helped me to think a bit more like a legal historian. Chapter I revises and expands on "Enemy Women and the Laws of War in the American Civil War," *Law and History Review*, August 2017, vol. 35, no. 3. Text from that article, copyright 2017 by the American Society for Legal History, is reprinted here with permission of Cambridge University Press.

The detour into legal history was one of the most rewarding parts of this project. I am particularly grateful to the colleagues who invited me to present my work on Frances Lieber at Columbia Law School's Legal History Workshop, especially Jeremy Kessler for fielding all my questions, and Sarah Knuckey, who introduced me to the scholarship on peace and conflict studies and showed me why this work on the nineteenth century still matters to people now. Rosemary Byrne at Trinity College Dublin showed me how these issues matter to human rights lawyers and sent me the United Nations resolution I used in the Epilogue. I would like to thank Sarah Barringer Gordon for the invitation to present at the legal history seminar at the University of Pennsylvania.

Over the time it took to write this book, I presented versions of the chapters at various other places, including Queen Mary, University of London and the Princeton Department of History's Modern America Workshop. I would like to thank Joanna Cohen, my former student, for hosting me for my time in London, and Anne Kerth and Matt Karp, whose comments at the Princeton workshop sharpened my thinking enormously.

At the end of the process I received needed encouragement and sharp advice from my editor at Harvard University Press, Joyce Seltzer, a legendary figure in the field of academic publishing. It is an honor to be part of her list, and I thank her for her support and friendship. I would also like to thank Pamela Haag, my copy editor, for the difference she made in the story I told, and Tim Jones, who designed the beautiful cover of *Women's War*. In the last round of revisions I benefited from the reports of two readers for the Press: Nancy Cott and another person who remained anonymous. This is not the first time that Nancy Cott's embrace of my work has made a difference in my life. She wrote for my tenure report a million years ago, when we did not know each other at all. My own advisors were not able or willing to support me but she did, and so did a number of other women in the profession, chief among them Drew Gilpin Faust and Christine Stansell. I owe a great deal to them and to the larger community of women in the history profession. Amy Dru Stanley's work has always informed mine and did again this time, as my citations show. Thavolia Glymph generously allowed me to read and benefit from her own forthcoming, brilliantly original book on women and the Civil War. My friend Elizabeth Colwill remains a pillar of support, and her pathbreaking work on France and Saint-Domingue continues to be an ongoing source of ideas and inspiration.

Finally, it gives me great pleasure to acknowledge the debt to my graduate students, whose work has advanced my knowledge so much over the past eight years. I am immensely proud of the dissertations and books they have written. Numbers of them are now published scholars: Aaron Astor, Dana Weiner, Joanna Cohen, and Erik Mathisen have all published books that started as dissertations. Many of my current students worked on aspects of this book or gave me the benefit of their readings of parts of it. Recent dissertations by my PhD students Abigail Cooper, Hope McGrath, Sarah Rodriguez, Emma Teitelman, and Alexis Broderick Neumann all enriched my thinking in different ways. Readers will see my intellectual debts to them marked in the notes. Serena Covkin, who was my honors student and is now a PhD candidate at the University of Chicago, did research on what became Chapter 1. Emma Teitelman worked as a research assistant on Chapter 3 and helped me navigate the dense terrain of Reconstruction sources and historiography. Alexis Broderick Neumann and I shared an interest in Gertrude Thomas and also sources that show up in Chapter 3. My intellectual relationships with my current PhD students at Columbia are no less rewarding. Kellen Heniford and Brooks Tucker Swett moved with me from Penn to Columbia. It is an enormous pleasure to supervise their dissertation work. Kellen helped me sort out a knotty problem in my thinking about race and Reconstruction. I have relied on Brooks immensely over the past year as I tried to bring this book to conclusion. Among other things, she procured all the art permissions required for publication of *Women's War*. She was also my sounding board and partner in developing a new lecture course on the Civil War and Reconstruction and served as the first teaching assistant for it. I thank her for all of it. The process, of course, is ongoing. I have two new graduate students at Columbia, Justine Meberg and Isobel Plowright, both beginning important work in women's history. I am deeply grateful for the intellectual companionship my students offer me and each other. I am very proud of the community they have formed and the way they sustain each other, even across distance and time.

I have far more personal debts, not all of which can be acknowledged fully here. My father, Sylvester McCurry, passed away just as this book was going to press. My debts to him go so deep it is a lifetime's work to figure them out. My mother, Margaret McCurry, continues to support me as she always has. She never needed to be told the value of women's history. Antonio Feros supports me in every way that matters. He has opened up a world of new ideas, experiences, and friends in the United States and Europe. His love is a gift and it shows me the way forward. One other unexpected gift I have recently received is the joy that comes with adult children. Who knew? Declan and Saoirse are both now in their twenties, well on their way in the world. They provide their mother the full and daily benefit of their fierce intelligence, wit, and humor and the kind of love that makes life worth living. I thank them for all their love and support.

This book is dedicated to my daughter, Saoirse McCurry Hahn, because it could only be for her. I offer it in awe of the bond of mother and daughter, and in recognition that it is in her capable hands, and those of the women of her generation, that our future rests. It is up to them, now, to secure the proper recognition of women's worth in every sphere of life, personal as well as political. I have great faith.

Index

black soldier's wife (*continued*)
91–92, 118–119; marriage promoted among, 84–85, 94–97, 104–105, 245n79; Militia Act on, 90–91; varied experiences of, 65–66. *See also* enslaved people; freed people
Blair, Montgomery, 76, 79
Blair, William, 222nn38–39
Blake, George, 22
Blodgett, Foster, 171
Bluntschli, Johann, 55, 230n85
Bradley, Aaron Alpeoria, 193
Browning, Orville, 89, 91
Bryant, John Emory, 143–144, 161–162, 163, 166, 168, 266n96
Buckley, C. W., 105
Bullock, Rufus, 174
Bureau of Colored Troops, 93
Bureau of Refugees, Freedmen, and Abandoned Lands (Freedmen's Bureau): agents, 163; and children retained by former masters, 144–145, 259n50; and civil rights for freed people, 143; and enfranchisement of freed people, 169, 170; establishment, 83, 113; and labor disputes between planters and freed people, 160–161, 163, 165; marriage and, 65; role in reuniting displaced people, 139–140; Sherman's Reserve and, 157; voter registration and, 169, 170
Burr, Virginia, 173, 261n64, 276n168
Butler, Benjamin, 7, 29, 75–77, 77–78, 80–81, 106

Cameron, Simon, 76, 77, 79
Caroline (former slave), 142

Cheves, J. R., 160
Cheyenne women, 26, 216n7
childbearing, 189–190
children, African American, 140–142, 143–145, 259n50, 260n55
Christian Recorder (newspaper), 139
Cimbala, Paul, 260n55, 266n91
citizenship, female, 21, 23–24
civilian immunity, 25. *See also* distinction, between civilians and combatants; enemy women
Civil War: author's approach to, x–xii; women's roles, 1–4, 203–204, 212. *See also* black soldier's wife; enemy women; Reconstruction
Clanton, Buddy, 146, 173, 177, 184
Clanton, Turner, 132, 147, 148–150, 150–151, 261n64
Clay, Henry, 121
Clear, Mary Jane (former slave), 99
Coates, Ta-Nehisi, 129
Coclanis, Peter, 264n81
Collamer, Jacob, 88–89
Columbus (former Clanton slave), 149
Colwill, Elizabeth, 71–72, 73, 239n26
combatants. *See* distinction, between civilians and combatants; enemy women; noncombatants
Confederate States of America: response to Lieber's code, 56–58; torture of women by, 58, 231n90. *See also* enemy women; Reconstruction; Thomas, Ella Gertrude Clanton
constitutional amendments, 121–122, 196, 250n103
contraband policy, 75–79, 80–82
contracts, employment, 161–163, 165

enfranchisement, 169–170, 171,
175–176, 269n106
Enlistment Act (1865), 113, 115–118
enslaved people: attempts by black
soldiers to save families, 106–108;
celebration of Union victory, 255n26;
denial of marriage to, 63, 234n2;
dilemma of refugee women and
children, 76–79; gendered recruitment
and sorting in Mississippi Valley,
97–101; humanitarian crisis of refugee
women and children, 78, 80, 83,
93–94; marriage promoted among,
84–85, 94–97, 104–105, 245n79;
military recruitment of men, 92–93,
97–98, 103, 113; photographs, *81, 102,
107*; plantation labor and refugee
camps for women and children, 98–99,
235n6, 244n69; Union treatment of
refugee women and children, 26;
women resistance to gendered policy,
101–103. *See also* black soldier's wife;
emancipation; freed people
—SPECIFIC INDIVIDUALS: Amanda
Walton (former Clanton slave), 149,
150, 151; America (former Thomas
slave), 136; Ann Summer, 106; Betsey
(former Thomas slave), 136, 140–141,
145; Caroline, 142; Columbus (former
Clanton slave), 149; Cyrus (former
Clanton slave), 149; Daniel (former
Thomas slave), 136, 140; Diania, 198;
Frances Johnson, 114–115; Geneva
(former Clanton slave), 149; George
Hanon, 111; Hampton (former
Clanton slave), 149; Henry (former
Thomas slave), 133, 134; Isabella

(former Thomas slave), 140, 258n42;
Isaiah (former Thomas slave), 172,
174; Israel Kelly, 165–166; Jim
(former Thomas slave), 136; John
Boss (former Thomas slave), 134;
Joseph Harris, 107; Laurence (former
Clanton slave), 149; Louisa and Israel
Smith, 99, 100; Lurany (former
Thomas slave), 147–148, 148–149,
150, 199, 261n64, 262n65; Mac
(former Thomas slave), 172, 174;
Mary, 145; Mary Ann Walker, 166;
Mary Jane Clear, 99; Milly (former
Thomas slave), 136; Milly Hopkins,
165; Mollie, 186; Nancy (former
Thomas slave), 136, 140; Ned
(former Thomas slave), 172; Patsey
(former Thomas slave), 136, 137, 167;
Patsey Leach, 115; Rachel Jones,
145; Reef Velard, 165; Sallie Crane,
139; Sarah (former Thomas slave),
140–141, 146; Spotswood Rice, 107;
Stephen Walton, 149; Susan (former
Thomas slave), 141; Sykes (former
Thomas slave), 133, 141; Tallulah
(former Clanton slave), 149, 150;
Tamah (former Thomas slave), 136,
137; Willis Thomas (former Thomas
slave), 163, 165, 167–168
Ewing, Thomas, 38

Ferguson, Jane, 37–38
Fields, Barbara, 191, 192, 252n9
Fields, Karen, 191, 192, 252n9
Fifteenth Amendment, 121–122
First Confiscation Act (1861), 79, 86
Fisk, Clinton, 114